First published in the United Kingdom in 2010 by BackPage Press

ISBN 978-0-9564971-0-9

Design and typeset by BackPage Press

Printed and bound in Scotland by Thomson Litho Ltd

www.backpagepress.co.uk

IN SEARCH OF ALAN GILZEAN

The Lost Legacy of a Dundee and Spurs legend

James Morgan

Born and raised in Northern Ireland, **James Morgan** is a sports journalist with The Herald newspaper in Glasgow. A lifelong Tottenham Hotspur supporter, he lives in Hamilton with his wife and son. This is his first book.

For Jim

CONTENTS

1

JIGSAW PIECES

This is the rumour as I know it. In the summer of 2005, a few Spurs internet messageboards started buzzing over a story which claimed that Alan Gilzean, the former Tottenham Hotspur, Dundee and Scotland footballer, had been living as a down-and-out somewhere in England's West Country. There was widespread sadness and dismay at news of Gillie's apparent decline. As a legendary Spurs player of the 70s, many of the contributors had witnessed Gilzean at first hand and there was genuine concern for his welfare. Relief soon followed, though, when another supporter assured fellow fans that while Gilzean had, indeed, fallen on hard times his son, Ian, had taken him back to Scotland to help him 'sort himself out'.

I read the story with a mixture of disbelief, sadness and incredulity, wondering exactly what set of circumstances might have contributed to Gilzean's decline. There were insinuations from a few other posters speculating about the role alcohol might have played. The more I thought about it, though, the more it seemed a bizarre, even ludicrous, tale. Aside from the very obvious concerns over the reliability of a story doing the rounds on an internet messageboard, something else didn't ring true. Why had the tabloids not picked up on it?

There was something faintly ridiculous about the whole suggestion, not least because Gilzean would have had some kind of pension from the Football Association and the governing body had a history of benevolent intervention in high-profile cases like that of Peter Marinello, the peripatetic Scotland international. According to one contributor, the story came from a friend of Steve Perryman, Gillie's former colleague at Tottenham Hotspur, who had attempted in vain to contact his old team-mate and discovered the awful truth. Even the extent of Perryman's involvement seemed unlikely and, as a start point for a book, it wasn't much to go on. A tawdry tale with little foundation or substance which nevertheless pricked my journalistic interest and prompted me to dig just a little deeper. This was a man who my father had idolised.

The search began where most cursory searches begin these days, on the internet. The first findings were limited to a few links to Tottenham supporter sites, an article by Hunter Davies in the New Statesman, a Wikipedia page. All in all, it was a meagre biography of a life less ordinary. I searched Amazon for books on Gilzean, there was nothing. I scoured the electronic cuttings section of three national Scottish newspapers to find what they contained on a man who had represented Scotland 22 times. There were five articles which either referenced Gilzean in passing or were a rehash of the information I had already gleaned. I visited the Scottish Football Association Hall of Fame website, where I found a Dane, Brian Laudrup, and a Swede, Henrik Larsson, but not Gillie. I hunted out some of my old Tottenham reference books, yet aside from the odd cameo appearance by way of a goal here, a flicked header there, the details contained were purely biographical.

The bare facts (according to the internet) were these: Alan John Gilzean was born in the Perthshire town of Coupar Angus on October 23rd, 1938 (I would later discover that two of these basic 'facts' were wrong). His playing career began in 1957 and lasted for 17 years. He made 190 appearances for Dundee, scoring 169 goals, including 52 in one season, a record which would stand until Larsson broke it 39 years later in 2001. In December 1964, Tottenham Hotspur paid £72,500 to take the then 26-year-old to White Hart Lane. He left Dens Park a hero but, as I would discover, under a cloud. At the London club, he played in 429 matches and scored 133 goals, forming two prodigious partnerships, first with Jimmy Greaves and then Martin Chivers. Having won five caps during his time with Dundee, he won a further 17 at Spurs. He scored 12 goals for his country.

He retired from top-flight football in 1974 and moved to South Africa, where he had agreed a contract with Highlands Park, a team from Johannesburg. There was no documentary evidence of his stay in South Africa, perhaps because there was little time to accrue any. Within months, Gilzean was home, becoming Stevenage Athletic manager before slipping out of football and the public consciousness. Some stories had Gilzean setting up a haulage company in Enfield which ultimately failed, some said he had parted from his childhood sweetheart and wife Irene, dates unknown.

These details were readily available to anyone who wanted to know them but this was the sum total of his life story in print or, more accurately, on screen. An anodyne list of achievements which was nothing more than a sequence of events, words and figures, and while those figures even now leave me somewhat agog, they told me nothing of Gilzean's character.

My initial conclusion was that perhaps there was more merit to the rumour about his plight than I had thought. Then in February 2009 came something of a breakthrough. Alan Pattullo, a journalist with The Scotsman, wrote a piece about Gilzean's semi-hermitic lifestyle on the eve of the Carling Cup final involving his old club Tottenham and Manchester United.

As Pattullo notes, "the trouble with such a withdrawal after years spent in the public eye is that it tends to encourage misinformation". But in the article were a number of details not previously in the public domain: he was living in the English seaside resort of Weston-super-Mare, so yes, he was in the West Country; the only former team-mate he kept in regular contact with was Bobby Wishart; Wishart and Ian Gilzean were both quoted and revealed that while Alan's recorded date of birth was October 22nd 1938, they weren't entirely convinced that Gilzean had yet turned 70. This seemed to encompass his idiosyncratic ways in one bite-sized anecdote.

Pattullo touched on the down-and-out story but informed readers that a friend of Gilzean's had phoned the Talksport radio station to shoot down the rumour. A friend, not Gilzean.

There were other fanciful claims. One Spurs website host revealed that his favourite Gilzean story concerned a football scout from Perth who also happened to book bands for the town hall dance. During one particular week, said scout had gone along to watch a young local football talent, but had been unimpressed and instead signed his cousin. A few days later the same scout, now acting in his role as would-be promoter, took a call from the manager of an up-and-coming Liverpudlian four-piece who was attempting to book dates for his band but the discussion stalled when talk turned to money. And so the story goes that this was the man who had turned down the chance to sign Alan Gilzean and The Beatles in the same week.

A fellow journalist told me another of dubious origin that still makes him laugh. Gilzean was a habitual visitor to a Greek restaurant in London's West End. Legend had it that one night Bill Nicholson took his players to the same restaurant as a treat and when the owner of the restaurant spotted Gilzean he immediately produced a bottle of Bacardi and four Cokes which he set down in front of the player before asking "The usual, Mr Gilzean?" This story, though, was not as difficult to give credence to. Writing in his seminal book The Glory Game in 1972, Hunter Davies made several references to Gilzean's capacity for booze.

The Glory Game provides the best snapshots of Gilzean's life, but he is mentioned barely 30 times in 296 pages. Those who have read the book will agree that his is a fleeting presence. It was an unprecedented work. Davies merely walked into the offices of White Hart Lane one day and asked if he could follow the team for a season. Bill Nicholson, the manager, agreed. When it was reissued in 1985, the synopsis described it as "a classic – probably the best book about football ever written".

It is a fascinating insight into the lonely, regimented existence of football life but it is far from a sensational account. As any fly-on-the-wall account should do, it spares no-one, but it is hardly explosive. Nicholson is depicted as a serial worrier, Eddie Baily, his assistant, as a sergeant-major type, obsessed with references to the army and war in general and Martin Chivers, the Tottenham striker, as a neurotic who has no time for supporters. Gilzean, however, hovers in the shadows.

The cover of my edition carries a picture of Chivers celebrating one of his two goals in the 1971 League Cup final against Aston Villa. In the foreground, a team-mate has leapt into Chivers' arms and in the background is Gillie, arms raised, with a broad smile across his face. He looks like someone's elderly father. Playing kit aside, he could easily pass for a middle-aged man who has taken the wrong turn for the toilets and stumbled out on to the pitch. His bald head is clearly visible but the lank strands of hair which hang around his neck are not so obvious and you can just make out the traces of grey peppering his sideburns. It is not a typical Gilzean photograph, though. Others from the early 1970s make him look like he could be a professor or a banker or a Dickensian villain – anything but a professional footballer.

His apparent decrepitude was entirely superficial. Gilzean was one of those players that everyone – from Jimmy Greaves, his striking partner at Tottenham, to Johan Cruyff, the legendary Ajax and Barcelona forward – had an opinion about, and those opinions usually started with a default phrase: What. A. Player. It made the absence of a book on his life all the more difficult to fathom.

I re-read The Glory Game in less than a week, taking notes of relevant mentions of Gilzean:

"Christ, I could go a cold lager," said Alan Gilzean, the only Scotsman in the Spurs first team. He was jogging with difficulty, the sweat covering his ample forehead. He hates roadwalking. He thinks footballers aren't meant to walk.

Alan Gilzean is the oldest Spurs player, but looks even older than he is because of his lack of hair. The club keeps his date of birth very quiet.

On the train home they had dinner and plenty to drink, half of them ordering lagers-and-limes, two at a time. Steve Perryman stuck to Coke. By the end of the journey Gilzean had several empty lager cans stacked in front of him.

They [the supporters] hadn't a bad word to say about any player. But Gilzean was clearly the most popular player. At the mention of his name, they burst into song, to the tune of the Christmas carol Noel, Noel. "Gilzean, Gilzean, Gilzean, Gilzean, born is the King of White Hart Lane".

The regular card players – Joe, Gilly [sic], Mike and Cyril – had got down to it the minute tea was over without looking at the weather.

For the home match against Everton, [Alan Mullery] turned up to watch with Samantha, his two-year-old daughter. Gilzean, in true Scottish fashion, did the doting uncle bit and pressed a ten-pence piece into her hand.

Alan Gilzean arrived late, looking as usual, unlike any of the other footballers. He was in an old-fashioned two-piece dark suit and white shirt. He slipped quietly in, as if it was a business call, and he had come to read the meter. There were none of the quick smiles or hurried glances in the mirror to check his hair and shirt, the way the younger ones had done. He was hardly noticed as he picked out a vacant seat and went straight to it, drink in hand. You could feel he'd been to many parties and had his priorities right. He wasn't going to waste time on any social chit chat.

This isn't the highlights reel of Gilzean's appearances in The Glory Game, this is pretty much all of them. Other players had entire chapters written about them but not Gilzean. Why had Davies steered clear of one of the most colourful players in the squad? And who was this person he was describing: a quickwitted, streetwise, borderline alcoholic? A terrace idol with an avuncular nature? An anachronistic, unfashionable social misfit who was a regular party-goer? The fleeting glimpses of Gilzean in The Glory Game merely muddied the picture. I had not expected mawkish sentimentality from Davies, clearly a journalist first and Spurs fan second, but this read like a series of vignettes which bordered on character assassination on the one hand and great affection on the other.

Years later in that New Statesman article, Davies went as far as to suggest that Gilzean did not like football, was dead lazy and would jump in his Jag to drive 100 yards to pick up his daily newspaper.

This bubbling cauldron of meat and bones only intensified my appetite.

I put in calls to old newspaper colleagues and old colleagues of colleagues. Within a few days I had numbers for some of the finest players in the histories of Dundee and Tottenham Hotspur. One number, though, continued to slip my ad hoc intelligence network – that of Gilzean himself.

It took months of searching but gradually I was able to piece together something resembling a picture of the man. Like a jigsaw purchased from a church hall jumble sale, though, many of the bits were missing.

Then one Saturday afternoon, a large brown envelope arrived in the post. The package was from Bill Hutcheon, the editor of the Dundee Courier, with whom I'd been in touch regarding the contents of the Courier's archive relating to Gilzean. He had sent me the lot. Contained inside the envelope were exactly 16 cuttings of Gilzean's life at Dundee and Tottenham. "Good luck with your research," wrote Bill. "You'll need it," I thought. And yet, having spent months mining paragraphs for a single nugget, this was a veritable gold rush. The articles were full of the kind of background information I had been crying out for.

Here was an interview in which Gilzean revealed he was player-secretary with Coupar Angus Boys' Club aged just 15 (Sporting Post 1962); next a feature on Gilzean which explained he had been a keen boy scout from the ages of 11 to 15 (The People's Journal, 1963); here was a story in which he was presented with a gold watch by his home town of Coupar Angus after scoring the winning goal for Scotland against England (The Courier and Advertiser, 1964); one picture showed him smiling and sipping champagne with wife Irene and former Dundee team-mates on his wedding day (The Courier and Advertiser, 1965).

Another, headlined 'It's Over: Gilzean joins Spurs' proclaimed the news every Dundee supporter had been dreading: "Shortly before one o'clock today there ended one of the longest drawn-out transfers in football history. Alan Gilzean, the Dundee forward, signed for Tottenham Hotspur."

I was left with an overwhelming conclusion. If Gilzean's decision to opt for a life of solitude was born of determination to keep his private affairs private then it was laudable, but that seemed at odds with everything that had preceded it. The man on the pages of the local newspapers of Perthshire and Tayside seemed far removed from the grizzled cynic found in the pages of The Glory Game, let alone the kind of man who could fall so far as to become a down-and-out.

Contained in this small clump of cuttings lay some part of Gilzean the man. They seemed as good a place as any to start his story.

2

SCOUTING FOR TALENT

It is a drizzly autumn morning when I drive into the car park at the Red House Hotel in Coupar Angus. Waiting for me, perched on his brolly, is the diminutive figure of Ron Ross, former sports editor of the Dundee Courier, raconteur par excellence and erstwhile school friend of Alan Gilzean. Ron has agreed to show me around the streets of the town where Gilzean learned his footballing trade. As we pound the cobbled streets of this once-thriving market town, built on requisitioned swampland by Cistercian monks, Ron replays sequences from more recent times.

Taking a right on to Forfar Road, we are soon standing at the wrought-iron gates of Foxhall Park, home to Coupar Angus Juniors and the football ground where Gillie first started to make a name for himself. One hundred yards away there once lived the answer to a quiz question: Neil Paterson. The former Dundee United captain stayed in an imposing house almost overlooking the ground. His other claim to fame? He won an Academy Award for his screenplay to the 1959 film Room At The Top.

At the Forfar Road end of Foxhall Park, a long row of tall poplar trees enclose the playing area; there are brown and golden leaves scattered across the surface of the neat park. At the far end lies the old Glasgow to Aberdeen rail track. Ron's memories come flooding back: "When the big games were on, you could see the signalman standing on his tiptoes inside his signal box as he strained to watch the match."

Ron recalls thousands passing through those iron gates for fixtures against the teams from the neighbouring towns of Alyth and Blairgowrie. "There were summer evenings here when you would be five or six deep in the crowd and there were some big teams that played here."

As part of the deal that took George Niven from Coupar Angus to Rangers, the Glasgow side played a friendly at the venue. Alan and Ron were among the heaving crowd who watched the locals succumb to a heavy defeat. There was a similar arrangement – and an equally large crowd – for the fixture that marked Telford Bannerman's transfer to nearby Dundee. Bannerman, who made the move to Dens Park some years before Gilzean, would prove less of a success at the club than his near contemporary, but he would eventually make his name at Brighton & Hove Albion. His young brother owns the Red House Hotel around the corner.

Gilzean honed his skills across Forfar Road on The Common, an area of land where children would play and local people would walk their dogs. It backed on to Coupar Angus School at one end and the headmaster's house at the other, enclosed by impressive sandstone houses on one side and a hedgerow on the other.

Every day after school boys would gather on The Common to play football. They would throw down their jackets and out would come the tennis ball. Alan and his cousin Billy Forbes were easily the best, often times dribbling through heavy mud with the ball glued to their feet. One summer evening when the boys were just getting started there was a screeching of brakes and a tremendous bang from the road.

An open-top tourer had attempted to overtake a lorry and pulled out in front of a fish lorry coming from Aberdeen in the opposite direction. When the boys heard the collision they immediately lifted their jackets and ran towards the road; the scene they discovered was not pretty. These were the days when cars were built without seatbelts and the car's passengers, two men and two women, had been hurled on to the road. "There was blood everywhere," says Ron. "There were people with contusions lying in the middle of the road. So we got our jackets and put them under the heads of the injured. One of the men in particular was in a bad way and was moaning and groaning. We did what we could as little boys and fortunately there were no casualties in the end. About two miles down the road I realised shock had set in and I ended up vomiting in the nearest field."

Gilzean is not Coupar Angus's only famous son. John Bain Sutherland, born there on March 11th 1889, went on to become one of American football's greatest college coaches with Pitt University after emigrating to the United States in his teens. He coached Pitt to four Rose Bowl appearances and, while what constituted national champions during the 1920s and 1930s was a grey area due to the diverse nature of the country's university structure, they had a genuine claim to this title in the years 1929, 1931, 1934, 1936 and 1937. He later took his talents into the professional arena with Brooklyn Dodgers and Pittsburgh Steelers. The city of Pittsburgh named a street after him when he died of a brain tumour in April 1948. Coupar Angus town council hung a picture of him in chambers. They gave Alan Gilzean a gold watch in recognition of his winning goal against England at Hampden Park in a British Championship match 16 years later. And that was that.

Back on the streets of Coupar Angus, Ron and I visit the Heritage Association in George Street. I enquire why the town has not thought of naming a street after Alan. "Do you not need to be dead for that to happen?" chuckles one man, who knew Gillie well. I ask if Jock Sutherland has had a memorial erected to him and the answer is no. Ron notes that the (living) author Rosamunde Pilcher has a street named after her in Ron's hometown of Longforgan, a few miles along from Coupar Angus.

One thought springs to mind: this is a country town where, for those who knew him, Alan Gilzean was and always will be the big lad from Strathmore Avenue who was good at fitba'. Another takes slightly longer to gestate: Stewart Imlach, the subject of Gary Imlach's book, My Father and Other Working Class Heroes, has a street named after him in his home town of Lossiemouth. Matt Hampson, the former Leicester Tigers and England Under-21 rugby player, has a school building named in his honour and he is very much alive. And if death is the only qualification for earning recognition from your town, what happened to Jock Sutherland's memorial?

Men and women over a certain age in Coupar Angus know of Gilzean, but newcomers and the young do not. Ian Mackenzie, a lifelong pal, feels that the town council should have recognised his achievements by naming a street after him, or putting a plaque up outside his former house. Norrie Currie, a former Coupar Angus team-mate, concurs. "We watch matches now and we will say, 'Look at that lad, he's not fit to lace Gilzean's boots,' and they say, 'Who's Gilzean?' "

There was a time when the name was known all over Coupar Angus and the outlying area. Most houses in Strathmore – the region in Perth and Kinross between the Grampian and Sidlaw hills – had an association with it. Willie Gilzean, Alan's father, owned a painter and decorators business in Gray Street and a sign bearing his surname hung outside his shop, a formidable old building which was formerly a bank before it was purchased by the Co-operative and later rented by Alan's father. It's the kind of surname you would remember, too. It resonates of old Scotland, of tribes and clansmen. The name Gilzean is said to come from MacLean and derives from the Gaelic mac gille Eoin which translates as son of the servant of John. (John is the middle name of Alan, his first son Kevin and Alan's father). In early times, the clan was known as Clan Gillean and over time metamorphosed into Gilzean. Today we pronounce the z but at some point in history it was almost certainly silent. That has not stopped a silent tug of war over the spelling of Gilzean's nickname. Dundee supporters insist on Gillie and even named a fanzine after him, Eh Mind O' Gillie ('I remember Gilzean'). Tottenham historians use Gilly.

In the early days, there was no confusion: Alan was Aga or Peenie to his pals. He was born at Perth Royal Infirmary on October 22, 1938, the youngest of four children Barbara Gilzean delivered. A year separated the oldest, sister Thelma (1928), from brother Eric (1929). A second son, William Macrae, was born in April 1936 but died after 28 days from infantile atrophy, a form of malnutrition.

Today both siblings live in Salt Lake City in the United States. Eric, a more than decent left winger in his youth, sought fame in London's West End after winning a talent contest at the Palace Theatre in Dundee as part of a trio with two other Coupar Angus lads who called themselves the Roed Boys. The trio were all set to leave for London when, at the last minute, one of the boys got cold feet. Eric and his friend Ron left for the bright lights and were soon working in a toffee factory to pay the rent. Eventually, Eric met a dancer named Audrey Ann from Liverpool, got married and emigrated to Canada in 1974. Now, he runs a Scottish memorabilia shop in Salt Lake City called Edinburgh Castle. Thelma has been in the States for years, too.

There are few Gilzeans in Coupar Angus today, a sad development given the long association it has had with the name. Willie was a well-known, distinguished figure in the community. As befitted a high-ranking member of the No.105 St John Operative Lodge of Freemasons, he was always well turned out, going to work every day sporting a bunnet and with a floral bow tie underneath his white overalls. He was an impressive public speaker and would be called upon to host Burns Nights.

Willie was born on December 3, 1902, in the family home at No.25 Causewayend in Coupar Angus. Two years later, on the same side of the street, Gillie's mother Barbara entered the world. Her address was No.53 Causewayend, the daughter of William McArthur Melville Forbes, a jute dresser, and Margaret Forbes, née Robertson. The public records show a long history of Forbeses marrying Gilzeans.

Gilzean spent nearly all his life in Coupar at 25 Strathmore Avenue, before the family moved to a substantial sandstone house, 2 Stuart Crescent, in the 60s. Standing outside the latter, I asked a young woman if this had been Alan Gilzean's house. She had no idea, she had never heard of him. She crossed the road and disappeared inside a house before returning with her father. "Ah ken, he lived in that hoose for aboot a year when his father passed away. That was aboot 10 year ago." Not for the first time in my search for Alan Gilzean, and certainly not for the last, I'm struck by how memory is unreliable: Willie actually died in 1993, Babs three years before him.

In the Athole Arms pub, a couple of hundred yards around the corner, Ron and I have lentil soup and roast beef sandwiches and ask about. One barmaid knows the name, she is a distant relative. "I've never met him. Perhaps once," she says smiling. Another has not heard of him but suggests "Roy Whytock might know something". But after a louder-than-intended telephone conversation, Gillie's former boys' club team-mate apparently refuses my invitation. "He's not in," says the barmaid.

An elderly man with a weather-beaten face approaches, followed by his huge Alsatian. "Si' doon," says the man as the dog makes its way towards me. He tips his pint glass back and takes a gulp from it. "Wha' do ya want to know about Alan Gilzean, like?" he asks. "Ah ken him, he used tae live aroon' the corner."

I ask the man for his name and he laughs. "Ye dinnae want ma name," he says. "Dinnae put that in yer book. Ah didnae really ken Alan Gilzean tha' well, just tha' he used tae live roon thaur."

I can't shake the suspicion that a tight-knit village is closing ranks.

What is known is this: Alan's footballing ability came from his maternal side. His father did not play, but took a keen interest in his son's career and would become a regular attendee at Dundee matches. After his son returned from school, he would tie an old football to a piece of rope and wrap it around a beam in the paint shop and Alan would perfect the leaping technique that would become his trademark.

Willie attempted to improve Alan's skills, but football ran in the blood in his mother's family. The name Forbes was synonymous with Coupar Angus Juniors, one of the top semi-professional clubs in the region. Junior football in Scotland is often confused in England with youth football, but it is barely a step down from the Third Division of the Scottish Football League. Many former full-time professionals see out their careers with Junior clubs who can boast attendances in the thousands for big games and who have rich histories of providing some of Scotland's finest players.

Six of Alan's uncles – Andrew, Jock, Doug, Drummond, Jim and Geordie – had Junior experience and most had trials for senior clubs. Doug and 'Drummie' played in what local amateur historians and knowledgeable barflies contend was the finest Coupar Angus side in the club's history. During the 1938-39 season, they won four trophies and the Angus Junior league and enjoyed a long run in the Scottish Cup. The 4,000 supporters who turned up to watch Coupar Angus defeat Kirrie Thistle to win the league that season still stands as a club-record attendance.

However, the side was dismantled at the outbreak of World War II, just a few weeks after that season ended. When the players returned at the end of hostilities, one member was missing: Drummie, whom many say was Alan's equal as a player, was killed at the age of 31 in 1944. "The Forbes family lived at Couttie Brig and that is where the great Drummond Forbes was born and grew up to be one of the greatest footballers to have graced the turf," says Ron, who has a friend in Tasmania who is still in touch with Eric Gilzean. "He was being watched by Rangers and Dundee when the war started. He was called up in the first draft and was killed early on in the fighting in France. The whole of Coupar Angus went into mourning."

Today a monument to former pupils who fell in the World Wars stands outside Coupar Angus primary school. Among the fallen, there are Grays, Laings and Dicksons, all names associated with the area. Coupar Angus, a primary and secondary school when Alan Gilzean was a pupil, would have held approximately 150 pupils. In total, the fallen number 91. It was some years before the football team recovered, too. Coupar Angus Juniors won just two cups in the four-year period following the end of the war and never again dominated in the way they had before Drummie died.

The countryside around Coupar Angus is famous for berry-picking and Strathmore remains one of the United Kingdom's most important fruit producing areas. The Preserve Works at the end of George Street was where fruit was turned into jam. Known as The Jellyworks, it was an important employer and, like many children in the region, Alan would have been out in the fields during the summer with his mother, brother and sister, helping to supplement the family income. Families in 1950s Coupar Angus could expect to make up to five pounds a week picking berries and, because it was casual labour, they didn't have to declare it.

"He wasn't much of a berry picker, Alan," says Ron McDonald, his old scoutmaster and family friend. "He could play football but he couldnae pick berries. His mother was a good berry picker and he would be working under her supervision, but he would probably play football at the end of the drill. All the kids went to the berries in Coupar Angus. That was where families made money to buy clothing and stuff like that. Berries, and picking potatoes in the autumn. Coupar Angus was surrounded by berries at one time; you can't see that now, other than a few tunnels. At one time, all the fields were berry fields. That was where you made your money; you got so much per pound, and if you were working with your mother she made sure you worked. You would start any time from 7 o'clock onwards, until 5 o'clock at night."

At school, he was of average academic ability and sport was his first love. He played in the secondary school team in first year, with much older boys. His football talent aside, he was a keen golfer and tennis player, and later excelled at cricket and was a top-order batsman and proficient fast bowler for Coupar Angus.

Ron Ross's first sighting of the 11-year-old Gilzean was in the playground: "There were about 200 boys chasing after a tennis ball. I thought I could play a bit but he was doing things with that ball that I had never seen before. He was small and so was

I, but he was doing magical things with the ball and I was mesmerised. I thought, 'What was that?' It used to annoy me, years later, when people said he was only good with his head when he went to Dundee. He could do anything with the ball."

Despite his good genes, Alan nurtured his talent daily, improving his left foot by knocking a tennis ball against a gable wall. When he tired of that, he would work on other skills. In an interview with The People's Journal dated November 23, 1965, Mr Dawson, Gilzean's old school caretaker, remembers him heading the same tennis ball against the same wall. Paraphrasing Mr Dawson, the article claims that "playing for the primary classes ... he was the daddy of the forward line and eventually [went] to the school team which, in the four years he was in it, won the Napier Cup twice."

The Napier Cup final of 1952 against Alyth at Foxhall Park was particularly memorable. A team including Ron Ross and Alan Gilzean quickly built up a four-goal lead over their local rivals. After half-time, Coupar Angus secondary's seemingly inexorable march to victory continued after the interval when they added a fifth.

"Then it went 5-1," says Ron Ross, "and suddenly it was 5-2. Hold on, now it's 5-3, and now it's 5-4. Someone, I think it was Gilzean, put the message around that we just had to kick the ball out of the park after that. We were clinging on for the last 10 minutes, Alyth were swamping us and were just kicking the ball as far away from goal as we could manage. We hung on for the win but Mr Sturrock, the teacher who took the school team, wasn't impressed with our tactics. At assembly on Monday morning, he told us as much and said there wouldn't be a trophy presentation and there wouldn't be any celebrations to mark the win. Can you imagine if that happened today? The parents would be in uproar."

Clearly, it was a strong team. The People's Journal carries a photograph of a young Gilzean sitting on a chair on what looks like the school playing fields. Standing beside him is a friend and team-mate, Hamish Rodger. The caption reads: "They were in the same class; played together in first the school team and the City Boys' XI; eventually progressing to the Juniors together. Hamish had a spell as a senior with Forfar Athletic, but is back playing for Coupar Angus Juniors."

The article captures a snapshot of 1950s life in the town, a sense of innocence pervading every sentence. It continues with more of Mr Dawson's recollections. "Asked if he ever had to check Alan for misbehaving in the playground he chuckled and said that if he ever saw Alan and his chums getting too high-spirited he just told them that they would land in the penalty spot – that being the headmaster's study. 'That was enough, they always simmered down then.' "

In 1950s Scotland, children sat the qualifying exam at 10 years of age to determine where they took up secondary education. Since Coupar Angus' primary and secondary schools were housed in the same building it made sense that Alan would merely shuffle along a few classrooms to begin the next stage of his schooling.

In the same article, teacher Eddie Sturrock recalls that Alan was football-daft but that "he was a good pupil and a sound wee laddie". Not that the young Gillie was a stranger to brushes with authority. He spent most of his childhood days in the company of Ian Mackenzie and, berries aside, it was fruit of a different hue that interested the pair. Alan and Ian would go "knuckling for apples" in the nearby orchards, always mindful of Sergeant Bob Mackenzie, Ian's father, and the strap on his baton. Sergeant Mackenzie spared no-one, least of all his son.

It was a Presbyterian upbringing according to Ian, but they were good times. "Aga, his cousin Scrag (Billy Forbes), myself and others went to local dances in Coupar, Blairgowrie and Alyth on Fridays and Saturdays, on occasions after a hostelry visit but not always, and on Sundays we went for walks," he says of their weekends.

They filled their week by swimming in the River Isla, golfing, playing tennis, cycling in the countryside around Balgersho and attending cricket practice. But above all was football; even when they took to the tennis courts it was to practise heading and keepie-uppies. "Our respective mothers, as were many at that time, were quite strong churchgoers and still had strong Presbyterian beliefs, hence the walks – possibly after church – and we were careful not to show any signs of our shoes having kicked a ball," adds Ian. "There was not that much to do in Coupar apart from the activities Alan and others enjoyed. Earlier years were dominated by scouting."

In those early years, Alan and Ian would form a lifelong friendship. They joined the scouts in 1949 aged 11. Alan would become patrol leader and enjoyed camping in the fields around Craighall in the beautiful Sidlaw hills overlooking Coupar Angus. Ron McDonald, his old scoutmaster, remembers a committed and popular young man who took to scouting with ease. "Alan was a great patrol leader. He won the Proctor Shield in 1955 for North East Perthshire for leading the Eagle Patrol at a jamboree at Craighall. He would have been judged on the standard of camping, food preparation and that sort of thing.

"The fact that he became a patrol leader means that he'd been selected by me because he had shown leadership skill. Many a scout never got to that stage because they didn't have the charisma. Alan had that, and when they played football they had one patrol against another, either in the scout hut, which was a very limited space, or outside. They all wanted to play in Alan's team because they all knew Alan was good."

McDonald recalls that Peenie – mindful of the scouting motto – would let setbacks bounce off him. "On one occasion, the scouts had to prepare food which the inspectors would taste and Alan decided he was going to prepare a trout in newspaper and cook it over the fire. So off he went to the river to wet the newspaper, but when he got to the river he realised he had forgotten the newspaper. He took some toilet paper and wrapped that around the trout and then dipped it in the river. The toilet paper was stuck to the fish but the inspectors didn't notice and ate it anyway."

Gillie did not have much luck with rivers in those days, Ron Ross recalls. "I was a member of Ardler scout group, but there were only eight of us. It was decided by our scout master that we would go on a weekend camp to a place called, would you believe, Tannadice, near Brechin, which was owned by Jock Neish, who was a well-known name in scouting circles. To bolster our numbers, two boys from Coupar Angus patrol came and joined us and that was Ian Mackenzie and Alan Gilzean. On the Saturday afternoon, it was Blackpool v Bolton in what became known as the Matthews Cup final. Stanley Matthews was coming near the end of his career and had not won anything. We got access to a radio in Colonel Neish's bungalow, I remember it especially because there were animal skins on the walls, and listened to the match … and that was the day Stanley Matthews won the cup.

"Later on we went walking along the river bank of the South Esk and we were larking about, swinging on trees and the like. Alan started to climb a tree but slipped on a branch and the next thing I knew he was in the river. Fortunately, we managed to fish him out, but he was a very sodden Alan for the rest of the day."

Ron McDonald knew that Gilzean had talent on the football pitch, but it was the little things like his unselfishness in possession and his dedication that impressed him most. Gillie would use the improvisational skills gleaned from the scouts to good effect to emulate his father's heading drill: "When he was in the scouts he would tie a rope to a beam in the scout hut; we had lots of very old sets of boxing gloves and he would take one of the gloves, tie it to the rope and attach it to the beam. He would jump up and head the glove and then when he had done that for a while he would shorten the rope and start again. Some of the other scouts would try to do it, but none of them would reach the height that he would. The wooden floor of the hut meant that he would get some spring because it had some give in it."

The highlight of his time in the scouts would come in 1953 when he attended the jamboree at Sandringham to mark the Coronation. Ian Mackenzie accompanied him on that trip and it was there that they met another scout destined for greater things: Roosevelt Brown, a member of a Bermudan scout troop. Brown, who later changed his name to Pauulu Roosevelt Osiris Nelson Brown Kamarakafego, campaigned for universal adult suffrage in his homeland and was an activist, a parliamentarian and a UN advisor in ecological and environmental engineering. He died in April 2007, and I wondered if Gillie had heard.

In the same year, Alan would make his debut for a newly formed football team. John Dawson, the school caretaker, suggested to Billy Forbes that some of the young lads in the town should club together and the Coupar Angus City Boys were established, with the help of Coupar Angus Juniors. "Mr Dawson was instrumental in getting the team going," recalls Norrie Currie, a team-mate of Gilzean's. "Those were the days when folk ran young teams. Nowadays that just doesn't happen anymore."

A measure of Alan's standing among his team-mates is the revelation that he combined playing with the role of secretary. He was young for a football administrator at 15, but if signing players was part of his remit then he knew what he was about. It was not long before the City Boys were sweeping all before them. One report in the Blairgowrie Advertiser from 1954 hinted at what was to come.

"An entertaining game was seen at Foxhall Park last night when a team of Coupar youths beat Scone City Boys by 5 goals to 1. Outstanding in the home side were Rodgers (left-back), Mackenzie (left-half), Gilzean (inside-left), Forbes (centre). First-half goals were scored by Whytock (2), and Forbes, Gilzean and Bannerman counting [sic] in the second period [...] In the opinion of many of the spectators Coupar Juniors should not lose sight of these local lads' talents."

Two years after their formation, the City Boys won the Perthshire Cup on the South Inch in Perth, defeating Errol 5-2 despite trailing 2-0 at half-time and playing into a gale in the second half. Gilzean scored two and Billy Forbes hit a hat-trick.

By now, Gillie was attracting the attention of scouts from senior clubs. He had two offers on the table by the time he played in a cup game at Easter Road against Edinburgh Thistle and was spotted by a Dundee scout. In a four-part interview with the Sporting Post in July 1964, Gilzean recalled that day. "I didn't score any. And my team, Coupar Angus Boys' Club, took a 6-0 tanking. It was a Scottish Juvenile Cup game at Easter Road against Edinburgh Thistle, for whom Johnny McLeod of Hibs and Arsenal was outside-right. They were much too good for us. But Dundee's East of Scotland scout seemed satisfied I'd make the senior grade. A week later Willie Thornton sent for me. I signed for Dundee in January 1956."

"Easter Road was like playing on Broughty beach that day, there was that much sand on it," remembers Norrie Currie.

Gilzean wasn't the only one who impressed. During that cup tie against Edinburgh Thistle, McLeod had given Coupar Angus Boys a torrid time. He had been wearing a pair of boots that were the same as the pair Alan had been wearing. Ian Mackenzie recalls: "The laddie McLeod had this pair of kangaroo skin boots and Alan had the same pair, but they were too small for him so he gave them to me. But when I tried them on they didn't fit me either. I found them years later in my loft. They had rotten away completely." The story reveals an inherent altruism in Alan that would not always be apparent to those who didn't know him. There were others. Years later, at Dundee, he would bring old leather footballs back from Dens Park and kick them on to The Common so that there were always plenty for the boys to play with, or spend several hours chatting to kids and signing autographs at Dundee Junior Supporters' club nights.

His performances for the City Boys – and those of others – were attracting attention further afield. Billy Forbes, Gillie's cousin, signed for neighbouring Alyth United, although he would play most of his career with Coupar Angus; Norrie Currie would join him in the same Coupar Angus first team and had trials for Brechin City and Forfar, while Ian Mackenzie would eventually find himself in Northern Ireland, where National Service with the RAF had taken him, featuring for Distillery.

Ron Ross says that these were heady days in the football history of Strathmore: "Billy Forbes was every bit as good a prospect as Alan, he was quicker. He did his National Service with the Black Watch at Queen's Barracks in Perth. Jim Baxter was with the Black Watch too, and they played in the same football team. He had trials with a few senior clubs but he ended up playing Juniors.

"It was a good time for Strathmore. Not only were there people like Alan Gilzean and Billy Forbes but also the former Rangers goalkeeper George Niven. Gordon Laing was another and, while he played football for Coupar Angus Juniors, his name is significant because he was third bat for Perthshire and Scotland. You would regularly see his name in the paper after he'd recorded another century."

The region was famous for many other footballing families. There were the Gray brothers, Davie and Tommy, who played for Rangers and Dundee respectively; the Brodies, of whom Eric played for Forfar, Dundee United and Shrewsbury Town, and the Kemps, Bannermans and Martins. There was something particularly special about Gilzean, though, and of all his pals he was garnering the most significant attention. Years later, he would tell the Sporting Post: "I did not play trials for any other side than Dundee, but before they booked me on a provisional form in January 1956, I had signing offers from Hibs and Cowdenbeath."

The discovery that Gillie turned down Hibernian comes as something of a surprise. As a boy he was so impressed with Hibs' Famous Five forward line that he decided this was the team he wanted to support, despite living a 100-mile round trip away from Easter Road. The Famous Five were one of the first phenomena in Scottish football. An Edinburgh Evening News supplement entitled Glory Days and published in 1990 described them thus: "April 21, 1949, was a red letter day for Scottish Football [...] the Famous Five were born. Gordon Smith, Bobby Johnstone, Lawrie Reilly, Eddie Turnbull and Willie Ormond – names destined to be memorised by all Scottish football fans because of their skill and artistry, not to mention their superb goalscoring achievements, played together in that formation for the first time. All five forwards reached 100 goals for Hibs in their careers."

The young Gillie would have been 11 when the Famous Five made their first steps as a forward line and was soon so enamoured with them – Turnbull was a particular favourite – that he persuaded several friends to take the train to Dens Park to watch Hibernian play Dundee. The date was March 7, 1952 and Ron Ross organised the trip. "Billy Forbes, Alan Gilzean, Tommy Galloway, Dave McFarlane, Roy Whytock and myself all went to Dens as far as I can recall, but there were possibly more, on the Blairgowrie Express to Downfield. From there we took the tramcar, which said Moncur Crescent on the front, to Dens. Along with 30,000 others we saw Bobby Flavell and Billy Steel score to give Dundee a 2-0 victory. The reason for the outing was that Alan was a fervent Hibs fan and wanted to see the Famous Five in action."

The decision to join Dundee thus seems puzzling, but was made with pragmatic considerations in mind as Gilzean told Jim Hendry in his book, Dundee Greats: "I had the chance to sign for about four clubs [...] but my father was very keen on Dundee and although I was not a Dundee supporter he reckoned I would not have problems like having to worry about digs." Later in the same book Gillie recalls being taken to watch Dundee as a boy. Dundee in the 1950s were one of the most exciting teams in Scotland and won two League Cups during the decade under manager George Anderson. While they may not have boasted the same number of headline names as Hibernian, they did possess the most expensive player in Scottish football.

"I saw Billy Steel play and he was fantastic," said Gilzean. "My dad used to take me to Dens – he divided his loyalties between Dundee and St Johnstone, supporting both, but obviously Dundee in the Steel era – there was a certain charisma about the whole club then. George Anderson was a charismatic figure; the bowler hat, the bow tie, the cigar and the walking cane. Then with Billy Steel in the team, he was the icing on the cake. Although I saw Dundee quite a lot, if anything, I was probably attracted more to Hibs, their forward line, the Famous Five [...] I was drawn to them for what real reason I have no idea. Nobody can say as a kid why they favour a certain team, but that was it and I was a kind of a Hibs supporter, and when I got the chance to go senior it was really between Dundee or Hibs."

It wasn't just football or Hibs that captured Alan's imagination, though. Cricket was another great passion. He told the Sporting Post in February 1962, five years after making his debut for Dundee: "Apart from this football life, I think I would have liked to become a first-class cricketer."

A report in the Blairgowrie Advertiser from 2007, recalling a series of matches in which Gilzean played 50 years earlier, confirms that he was adroit with the bat. "Gillie was obviously good at most ball sports [...] he could really crack a ball," reads the article. "Coupar played NCR from Dundee at Larghan Park on July 7, 1957 and an A. Kinninmonth is listed, so I suspect that he was Alex Kinninmonth, who also played for Dundee FC [...] Although Coupar lost that day, Gilzean was 33 not out [...] On Wednesday, July 10, Alan Gilzean was again among the runs when he scored 40 undefeated against a strong Blairgowrie side."

In summer, Alan would bring a side made up from his Dundee team-mates across to play his home town. One report explains that a match between the two sides was organised to raise money for charity. "Dundee footballers provided a bright evening's entertainment at Coupar Angus last night when they took part in a cricket match which raised £6 8s 9d for the Toc H old folks fund. Not surprisingly county cricketer Alan Cousin led with a breezy knock of 44 which included two 6s and four 4s. And Alex Stuart showed he was no newcomer to the game with a bright 23."

Gilzean is not noted in the report but he is listed in the scoreboard. His dismissal for one could perhaps be put down to the excitement of facing his hometown club.

Ian Mackenzie says he was a more than useful golfer too. One photograph, taken at Hazlehead Golf Course when Alan was 21 or 22, shows him sitting on the tee box, head turned and holding his ball to the camera with a grin on his face. For Ian Mackenzie, the picture holds fond memories of their first match at Alyth.

"We shared my dad's hickory shafts and a motorbike to get there. Alan could play a reasonable game of golf. Probably before he lost the ball. His first game would have been at neighbouring Alyth. He scored 100 and me 102," he says.

Alan left school and went to work as a despatch clerk with Coates and Company, a carpet manufacturers in Perth. He continued to live at home and would commute by bus. He found the work boring but learned shorthand and how to use a typewriter. Ron Ross says that he would meet Gillie regularly coming off the bus as he was getting on and they would exchange hellos, and that he would see him at one of three town hall dances every Friday night. "I think that's where he met Irene," says Ron as we continue our walk through the streets of Coupar Angus and past the town hall. Irene Todd, who lived at 31 Hill Gardens in Coupar Angus, was Gilzean's childhood girlfriend and later his wife. Asked, in 1963, how she met Alan in an interview with The Sporting Post, she said: "I've really known him all my life – I used to stay around the corner from him, but he was just one of the boys – I thought nothing about him until I met him at a dance a few years ago and we became friends."

Ron and I arrive at Willie Gilzean's former paint shop, an impressive building with intricate plasterwork. The windows are screened by modern blinds, but it seems deserted otherwise. "You could see the sign above the door as you approached from the entry at Brodies Yard," says Ron Ross. "It barely looks as if it's used now."

Having been signed for Dundee by manager Willie Thornton after impressing in a trial at the start of 1956, Gillie was immediately shipped off to play in the club's Junior team, Dundee Violet. His stay was shortlived. "I played one game for them," he would later recall. "Then, anxious to be with my pals in Coupar Angus Juniors, I asked to be transferred to my home club."

"I was told they tried to farm him out to Millwall," says Norrie Currie, but instead, "he signed a Junior form before he went senior" and moved to Coupar Angus. He spent the 1956-57 season at his hometown club, where the highlight was his performance in the Arbroath and District Cup final against Arbroath Vics at Strathmore Park in Forfar. Gilzean scored four as Coupar Angus won 5-2.

His efforts had not gone unnoticed at Dens Park. Thornton was in the final stages of building a team by sweeping up the best young talents in the Junior game. The process had begun in earnest in early 1955 when, following three successive defeats, there were urgent calls for an injection of new blood. The club had lost numerous players to National Service in Ian Stables, Jackie Stewart, Dave Sneddon and George Carmichael, and within 12 months Thornton had raided the Juniors for Alan Cousin (Alloa YM), George O'Hara (Shettleston), George McGeachie (Falkirk High), Bobby Cox (Osborne), and Doug Alexander (Westrigg Bluebell). They would be the first tranche of signings who would become known as Thornton's Babes. Cousin, McGeachie and Cox would all contribute when Dundee won the league in 1962. Cox and Cousin were key members of the team. Contained within the next wave of cherub-faced arrivals were other integral members of a side that would reach the European Cup semi-final.

This fresh batch included a gangly youth from Coupar Angus who would make it all happen. Gillie had signed a provisional form with Dundee in January 1956, but it would be another year and a half before the call into the first-team squad would come from Thornton, and a further two years before he made his debut. Gilzean, meanwhile, soon received another call-up, this time from Her Majesty's Government and the Ministry of Defence. In 1957, he was given notification that he would have to perform National Service, which he would spend working as a clerk. The shorthand and typing skills learned at Coates and Company came in useful in the Royal Army Service Corps at Farnborough. He would eventually rise to corporal.

Chroniclers of Dundee's history claim that after making his debut for Dundee, a 4-1 defeat to Motherwell in the League Cup in August 1959, Gilzean had to dash back to Aldershot at the final whistle. In an interview with the Sporting Post, Gilzean says that he was based in Farnborough, yet most accounts claim he was posted to Aldershot, four miles away. In later interviews, he says Aldershot. The proximity of the two suggests they were perceived by Gillie as one and the same.

Returning south was never a happy time. Norrie Currie recalls that Gilzean's heart would sink as his leave neared its end. "That old perforated eardrum is starting to play up again, Norrie," he would tell his old Coupar Angus team-mate, only partly in jest. Ian Mackenzie remembers once pretending to be Gillie's father and phoning his commanding officer to say that Alan would be late back because he was sick.

This seems to have been at odds with other men from his generation. Ron McDonald, his old scoutmaster, claimed National Service was "what made you. Here you were in this country town and suddenly you had the opportunity to go travelling." It was not welcome news for Gilzean, however, and Willie Thornton, speaking many years later, says he had to convince his young player that it was for the best.

"He came to see me one day and he was pretty upset. He was only 18 at the time, and he had his call-up papers for the army in his hand. He told me he didn't fancy the idea too much and asked me what he should do. I pointed out to Gillie that he would be in uniform for a mere two years, and that he probably wouldn't spend that time avoiding flying bullets. I then told him I had had six years of the army – during which time I was mostly ducking. He got the message and off he went. He was posted to the south of England and I arranged for him to have a spell with Brighton. Alan came back from National Service a mature character – and he didn't half reflect it in his football. He went from strength to strength from then on."

Like many footballers who were called up for National Service, Gilzean played for his unit side, which included Ron Yeats, the Dundee United and Liverpool centre-half. The rivalry between Dundee and Dundee United meant that banter between Gilzean and Yeats was rarely in short supply. Later, prior to a derby when Gilzean knew he was due to start and thus face Yeats, he wagered a bet with the United defender that Dundee would win a league match against their newly-promoted city rivals. United won 3-1 and Gillie lost half his army pay. For the return game at Dens Park, Yeats suggested that they go double or quits and this time Dundee won 3-0.

Yeats was not the only famous footballer sharing Gillie's barracks. Also present was Jackie Plenderleith, the then Hibernian centre-half who would later go on to play for Manchester City and Queen of the South, and Alex Young, who starred in Everton's First Division title success in 1963.

Alan was also playing for a local football team, Aldershot, but did not make a single first-team appearance. It proved something of a missed opportunity for the

Division Three (South) club, as the club historian pointed out in the match programme for the last game of the 2008/2009 season against Chester City:

*His then Scottish club Dundee arranged for him to be loaned to us and on the
payroll at £5 a week. At the time we were struggling to ensure we finished in
the top half of the old Third Division (South) which was about to be sliced
in two with the formation of Division Four. Sadly we failed to make the cut.
Possibly because it was late on in the season, Gilzean did not get a game in the
first team. The following season [...] Gilzean was still locally based and in
fact turned out for the Shots – alas in the reserves and more often as not in the
A team in the Hampshire League. At this distance and with hindsight it would
be easy to say he could have made a difference, but a chance in the first team
would surely not have been a waste of time. He went back to Dundee, helped
them to win the Scottish League and propelled them into the European Cup.*

Pat Liney, the goalkeeper in Dundee's league-winning team in 1962, remembers that things might have been different for Aldershot had Gilzean, who was disillusioned at his inability to break into the Dundee first team, got his wish for a
transfer from Dens Park at the end of the 1958-59 season: "He came to me one
day after training and said he wanted to get away because he would get a game with
Aldershot. We were in the reserves and we were just finding our feet, but you could
see that Alan had something about him."

But Gilzean stayed where he was. Pat Liney wasn't the only one who could see
that Alan did indeed have "something about him", and while Gillie might have imagined that he needed to leave Dundee to further his career, he wouldn't have to wait
much longer for his big break.

The next time Ron Ross saw Gillie on the bus from Coupar Angus to Dundee
they discussed their careers and prospects for the future. Ron had just taken a job
with DC Thomson, the newspaper conglomerate, while Alan had, by now, broken
into the first team at Dens Park.

"He was on his way to play for Dundee against Ayr United and I was going to
watch. He told me he was earning £25 at Dundee. Thinking back, the pay differen-
tial between now and then was amazing. I was on £18 as a compositor."

And while the wages earned by both men were comparable, their lives were not.
Gillie was now a full-time professional footballer playing in front of thousands every
week. His simple, pastoral life was fast becoming a thing of the past.

3

Every Picture Tells a Story

On a wall in a well-lit corridor, deep in the inner sanctum of Dens Park, hangs a picture. The casual observer might walk past it, situated as it is among a host of other old photographs and caricatures of former players, like the great wing-half Doug Cowie or the dashing inside-forward Billy Steel. But this picture might be the leitmotif of a life story, that of the footballer who never wanted the limelight; one who shunned it, even. Alan Gilzean once said that "when I've finished playing, that's it. I couldn't stand the aggravation of being a manager, having fans, directors, press, everyone after you. No thanks". Shortly after retiring from full-time football, he took over as manager of Stevenage Athletic, but for now let us be unequivocal: this picture tells, in full monochromatic detail, the story of Alan Gilzean.

It is Saturday April 28, 1962. The players of Dundee Football Club are gathered on the balcony of the city chambers, the occasion is the presentation of the new league champions of Scotland to an adoring public. There's Alec Hamilton in the foreground, his blond hair freshly crew-cut and a boyish smile spread over his face. Ian Ure, the giant centre-half, also has a typical 1950s haircut and Cheshire Cat grin. Hugh Robertson has a bottle of champagne in his right hand. Bob Shankly is right at the front, taking the acclaim of the crowd below. He is flanked by his captain, Bobby Cox, who appears to be falling backwards, and Pat Liney; one figure, it might even be Gilzean, is obscured by Shankly's outstretched right hand. Indiscernible figures lurk in the background; one of them might just as easily be Gillie.

He was never one to milk the applause or bask in the limelight. Look at other photographs from the time and Gillie is nearly always in the background, smiling nervously. Perhaps he found himself in the back row because he was taller than his team-mates, but at 5ft 10in he was hardly a giant. More probably, his extra few inches made it easier for him to hang in the background until the snapper made it easy for him by telling him to bunch up beside Ian Ure or Bob Seith.

Today, former Tottenham colleagues have lost touch with Gilzean. Ask them about him and their first words, invariably, will be: "Where is he?" At one time, he was a regular attendee at Dundee reunions, but the last anyone saw him was at Bert Slater's funeral in 2006 and he was a no-show the night he was inducted in the club's hall of fame in February 2009. His son Ian picked up the award and explained that his father was ill. It fuelled the intrigue about Gilzean. While his decision to stay in the shadows has baffled some of his former team-mates, it has not surprised others who talk of a fiercely private man who preferred others to take the acclaim.

Kenny Cameron, who played in the same forward line, remembers Gilzean's reaction after his seven-goal haul against Queen of the South in 1962 with misty-eyed amazement. "We were in the dressing room after the game and he was just sitting there as if nothing had happened. Players were congratulating him and he just shrugged his shoulders and said, 'That's just part of the game.'"

Hugh Robertson says that was typical. "He was very modest. If it had been Hammy, he would gone through every goal a hundred times. When we played Anderlecht in the European Cup, Kenneth Wolstenholme, the commentator, was staying in our hotel and one morning at breakfast he asked Hammy, 'How do you rate as a player?' Hammy replied, 'I'm the best in the world.' And the thing is, at that time he probably was. But so was Gillie."

There is another explanation why Gilzean refused to take any credit on that day against Queen of the South. In an insightful, though heavily ghosted, four-part interview with the Sporting Post in 1964, he says he was embarrassed. The interview is interesting because it is one of the rare times he spoke to the press, even though it is written up by the reporter. The interviews represent approximately 8,000 words that he was happy to sanction as an account of his time at Dundee.

"The most goals I've ever scored in one game was seven," he says. "And I didn't feel too happy when it was all over. We were playing Queen of the South and were leading 3-0 when George Farm dived at my feet to save. His head hit my knee. What a smack! George lay still – out cold. He was carried off on a stretcher and taken to the infirmary. After the game, I went to the [hospital] to see George […] As soon as I got to his bedside, George said, 'I've heard the score, Alan. How many did you get?' It was just about my most embarrassing moment ever to tell him – seven."

Therein lay the difference between someone like Gilzean and Hamilton, notes

Pat Liney, the goalkeeper from that title-winning team. One thrust himself into the spotlight, the other spurned it. Former colleagues recall that when Hamilton retired he went to South Africa, took a job playing piano in a nightclub and one evening continued tinkling for so long that he was eventually wheeled out of the club, on to a removal van and driven off. Gilzean disappeared too, but unlike Hamilton, who eventually returned to Dundee, his whereabouts were less well-documented.

These were the days when the Scotland national team was often picked by a coterie of selectors and a handful of esoteric journalists and sometimes it quite literally took extraordinary behaviour by those players playing outside of the Old Firm to get noticed by the selectors. "Hammy played for a provincial club and he got quite a few caps, but he was also an extrovert," recalls Liney. "The press loved guys like Hammy because they gave them stories. There was a shyness or inhibition about Alan. He would rather push someone like Hammy to the front and then follow him. He wisnae a patter man, he did it on the field."

Hamilton was a character who could relieve the tension inside the dressing room with his light-hearted asides and gallus cheek. One story has it that during a match against Rangers at Dens Park, the visiting team's inside forward, Ralph Brand, went up for a header and came off second-best. Dazed and nursing a headache, the shout went out from the dugout for him to move out to the left wing until he recovered. "The poor laddie was concussed," recalls Alan Cousin. "When he got over to the left wing, Alex Hamilton was standing waiting on him and Brand said, 'I know your face, where am I?' and Hammy replied, 'You're at Dens Park, you're up against the best full-back in Britain and you're no' getting a kick of the ball.' "

Bobby Seith, another from that Dundee side of the early 60s, sheds some light on why Gilzean was so often the errant party in photographs of the day: "He had a quiet confidence and did his talking on the field. Gillie, Bob Seith and Bobby Wishart would hardly be seen in team photos," says Seith. "Craig Brown, George Ryden and Alec Hamilton always seemed to get to the front. On one occasion Bobby Wishart said to me, 'Let them all get settled and we'll run to the front,' but we couldn't get there before the photograph was taken. Over and above that, it was always the same guys at the front – usually the ones who didn't get many games!"

Few people fit black and white descriptions, however. Gillie was introspective at times, an extrovert at others. The pitch was his stage and when the production had ended that was it; he was still Alan Gilzean fae Coupar Angus.

But we are getting ahead of ourselves. Let us return to that title-winning team.

There was a wonderful sense of camaraderie among the players of the Dundee side that won the league in 1962, the only time the club has done so. Gordon Smith,

Bob Seith and Bobby Wishart were the elder statesmen. Alan Cousin, Craig Brown and George McGeachie were teachers, but merely the cream of a group of intelligent men who would spend coach and train trips working on crosswords or reading newspapers. Ian Ure had attended Ayr Academy, not the usual breeding ground for career footballers, and gave up rugby to play for Dundee. Robertson and Hamilton were streetwise and quick-witted; Gilzean enjoyed their company and they enjoyed his.

"He was witty, he had some good one-liners," recalls Brown. "A lot of players are like that. He reminded me of Kenny Dalglish, a dry humour that's for sure. He could hold a conversation with a smile and he could make you smile."

One of Gilzean's favourite gags at Dundee was ribbing the combustible Ure. "At Dens, we had a communal bath," continues Brown. "Everyone bathed together and it made for great banter. We would play this game: the Scottish international good-looking team versus the Scottish international ugly team. Gilzean would be sitting there holding court in the bath and he would always read out the team: it would include players like Davie Provan of Rangers and when he got to centre-half he would say, 'Centre-half … Ian Ure … Dundee … captain.' Then he would run through the good-looking team and when he got to centre-forward he would say, 'Centre-forward … Alan Gilzean … Dundee … captain.' "

Bobby Wishart remembers that "Hammy's gang of Robertson, Ure and Gillie were always up to something. He always liked to wind the other lads up, especially Bobby Cox, about how many caps he had won".

Cox was never picked for Scotland, despite many team-mates suggesting he was Hamilton's superior as a defender. Eric Caldow, the Rangers left-back, had a monopoly on the position. Gilzean would earn just five caps at Dens Park and cited his international career as one of his main considerations when he left in 1964.

Ian Ure is particularly scathing of the international set-up during the 1960s and says that the bias towards Rangers and Celtic players was a major reason why he and others did not win more caps. In 2002, he told the Evening Times: "My career with the national team ended when I moved to England in 1963. It was a shame because, after a couple of seasons down south, I was a much better all-round player […] Basically, the Scotland team was picked by the press back then. John McKenzie of The Express, Malky Munro of the Evening Citizen and Evening Times, and Rex Kingsley of the Sunday Mail were the selectors."

Dundee's 5-1 win over Rangers from the championship-winning season is a case in point. In the aftermath of Gilzean's epic performance at Ibrox on that foggy November afternoon in 1961, there was a growing clamour for him to receive a call-up for Scotland's World Cup qualifying play-off with Czechoslovakia at the end of that month. Cyril Horne, writing in The Glasgow Herald, put forward his candidacy to start the match: "Not only did Gilzean, who has been an under-23 cap, score four times but he was within inches of scoring four more, and in every aspect of forward play was the superior of Brand, Rangers' inside-left," wrote Horne. "Furthermore the collapse of Rangers, which was not surprising to those who have watched the recent deterioration of their play in recent weeks, seems to suggest that some of their players are no longer in the form or mood which makes internationalists."

Yet when the Scotland side took on their Czech counterparts just over a fortnight later, there was no place for Gilzean and a starting spot for Brand and Eric Caldow and Jim Baxter, his Rangers team-mates. Dundee, top of the league, were represented by Ure, Hamilton and Hugh Robertson, the left-winger. Ure and Hamilton had played before but Robertson's inclusion was necessitated though injury.

"I played just one game for Scotland and that was because Davie Wilson of Rangers was injured," says Robertson. "When Davie Wilson came back from injury I was out. There were three or four left wingers who were good enough to play for Scotland at that time but they never got a look-in."

The Old Firm bias particularly irked Ure, who won just 11 caps yet was widely acclaimed as the best centre-half in the country. When I meet him on a sunny June day at a hotel opposite Kilmarnock's Rugby Park stadium, he is as indignant as he might have been had the snub occurred that week.

The hotel is a monument to football's corporate behemoth, a sterile, modern building with an interior of smoked glass, pine floors and posters of Kilmarnock players. At the steps leading to the mezzanine cafe, a few punters are queueing for tickets, whether for a cabaret night or the football team, I'm not sure. Someone I imagine might be Ian emerges from the toilets opposite me. He's tall and bespectacled, his hair balding in the middle and long at the sides. When our eyes meet there is a brief flicker of recognition and he mouths 'James' at the same time as I mouth 'Ian'.

Before we start the interview, I repeat the sales pitch that is fast becoming a mantra. Gillie ... rightful place ... SFA Hall of Fame. But if I had my fears that Ian would prove a difficult interviewee given his reputation for being an uncompromising and aggressive footballer, I need not have worried. Within seconds he is off. He rails against the demise of Scottish football, the standard of play at Kilmarnock and schools football.

"There was a dispute with the government over pay and, when it ended, the money the teachers were being paid for taking kids on a Saturday was scrapped. It ruined football. You would go to the old Ayr Racecourse on a Saturday morning and it would be black with schoolkids, now you're lucky if you see a single match there.

The only games that are played between schools now is when one teacher phones up another and they challenge each other to a match. That happens about once a year. My wife's a teacher and I speak to colleagues of hers all the time who would love to take a football team, but they won't do it for nothing. Why should they give up a third of their time off and not get paid for it?

"Now all the best kids come to clubs like this one and there is no provision for the ones who might not get picked up at a young age. I come here some Saturdays and I can't believe how poor the standard is. It's dreadful. People say to me, 'Ah but the players are much fitter than in your day,' and I think to myself, 'If I couldn't play in that I would cry.' You have 15 players bunched around the ball, they're heading it into the air between each other and not one of them will get it down and try a pass or spread out. It's like schoolboy football."

It wasn't like this in Gillie's day, but despite his scoring record and sure touch with head and feet, he still only won 22 caps. Was there a deficiency in his make-up? Ure has his own theories. "The most complete player I ever played with or against was Dave Mackay. You ask Gillie, if you see him, who his favourite player was. I bet he says Mackay." I make a mental note to do just that. "It was an outrage that he didn't win more caps for Scotland but he played left-half and who played left-half for Scotland? James Baxter. And who did James Baxter play for? Rangers. In those days, Scotland should have lined up with Baxter at inside-left and Mackay at left-half.

"I hated playing with Baxter. Don't get me wrong, he was a good player, but he would go on these runs up the park and then he'd lose the ball, and suddenly there would be guys coming at you from all directions. You'd look 40 yards upfield and there would be Baxter lying flat out on his arse.

"The bias against provincial clubs was disgusting. The selectors were old buffers in blazers, the sort who would spend international trips drinking at the bar. Then on the odd time they would come to watch you and you had an average game you wouldn't get into the squad. A Rangers or Celtic player would play three or four good games and suddenly everyone would be touting them for a place in the Scotland team. I believed that young players should have to serve an apprenticeship before they won a cap."

Ian invites me back to his house for a coffee. It's a detached art deco-type building, a stone's throw from Rugby Park. His cat Puss Puss eyes me suspiciously. "I miss the game, it was wonderful, but I do wish I had made more money from it. Everyone had a rough idea what everyone else was on, but it wasn't a fortune. We were purely exploited in those days. One day I sat down and I worked out my wages over the years and I added a bit on for bonuses. Do you know I worked out that John Terry earns in three days what it took me 16 years to earn as a player? I earned £65,000 over my career.

"I was one of the 10 best-paid players in the whole of Britain when I signed for Manchester United in 1972 and I was on £120 a week. Don't get me wrong, in those days we lived well but we were maybe only three times better off than your average tradesman. We had a decent standard of living, you could buy a decent car for under £1,000 and a house for £5,000 or £6,000. Do you know there is a Junior player at Irvine Meadow, just down the road, who earns £2,000 a week and has a hospitality car with his name on it?

"When I finished playing I trained at Jordanhill College between 1979 and1980 and got my social work qualifications. It was bloody hard going back to school after all those years. I went into the prisons and was at Barlinnie for 11 years and then was in Lowmoss until two years ago. I worked two years over my retirement and I would have stayed if they had wanted me, but the prison closed."

I wonder whether Ian has become disillusioned with the game, but he says he has not and I believe him. His wife, Janet, wears his league winner's medal as a piece of jewellery around her neck and he opens a drawer to a treasure trove of his old football shirts – one is a swap, the shirt John Charles wore for the Italian League in a match against the Scottish League in 1961. By chance the previous night I had been looking at a website which sold vintage football jerseys. A signed shirt worn in a match by Andy Turner, a one-hit wonder who made just 21 appearances for Spurs at the start of the 1990s, was priced at £350. What price a John Charles original?

Or even a Dundee league winner's shirt? The club still put on reunion nights for the old players from that team but Gilzean has stopped going. "He was a funny guy. He and wee Hugh Robertson. He was always winding Shug up about his sayings. Hugh was from Auchinleck and Gillie used to wind him up about his accent. But he just seems to have disappeared, he hasn't been to the last few Dundee reunions and when we meet up all the players ask, 'Where's Gillie?'"

It is an illuminating conversation not just because of Ian's candour about his own career, but also his recollections of Gilzean the player.

"He could make a decision in the air, you would see him readjust and he would judge whether there was a direct header on goal or whether the chance was too diffi-cult and he would pinpoint it to someone running in for a shot and nod it down. He had a great left-foot shoot and he could strike the ball really precisely from distance. It surprised me when he came down to England that he did so well because I thought he was a bit soft for England. I used to think, 'How will he cope down here?' But he did. He was a thinking player. He had great wee flicks and was good with both feet."

I tell Ian that Gillie has never been back at White Hart Lane. "I've never been back to Manchester United or Arsenal. A young girl from Arsenal phoned me one day to ask if I would go along for the opening of the Emirates Stadium and I told her I would love to. When I asked if I would be able to claim expenses for return flights to London and an overnight stay in a hotel she said, 'Oh, I'll have to get back to you on that Mr Ure.' A few days later Arsenal phoned back to say that the club would not be paying expenses. I told them to shove their invite up their arses. It wasn't the money, it was the principle – they are paying guys thousands of pounds a week and all it would have taken was two or three thousand for flights and accommodation for former players. George Eastham lives in South Africa and they invited him too. He didn't turn up either. I could well afford the money but I thought, why should I? I would have been out three or four hundred quid by the time I'd had a drink with the boys afterwards.

"Arsenal once had an old-fashioned Corinthian attitude. You weren't just a lump of meat. The board had elevated positions in society, city of London types, wealthy men, but wealthy men with morals. Now it's a corporation. If that had been the old board they would have said, 'We will pay all the expenses.' "

Before I leave Ian, Janet, Puss Puss and the John Charles vintage football shirt behind, he tells me a final story about Alan. "Something came back to me when I was in the shower this morning. I went up to stay in Alan's house overnight in Coupar Angus. The next morning I got up and it was dark outside. It was a winter's morning and I went downstairs and opened the curtains and there was this great big stag in his garden. They used to come down off the hills and eat the kale, cabbage and brussels sprouts growing in the gardens. That image comes back to me quite a lot."

Many months after my meeting with Ian, I discover that the long-sleeved No.9 jersey which Gilzean wore for Tottenham's 1967 FA Cup final win over Chelsea was sold at auction in May 2009 for over £6,000. He had simply given it away to a relative of a boy who worked at White Hart Lane.

I meet Pat Liney, the goalkeeper in Dundee's title-winning team, on a drizzly summer's day in the car park of a sprawling Tesco, a few hundred yards, as the seagull flies, from where the Discovery, the boat Captain Scott sailed to the South Pole, is moored in perpetuity. Pat's a cheery wee character and he's all smiles. He's been waiting for a few minutes, but greets me as if he's just been reunited with an old friend. "Hi James, how are you? There was a Jaguar which drove past me about five minutes ago. The number plate was JJM 1 and I thought, 'Here he is now.' "

"Perhaps when the book sells its millionth copy."

During a phone call a few weeks earlier, I explained to Pat that the purpose of my book was to give Alan his rightful place in British football history and that I was trying to get him inducted into the Scottish Football Association's Hall of Fame. He is so enthusiastic about the idea that he has promised to show me around Dens Park when our interview finishes. But for now, over cups of tea and Kit Kats in the cafe inside, we talk football, Gillie and 1962.

Pat was one of the unsung heroes of Dundee's league-winning campaign. His penalty save in the penultimate match of the campaign, in the derby against Dundee United, ensured they entered the final game against St Johnstone requiring only a draw to secure the title. Pat smiles as he recalls Gilzean's feats in the air.

"The way he played, he was a natural. I hated playing against him in practice, because if a ball came into the area you knew he was getting it. Not even Gordon Banks, who was a world-class keeper, could stop him in the air. There is a famous photograph of Banks, his arm fully outstretched attempting to punch the ball, against Scotland in 1964 and Gilzean is above him, nodding in the only goal. In the end I just used to try to catch the header and forgot about going for the cross."

Today, Pat fits car radiators. I'm struck by the inequality between a footballer's life today and the era of these men. It would be quite easy to give up on life, hit the bottle and slip blissfully out of the public's glare.

Pat, who finished his career in England with Bradford City before becoming a sales rep, carried on playing sport until well into later life. He turned his hand to rugby when his son took it up, just to keep active. "I played football on a Sunday until I was 60, I used to play in the works team. I would travel from Bradford to Manchester, 40 miles over the Pennines just to get a game. When I came back to Dundee I played rugby for Blairgowrie until I was 47. My son was a good player, he had played for the county in England and we helped form the team in Blairgowrie. I used to give him a lift to training and games and would sit in the car and watch. One day they were short of players and asked if I would help out in the first team. I said yes, and that was me in the team from then on."

I suggest he was trying to fill a void. "You know, I've never thought about it like that. I was trying to fill a void in my life. It's not about proving to the world that you can still do it, but about proving it to yourself. Even now, the boys in work ask if I need a hand lifting a radiator and I tell them I can do it myself."

Pat used to see Alan at Dundee reunions but Gilzean doesn't attend them any more. "I heard he wasn't well," says Pat. "The last time I saw him was at Bert Slater's funeral and we all had a cup of tea. He said he wasn't drinking. I'd love to see him again. He was a bit like myself in that he came from a small community; you're not aware of the big city and suddenly you're getting thrown into the limelight. He could either have gone like Ronaldo or George Best, but he maybe retreated into his own wee world. He might feel, because of the circumstances in which he left here, the fans might hold it against him but they don't – they still love him here."

Dens Park still has the feel of an old football ground. The corridors are painted in red and blue halves and the carpet bears the club insignia. A montage at the entrance bears the faces of a bygone era. Few of those captured are modern-day heroes, save for Claudio Caniggia, the former Argentina and Roma striker who briefly illuminated Dens Park at the end of the 1990s and who was inducted into the club's hall of fame on the same night as Gillie in April 2009. This is a club which can't escape the ghosts of 1962. The walls are adorned with their portraits, each detailing the goal and appearance records of their subject. One long corridor contains row upon row of inquisitive eyes, some steely, others smiling but all possessing an ethereal quality. How many players since Dundee's glory days have had to make that walk past these ghosts following a humiliating defeat; how many are even aware of their legacy?

Inside one room, I remark that there are quite a lot of pictures of Charlie Cooke. "This is the Charlie Cooke lounge," says Pat. Cooke played 59 times for Dundee and scored 11 goals, and he has a lounge named after him. Gillie played 190 games and scored 169 goals – what's that about? "Ah, you've noticed," says Pat.

"He was a fucking hero to me and I played in the same team as him." Pat's words take me aback and not because of the profanity. How many players, from his era or this one, would admit their hero is a contemporary?

But then there were plenty of heroic feats. Gillie's career at Dundee started slowly, interrupted as it was by National Service. When he was finally given his debut by Willie Thornton in a League Cup game against Motherwell on August 22, 1959, it ended in a 4-1 defeat and a dash back to his barracks. By the time of his next appearance, against Rangers the following February, Dundee had a new manager. Thornton resigned a week after handing Gillie his debut because of his wife's ill health and took up the manager's position at Partick Thistle.

His replacement was the brusque, no-nonsense Bob Shankly, who had beaten his brother Bill, then manager of Huddersfield Town, to the job. Bob had impressed the Dundee board with his work at Third Lanark, who he had guided to the 1959 League Cup final (they lost 2-1 to Hearts) in the weeks prior to his unveiling at Dens Park. How things might have differed had Bill, whose application for the post arrived on the day Bob was appointed, and not his brother taken the reins is a matter for conjecture. But it is sufficient to say that Bob and Dundee were to prove a very good fit.

During the transitional phase of Shankly's early reign, Gilzean was undergoing a fairly hectic schedule, travelling north from Aldershot on Thursdays, training with the first team on Fridays, playing with the reserves on Saturdays and returning south on Sundays. Nevertheless, these were exciting times; Thornton's groundwork was beginning to bear fruit and Dundee had built a formidable group of players.

Hugh Robertson, the left winger in that great side, recalls looking around the reserve team and first XI at the time and thinking they were destined for greater things, a hunch that was only realised fully during that 1961-62 season. "There was a real sense of excitement about the team at that time. I think Dundee were lucky in getting the young players they did: Alec Hamilton, George McGeachie, Ian Ure, Alan Gilzean, myself and Alan Cousin. There was a good blend of young talented players and older heads, people like Bobby Seith, Bobby Wishart and Gordon Smith, who were all tremendous players and had plenty of experience."

In his second match, Gilzean performed creditably in a 0-0 draw at Ibrox. His National Service was at an end and Gillie was back at Dundee – and back at 25 Strathmore Avenue. The return to normality had a stabilising effect on his performances. The following week, he scored his first senior goal for the club, against St Mirren. Fittingly, given the number of times he would score with his head, Gilzean's goal was a well-placed header, the opener in a 3-1 win.

Dundee's title challenge had long fizzled out by that stage, however, and Gilzean was powerless to prevent their exit from the Scottish Cup at the hands of Hibernian on Monday, February 29. A match that had been postponed seven times finally went ahead, and very soon the pitch was a quagmire. Hibs coped best and won 3-0.

From then until the end of the season, Gilzean served notice of his potential at a time when Dundee were crying out for a new striker. Norrie Price, in his book, Up Wi' The Bonnets, describes Gilzean's end-of-season form: "In late March, Bob Shankly returned from a scouting mission to find that the Dark Blues had trounced Hibs 6-3 at Dens Park. Andy Penman had scored three but Alan Gilzean had been a revelation in his new role at centre-forward. In 90 seconds, he thundered home Dundee's opener and generally impressed with his clever distribution and powerful shooting. The big Coupar Angus boy added another six goals in the remaining four games and an unbeaten seven-game run saw the Dark Blues finish fourth."

This was real evidence that Dundee were capable of putting together a title challenge. There had been significant changes in personnel during the preceding years as Thornton's policy of signing young talent had taken root and others were transferred for large sums or released. Notwithstanding the sale of influential performers like Bill Brown (Tottenham Hotspur) and Jimmy Gabriel (Everton) and the phasing out of old hands from the George Anderson era such as Dave Curlett and Albert Henderson,

Dundee had amassed a formidable squad as the 1960s hovered into view. Liney had been signed from Dalry Thistle in 1957, the same year future Scotland international Robertson joined from Junior side Auchinleck Talbot. Next to arrive was Ian Ure, a promising stand-off for Ayr Academy in schoolboy rugby who played in the same XV as Ian 'Mighty Mouse' McLauchlan, who would captain Scotland at the sport, and Mike Denness, who would do likewise for England at cricket.

The lanky centre-half would also represent his country, just three years after signing for Dundee from Ayr Albion in 1958. His rapid progress was the result of many hours spent working with a ball in the gym. Ure had been inspired by the skills of Real Madrid when he attended the epic European Cup final of 1960 in which the Spanish side beat Eintracht Frankfurt 7-3 at Hampden Park.

In January 1959, another youngster arrived, Andy Penman. The 15-year-old right-winger had been homesick at Everton and when he returned home Thornton moved quickly to sign him. Within a month he made his debut against Hearts to become the youngest player ever to represent Dundee, a record he still holds.

It was into this milieu that Gilzean arrived back from National Service: a young, vibrant group of players who enjoyed football and life in general. There was a growing anticipation that this was a team that could go places and at the start of the 1960-61 season, Shankly carried out a rigorous assessment of his squad and decided that Bobby Seith would be his only new arrival. The 29-year-old had captained Burnley on their way to the First Division title in England, but with a third of the season remaining had a falling-out with the club's chairman Bob Lord.

The League Cup, drawn in sections and played home and away until the knock-out stage, began very impressively as Dundee despatched Raith Rovers (5-0 and 3-0), Aberdeen (4-1 and 6-0) and Ayr United (2-1 and 3-0) to reach the quarter-finals. Twenty-three goals and six straight wins confirmed Dundee as one of the country's top sides, and Gilzean had been lethal, scoring six against Raith, five against Aberdeen and two against Ayr.

Previous Dundee teams had played similarly attractive football to Shankly's but now there was someone to finish off the good work, and Gilzean's statistics were staggering. In his first 18 senior games, spanning the end of the 1959-60 season and the start of the following campaign, Gilzean scored 24 goals. In the first eight matches of 1960-61 he found the net 16 times. He scored four hat-tricks in that run as defences struggled to cope with his aerial ability and powerful shooting with either foot.

"He was just a natural goalscorer. I was playing centre-forward at the time, but Gillie was our main goalscorer, and a good footballer too. He was good with flicks, good off either foot and absolutely superb in the air. He took some hard knocks in clashes with heads," recalls Alan Cousin, Gillie's strike partner as he was breaking into the team and the man who would make up the other half of Dundee's centre-forward partnership when the club won the league the following season.

His efforts had not gone unnoticed in England. The Daily Mirror reported on September 21 1960, under the banner headline "Arsenal will bid £65,000" that "George Swindin, manager of Arsenal, checked on the fitness of £40,000 buy Mel Charles yesterday morning then rushed north to make two bids. Targets of his trip are Alan Gilzean, 21, goal-getting Dundee centre-forward, and George Eastham, the young England inside forward whose dispute with Newcastle will soon be over."

Eastham had gone on strike at Newcastle over their refusal to grant him a transfer. He finally got his move to Arsenal in October 1960 after Newcastle caved in over his threat of legal action. His fight ultimately would spell the end of the retain and transfer system, which weighted player ownership wholly in favour of the clubs, and end the maximum wage. There would later be an echo of Eastham's actions in Gilzean's determination to leave Dundee, but it is intriguing to note that there was interest in his fledgling talents as early as 1960 and from Arsenal, of all teams.

The report continues: "Swindin has arranged to attend the Scottish League Cup semi-final between Dundee and Rangers tonight. He's ready to splash about £15,000 for Gilzean and £50,000 for Eastham [...] It will need a lot of Swindin's persuasion to make Dundee sell Gilzean. Manager Bob Shankly said last night: 'I am building a team not destroying one.'

"Gilzean, who has 14 [sic] goals this season for Dundee, set himself on the road to fame when he was only 15. He founded a team called Coupar Angus Juveniles [...] and made himself secretary, signing on the other players. He was spotted with them, signed by Dundee and later guested for Aldershot when serving with the RASC. Now he's back in Scotland and still has the same keenness he showed as a boy."

Arsenal did not follow up their interest. Gillie, playing out of position at left-half, spurned a chance to impress Swindin when he missed a penalty in the second leg of the 5-3 aggregate defeat to Rangers in the League Cup quarter-final. Despite his failure to shine in front of an English First Division manager, there was much to encourage him at Dundee, not least the start Shankly had made at Dens Park.

"Shankly was an honest man and he quickly gained the players' respect with his knowledge of the game," Gilzean once said. The respect was mutual, with Shankly admitting years later that: "Alan was one of the most decent professionals I ever met. His enthusiasm and vim in his work were a pleasure to see."

At Tottenham, Gillie saw similarities between his manager, Bill Nicholson, and Shankly. Kenny Ross notes in his book, Dundee: Champions of Scotland, that

Gilzean was intrigued by the fact that neither man was a particularly skilful player, but both demanded attractive football. "Shankly and Bill Nicholson were both hard workers, extremely honest and hard when they needed to be. Both had a drive to win things and do it if possible while playing flair football."

Gilzean knew all too well, as demonstrated when urging his young team-mates to kick the ball to touch in the Napier Cup final in 1952, that pragmatism as much as flair was the key to success on the football pitch.

What happened next in Dundee's season proved to him all the more that Shankly was the right man for the job. Five straight wins in September and October sent them top of the league, and Gilzean was rewarded with a call-up to the Scottish League representative side for a fixture against the League of Ireland, a match he played in alongside team-mate Penman.

But by the start of the next month Penman had broken an ankle and with Dundee lacking the right winger's pace and penetration, results took a slump. An attempt to replace him with Gordon Smith from Hearts was made, the second such attempt in a year. When he rejected the opportunity to link up again with Sammy Kean, his old coach from the Famous Five days at Hibs, and Dundee lost five on the spin, Shankly bought the Aberdeen inside-left Bobby Wishart for £3,500. It had an immediate impact. The 29-year-old scored twice in front of 22,000 supporters in a 3-0 victory over Dundee United in his first match and while Dundee remained in mid-table as they entered the new year, there was plenty to cheer in a 4-2 home win over Rangers, the league leaders. There was personal satisfaction for Gilzean, who scored twice in a performance which attracted the notice of the Scotland selectors and he was included in the Under-23 squad for the international match against England.

Much encouragement was drawn from the defeat of Rangers and there was plenty of optimism as Dundee went into their Scottish Cup second-round match against the same side and at the same venue, three days later. However, the would-be champions raced into a four-goal lead and won 5-1.

Wishart's arrival would have a significant impact on Gilzean and expedited the decline of stalwart Doug Cowie. The left-half had made over 300 appearances for the club but it was clear his time was nearing its end and when Wishart was drafted in at left-half as the season drew to a close it meant a return for Gillie, who had been filling in for the injured George McGeachie, at his favoured inside-left slot. Wishart's presence would mean more than just a positional change for Gilzean. He had won a league medal with Aberdeen in 1955 and, while he added an experienced voice in the dressing room to replace Cowie's, on a personal level he became something of a mentor to the 20-year-old Gilzean, forging a friendship that exists to this day.

"Bobby Wishart was a good talker off the pitch and he was a good talker on it, and if he had something to say you listened to him," Hugh Robertson recalled. "He probably did take Alan under his wing back then without him noticing it. But it was the same with Gordon Smith and Bobby Seith."

There was still time for Dundee to flirt with relegation before a hat-trick of home wins – in which Gilzean scored three times – helped them secure a 10th-place finish. It had been an extremely productive first full season in top-flight football for this relative greenhorn who just a season earlier had been playing sporadically for Aldershot's B team or his army unit and training one night a week with Dundee.

His 32 goals in 42 games in all competitions included four hat-tricks; the longest he went without scoring was three matches. This consistency was no accident: "I would often go back to Dens after lunch to practise ball control and try to improve my heading work," he recalled.

Hugh Robertson would join Gilzean to work on moves and says there was no question that it brought about an improvement. "Alan and I would play a lot of one-twos together. After training in the morning we used to go back to Dens Park and practise in the afternoon. There would be quite a few of us, Craig Brown, Gillie, Ian Ure, Alec Stuart, Alec Hamilton, Kenny Cameron, Tommy Mackle, myself and a few others, and we would play five-a-sides. We weren't allowed on the park so we used this area off to the side which was about 20 yards by 40 yards wide, and we would just work on one-twos. The number of them we played in that wee area was unbelievable. Some of it must have rubbed off in games."

Bobby Seith would stay behind and work on corners, free-kicks and other drills. Gilzean's aerial ability was always at the forefront of Seith's mind when he set up a practice session. "He was so good in the air that you had to bring that into the equation," says Seith. "The great ability of anybody in the air is almost the ability to hang there. And they seem as if they are on a platform, Nat Lofthouse, Tommy Lawton, all the greats were able to do that. I would rate Gillie among the best ever in the air."

We see a picture then of a young man coming to the peak of his powers, someone not content to rest on his laurels and who was constantly striving to better himself on the training ground. Gillie's fastidious approach to his profession was not in vain, though, because all of that practice was about to pay off.

4

A League of his Own

June 2009: I've arranged to meet Alan Cousin at 11 o'clock outside Recreation Park, the home of Alloa Athletic. Not for any symbolic reason but because it is the one place in Alloa that I have been to before. Pulling into the car park beside the ground and alongside Alan's red Citroën I'm immediately aware of his advancing years. Having spent the last few months looking through books about Dundee's league-winning team, the imprint in my mind is of young men captured in time.

"Well, that was good," he says as I open the front door of his car at one minute to 11. "Yeah, the sat-nav worked a treat," I reply, "although at one point it had me driving across water instead of the Clackmannanshire Bridge."

Alan chuckles. He's dressed like he's just stepped off the golf course. He's wearing a green jumper and a Tattersall check shirt and looks every inch the country gent. "Jump in and I'll take you into the town for a coffee."

Alan Cousin is worthy of a story in himself. Signed from Alloa YM in 1955, Gillie's strike partner in Dundee's league-winning team combined studying for a Classics degree at St Andrews University with rampaging through Scottish First Division defences. Pat Liney told me that Alan taught him to work out the cryptic clues to crosswords by using the scant Latin Liney had learned at school. Education came at a price, however. He was turned down for a bursary by the Dean of Faculty because he refused to give up football and had to train on the beach at St Andrews with a warning from Bob Shankly ringing in his ears: "If ever you drop your fitness levels you'll be training elsewhere, Dundee United or Falkirk or someone else". Later, when he graduated and started teaching at Alloa Academy, work colleagues would join him on training runs to keep him company. It is a testament to how well Cousin looked after himself that he played hockey, tennis and cricket for many years after he retired from football. At 70-something, he is as fit in mind as he once was in body, and that still seems to be in pretty good working order.

"I've been for a round already this morning with two of my friends; we play 14 holes every day at 7 o'clock providing it's dry," he says, as we leave Recreation Park. On our way to the coffee shop, Alan tells me that he had heard rumours that Gillie had set up a haulage company and lost his business but that he knew little more than that. He too, hasn't seen in him in many years.

No one stares at Alan inside the half-empty cafe. The staff smile and are courteous, but he is merely another elderly gent, one of a dozen they see in any given day. They have no notion that he was once a famous footballer. We misjudge the elderly, us younger folk, imagining them to be too rooted in their ways. Alan orders a mocha, as he positions himself in a chair and prepares to defog the mists of time. "He was a funny chap, Alan. He was good fun in the dressing room. It was the usual kind of ribbing that would take place in every dressing room, I suppose. But I only saw things like this on match days."

Cousin recalls an occasion when Gillie was asked by someone in Coupar Angus to give a talk. Who better than a Classics student at St Andrews to lend advice? "I was president of the local YMCA and very often I would be asked to go to men's groups to give talks and so forth. So I had one or two speeches written out about trips abroad and the European Cup run and I remember Gillie was asked if he would give a talk in his hometown. He knew that I had given a few speeches so he came to me and said, 'What will I say?' I said, 'Look, I have a speech written out in a book, so I'll give you that.' I think he did it very well because it was a great success and one day, not long after, he came back to me and said, 'Listen, can I borrow that book again?'

"He was a lovable rogue, that was his persona. He was reserved until he got to know you. He had a pawky sort of humour. He was quite accomplished at dishing out insults. He was good fun and, because things were going so well for us, there was a lot of fun. Don't get me wrong, it was a very strict regime, but it was great fun."

I ask about John White, the Tottenham midfielder who was killed when he was struck by lightning on a golf course in 1964. Gilzean starred in a benefit match for White's family for a Scotland XI against Spurs at White Hart Lane, the two roomed together on Scotland trips and, when Gilzean arrived at the London club, he was an inside-left, the position White played. Only Bill Nicholson's glaring need for a presence at centre-forward dictated that Gillie would spend long spells of his Tottenham career at that position rather than his favoured one.

"Of course, John White started his career at Alloa, you know." I tell him that I didn't, that I thought White began his playing days at Falkirk. All through the course of my investigation into Gilzean, I have been aware of little things clicking into place: my brother and Gillie's son both playing for Glentoran; Gillie joining Spurs on the same date in 1964 as my father would die in 1999; him making his senior debut for Dundee on the same date that I got married; scoring his first goal on the same date as my brother's birthday. I have never been one for mysticism but there is something unerring in the regularity of the coincidences – or perhaps I am trying too hard to find them? What is certain is this: Gilzean scored two goals in a 6-2 win in White's memorial match which, it is widely accepted, finally persuaded Bill Nicholson that he was worth signing after a long and diligent pursuit.

Ahead of the 1961-62 season, Doug Cowie left Dens Park in acrimonious circumstances; a 16-year association with the club was brought to a halt when Shankly told him he was being given a free transfer. Cowie, who intended to commute to Greenock to play for Morton, was then told he would not be allowed to train with the first team, despite believing there had been provision in the deal for him to do so. It infuriated Cowie, who felt hurt by the snub. Shankly vindicated himself by saying that Cowie was free to train at Dens Park, just not with the first team.

As Kenny Ross notes in Dundee: Champions of Scotland: "Shankly balked at the idea of letting any non-Dundee player train with his first team. He issued an instruction that only DFC players would be welcome at Dens in the mornings, although guests would be permitted to train at the ground in the afternoon or evenings." Cowie claimed that he was being denied access to the ground even after hours and instead went 300 yards down the road to Tannadice to train with Dundee United.

It wasn't just Cowie who felt saddened by the manner in which he was jettisoned, his fellow team-mates too were given a quick and brutal lesson in the dark arts of football club diplomacy. Ian Mackenzie, Gillie's lifelong pal, recalls that Alan held Cowie in high esteem and used to relish playing with him. "He played balls into Alan that meant he didn't have to check his stride, beautifully lofted passes that he could take on in one move." Years later, Gilzean would say: "I always considered it a privilege and a pleasure in my first season to play alongside Doug Cowie. To me he was one of the greatest players to have played for the club. He was fantastic."

As one old head departed, another arrived in the shape of Gordon Smith. The right-winger had been courted by the Dens Park hierarchy on more than one occasion, but despite three league medals with Hibernian, one with Hearts and 18 international caps, there were doubts expressed over the wisdom of his signing at the age of 37. Hearts had just released Smith and there were questions raised over what he had left to give. Nevertheless, Dundee had brought in a charismatic figure. Gilzean had worshipped him as a boy, and he was not the only member of the team who had. Pat Liney says he was the Cristiano Ronaldo of his day. "I've got Gordon's autograph on the back of a cigarette packet," he said. "Every football book I had when I was a young boy had Gordon in it. He was a handsome man; he looked like an actor."

Cousin recalls the sense of expectation on Smith's arrival among the young players who had idolised him. "I think we were all slightly in awe of Gordon. He had done everything in the game. I hesitate to say he was someone like George Best, because he was so unlike him in every way except ability. There was definitely an aura about him but there wasn't anything deliberate in it," Alan pauses, before adding with a chuckle: "Mind you, he did drive a Porsche.

"Gordon is bound to have known that he had something special. I was about 13 when my elder brother returned from Edinburgh one day to say that he had seen Gordon Smith. I asked him how he knew it was Gordon Smith and my brother said because a crowd of 11 or 12 boys were following him down Princes Street."

Gilzean's Tottenham team-mates talk of his thirst for a drink. It is clear that heavy drinking at Spurs took a rapid increase in the season after the club won the double in 1960-61, and was a way of life by the time Gillie arrived in north London. It was, as Steve Perryman would later tell me, "what everyone did".

There is little doubt the players at Dundee also enjoyed socialising after games. Ron McDonald, Gilzean's old scoutmaster, remembers meeting him and his team-mates for late-night sessions more than once, but one occasion stands out. "He used to drink with his Dundee mates out at the Kinloch Hotel. And, of course, he would meet up with my brother and lots of us out at the Kinloch. The lady at Kinloch used to go to bed and she just left the bar open, you just helped yourself and you would go and make your own supper in the kitchen – she got paid for it eventually – but Alan is there at the bar and he says, 'Right, who ordered the brandy?' Nobody had ordered the brandy. Alan took the glass and he threw the contents into the open fire and the flames shot right back to the glass. Of course, the fumes were overpowering. And that's one of the things I always remember about Alan Gilzean."

But the consumption of alcohol does not seem to have been as rife at Dens Park as it was at Spurs. Or perhaps it was hidden better then, and subsequently not talked about now. Pat Liney claims that a number of players drank orange juice the night Dundee won the league so as not to cloud their memories of the event. Smith, who was teetotal, was a big influence and it is unlikely he would have sat idly by if he felt drinking was affecting performances. "He was someone who had done it all before," says Alan Cousin. "He was very instructive and would be very careful to tell us what to eat – to have plenty of fibre and the like. He looked so young and people couldn't believe it when they found out he was 39.

"Once in New York when we were playing in some summer tournament, we went to a bar for something to eat and the barman came and spoke to us. 'Are you guys, from Scotland?' he asked. 'I was in the US Air Force, I was stationed at Turnhouse Airport, the old airport at Edinburgh. I remember there was a great soccer player who played in Edinburgh. What was his name, Gordon something?'

"To which I replied, 'Gordon Smith? He's sitting over there.' 'No, no,' said the barman. 'He was much younger than that.'

" 'That's Gordon Smith sitting there,' I repeated to the disbelieving barman."

Talk to Dundee players of the time and the picture that emerges of Smith is of a dedicated professional who would go to extraordinary lengths to give himself an edge. Many years before clubs started to adopt scientific methods, Smith was a trailblazer. He would wade in the sea at Broughty Ferry because he believed salt water helped speed up the rehabilitation of injuries; he would perform yoga to help his flexibility and he would urge his team-mates to avoid the twin "killers", salt and sugar. " 'Don't put sugar on your cereal boys, a few raisins, yes …' he would tell us," says Cousin.

It didn't take Smith long to win over those who doubted his worth to Dundee. Gone was the speed which would take him past players to the byeline, but instead Smith developed a knack of cutting back on to his left foot and delivering pinpoint accurate crosses. His introduction to the squad came on a pre-season trip to Iceland, and it did not take long for him to make an impression. A 20-strong party flew from Renfrew to Reykjavik on July 4, 1961 but had to wait for four hours before departure because seagulls got caught in the engines.

They played KR Reykjavik first, a game in which Smith marked his debut by scoring the opener in a 3-1 victory. Gilzean watched from the sidelines as he had undergone minor knee surgery that summer, but he was deemed sufficiently recovered by the time of the next match, on July 12. Dundee's opponents were the Icelandic champions, Akranes, who contained eight internationals in their line-up, but they proved no match for their Scottish opponents, who were convincing 4-0 winners. The Icelandic press claimed that behind the great Moscow Dynamo team of the 1950s, Dundee were the best side ever to play in Iceland.

Smith caught the eye of the Scottish press and when Dundee completed their schedule with a 3-1 over the Icelandic national team with goals from Gilzean and Hugh Robertson (2) it was clear they had much to cheer them. With the start of the season just a week away, Shankly gave his players time off, but for some the thought of spending so long without a ball with the advent of the season upon them was inconceivable, and they entered a team for a five-a-side competition involving Dundee United, Montrose, Brechin City and St Johnstone at Gayfield Park, the home of Arbroath. The Dundee contingent was made up of Bobby Cox, Alec Hamilton, Hugh Reid, Bobby Seith and Gilzean, each taking turns to go in goal, and they won the tournament to further raise team spirit after the Iceland trip.

Several players lodged together with the club's landlady, Mrs Garvie, in Dundee. On occasion Gillie would bunk in with Ian Ure if it was too late for him to drive back to Coupar Angus. Bobby Waddell, the reserve centre-forward from that squad, remembers his digs unfavourably. "I stayed with a wee old couple. There would be one bed in your room and you'd share it with another fella, sometimes two. There was a toilet, no bath; you got washed in a galley kitchen, which was tiny. There was a sink at one end where you had a shave and washed your face, and a cooker at the other and that was it. I couldn't wait to get out for a walk most evenings. Monday was always the cafe, Tuesday or Wednesday you went for a meal, Friday you went to the cinema and Saturday was the dance. Gillie was lucky, he didn't have to live in digs. He stayed at home. Andy Penman was lucky too, he had his own wee cottage near the mountains. He liked his own company, Andy."

Penman was a rarity in that respect. Often the players would meet in Dundee after training and stand at Samuel's Corner in Reform Street chatting with each other and watching the girls go by. Gillie, Ian Ure, Hugh Robertson and Alec Hamilton tended to chum around together, but in football there is a friendship that transcends normal workplace relationships – that idea of entering the battlefield as one, whatever the strengths and weaknesses of your colleagues. There is something almost familial about the game in that sense – you can say what you want about your siblings but heaven forfend anyone else doing likewise.

Togetherness and great ability proved a potent mix. Dundee were a machine in their title-winning season and, while they showed signs of wear and tear towards the end, they found another gear when it mattered. The jokes the players shared would prove crucial and Gilzean delivered them as adeptly as he did goals. "I remember us discussing a certain player at Dundee and we were saying, 'Such and such has a great left foot, there's plenty of goals in there,' " recalls Cousin. "And he said, quick as a flash, 'There must be, because none have come out yet.' "

Despite the impressive pre-season tour, the 1961-62 season started sluggishly for Dundee. Pitted against Third Lanark, Airdrie and Rangers, the champions and hold-ers, their draw in the League Cup was tough, but after a league double over Rangers the previous season there was cause for optimism. It soon dissipated following their miserable performance in the opening game. Dundee beat Airdrie 2-0, but it was a woeful performance and Shankly sighed: "The boys just had one of those days."

Cousin recalls Shankly would spare no-one when things had gone wrong: "[His ability to motivate] was the great strength of the man. He was as straight as an arrow and very blunt. 'That was gey pair,' he would say if we had played particularly badly. He had an air about him; you would not like to have got on his bad side, but he was kindly as well. When he came up we were an emerging side and he was aware of that. He was good tactically, too."

Nevertheless, Shankly was unable to provoke a positive reaction for his team's visit to Ibrox, where Dundee had not lost a league game since 1957, four days later. There were mitigating circumstances; Gilzean's knee injury was still causing him problems, having aggravated it in the five-a-side tournament, while Smith had a broken toe, but it was enough to question whether Dundee were capable of a championship challenge. Ralph Brand scored twice inside a minute as Rangers raced into a 2-0 lead before goals from Cousin and Penman left the teams level at the interval, but Davie Wilson and Jimmy Millar scored after the break to secure a 4-2 win for Rangers.

A 3-2 defeat at Third Lanark put paid to any hopes of progressing from the group, but there were minor pluses for Shankly. Smith made his competitive debut and scored his first goal for the club, though he had not demonstrated any real understanding with Andy Penman, his inside right. Perhaps of more significance was Gilzean's return. He shook off the niggling knee injury and scored his first goal of the campaign, nodding in from Robertson's cross. It was little more than a consolation, but gave the statisticians something to reflect on: it was Gillie's 40th goal in only his 50th appearance and he was emerging as the most potent, feared striker in Scotland. His partnership with Cousin was blossoming and the pair were beginning to strike up the kind of understanding that, since Cousin did not train week to week with Dundee, could only have come from intuition.

"There is no doubt that he was the goalscorer," says Cousin. "I scored a lot of goals, but he was exceptional in the best possible sense, and he was wonderful in the air. We both had similar builds and were really centre-forwards, despite Alan being listed as playing at inside left. I was the one who came back to help out midfield. It wasn't that he didn't want to come back, it was because we knew that he would be a positive threat in just about every match.

"I suppose we were a bit like [Alan] Shearer and [Chris] Sutton when Blackburn won the league. I would not describe us as being overly physical; we were great in the air, fast too, but not like Shearer in that he could throw his weight about. Indeed, Alan [Gilzean] suffered once or twice with cuts and bruises."

The respect was mutual. Gilzean was acutely aware of the sacrifice Cousin made on behalf of his team-mates on the pitch and, to a lesser extent, off it. "Alan Cousin was very much underrated," said Gilzean. "He had two options, of course; he was at St Andrews University going for his first class honours MA and obviously his academic career was more important to him than football. We only saw him as a full-timer during the school holidays but he was a great player and a fine fellow.

"I am sure if he had dedicated himself to football he would have been every bit as good as I was and maybe even better, because he had fantastic pace. He was only part-time, but stamina-wise he was fantastic and that, more than anything else, looked after the guys behind him, guys like Seith and Wishart."

Cousin's role is one of the great unheralded stories of the 1961-62 team and his 15 goals more than helped the team when Gillie went through a fallow period. He was on target when the league started the following week against Falkirk at Brockville, a match which proved something of a defining moment in Dundee's season.

Shankly stuck with the same side that had lost to Third Lanark and it was a judicious choice. "They would soon become household names for, with few exceptions, they would be first choices thereafter," notes Kenny Ross in Dundee: Champions of Scotland. "Gordon Smith rediscovered his rhythm and dashed up the wing with his old accustomed style, scoring his first league goal for his new club." The Dundee Courier declared the Gay Gordon "back to his gayest". He scored one and set up two others as Dundee won 3-1.

Gilzean, in contrast, looked unfit and turned in a quiet display. His injury was giving cause for concern, but within three days he was back among the goals against Airdrie, where something portentous was to occur. Dundee won 5-0 with Gordon Smith again in scintillating form. He scored one but twice, shortly before the end, his excellent crosses found Gilzean's head to complete the rout. It signalled the beginning of an extremely profitable partnership. Hugh Robertson, the left winger, estimated that 90% of Dundee's crosses during Smith's time at the club came from the right. He remembers Smith attacking the byeline, whereas Brown recalls him cutting back on to his left and floating crosses. What is not in doubt is that Smith and Gilzean forged a formidable double act.

"Gordon Smith and myself were two completely different types of wingers," said Robertson. "I was more direct and would play one-twos and cut in for shots, but he just beat his man, got to the line and put his cross in. I would say six times out of 10 when he did that Alan scored a goal." The sums probably don't quite add up, but Smith was clearly a hugely significant creator for Gilzean. "The understanding between [the pair] was like telepathy," recalls Bobby Seith. "Things just happened."

There is an unquantifiable element to this type of connection between certain players; one imagines it comes from a higher state of consciousness, an innate understanding of what is possible. Alan Gilzean would laugh at that, shrug and say it's just part of the game. And he would be right to a certain extent but it wouldn't explain why so many of his goals arrived via Smith's boot and not, say, Robertson's.

In his four-part interview with the Sporting Post in July 1964, he recognised the part played by Smith on the announcement that he was hanging up his boots: "Gordon's decision to retire this week made me realise what a pleasure it was to be associated with this great footballer. He was so accurate in his crossing, I knew almost exactly where he was going to put the ball. It sort of floated across, making connection very easy. Gordon was a great reader of the game, too. If things didn't go well with us in a first half, he'd get the forwards together in the dressing room at the interval and start a sort of inquest. We would all give our opinion about why things were going wrong – and improvement often followed."

Alan Cousin recalls that Gillie would rarely let Smith see how impressed he was. "Gordon Smith would put in these great crosses from the right and Gillie would head them in at the back post," says Cousin. "Then when they were on their way back to the centre circle for the kick-off you would hear another example of Gillie's humour. He would turn to Gordon and say, 'Can you not get the laces facing the other way when you put those crosses in so that it doesn't hurt my head?' "

Speaking to Jim Hendry in Dundee Greats many years later, he said: "Gordon Smith was just fantastic and the contribution he made was tremendous. He was an internationalist, a world-class player and I believe he never got the caps he should have had when he played with the Hibs; it is amazing when he moved to Hearts and Dundee he got championship medals with each of them too. He was a great influence, and obviously the other four in the forward line were all youngsters, and so his influence was very welcome."

While the rest of the team prepared for the second fixture of the new season against Dundee United, Gilzean and Alan Cousin were selected by the Scottish League to face their League of Ireland counterparts at Dalymount Park in Dublin. The game ended 1-1, but appears to have been something of a toil for Gillie. Reports gleaned from the Scottish Football Association's archive mention him just three times and in pejorative terms: "The hefty Hughes and Gilzean strangely [failed] to impress in the heavy going [...] although both appeared cumbersome, [they] were the only Scottish forwards to get in worthwhile shots at goal in the first half." His insipid performance is complete when his poor clearance from a corner leads to the League of Ireland's equaliser 18 minutes from time.

It must have come as some relief to Gillie that Dundee's next game was a derby match with United. Yet, despite Dundee's 4-1 victory, he was off target and when he finally scored again, the following week against Aberdeen, it was merely the consolation in a 3-1 defeat. That ended a three-game run without scoring, but any lingering doubts about his ability in front of goal ended in his next match, against Hearts.

Hearts 0 Dundee 2 – Tynecastle, September 23 1961
  Thank goodness for Alan Gilzean. A dreary match is brought to life when Dundee, all in white, finally wake up and their big striker scores […] Penman gets the ball on the line and chips it across goal. Keeper Marshall parries, only for Gilzean to come rushing in and bury the ball from six yards.
  After 70 minutes, Gilzean scores again […] Smith's crossfield pass, Robertson's thrilling run and cross followed by a flick of Gilzean's head make it 2-0.
  – SFA Archives

The wins came thick and fast thereafter. Dundee swept into a five-point lead over third-placed Rangers – the champions and favourites who had two games in hand – and fourth-placed Celtic, courtesy of an eight-game winning streak which brought seven goals for Gilzean. Kilmarnock, on 13 points, were second. The highlight of that run was the 4-2 home win over Motherwell, a game which Gordon Smith said was "the greatest exhibition of football I've ever seen in a club game".

There are pivotal moments in any season and while we are oft-reminded that the league rewards the tortoise not the hare, six fixtures undoubtedly encapsulated Dundee's league winning season: three in consecutive weeks against Celtic, Rangers and Raith Rovers in November and three during the title run-in against Rangers, Dundee United and finally St Johnstone as Shankly's side lurched from one abject defeat to another before finally recovering their composure. Throughout good and bad, Gilzean's goals or, at times, lack of them, correlated exactly with Dundee's fortunes.

Dundee's first major test arrived in the first week of November when Celtic arrived at Dens Park, looking to close the gap. Celtic supporters clashed with Dundee fans in streets and pubs around the city. (One macabre footnote was the suspicious death of a Celtic fan in police custody, which would later be blamed on crushing in the crowd).

Dundee 2 Celtic 1 – Dens Park, November 4, 1961
  An enthralling match at Dens Park is lit up by Smith who, though not the marauding player he was once, is the best passer and crosser on the park.

*Prompted by their right-winger Dundee take the lead in the ninth minute
when Wishart's shot through a ruck of retreating players gives Haffey no chance.
Celtic equalise soon after when Carroll outpaces Hamilton and shoots so
powerfully and accurately that Liney's attempt to save is merely a token gesture.
Celtic look like the stronger team in the second half and inside-left Divers is
principally responsible for them not taking a 2-1 lead [...] they are made to
pay when Gilzean heads the deciding goal from Cousin's cross. It is a fair result.*
    – The Glasgow Herald

Bobby Waddell told me I had inflated the significance of this match, since Celtic
weren't the team they later became and, "everyone could beat them". But it was another
game in which Gilzean would emerge as Dundee's hero. That season he scored the
winner, all of the goals, or decider in eight games. He scored 16 of Dundee's 54 goals,
in 29 appearances, missing five league games through injury or illness.

There was no doubting the importance of Dundee's next match: a trip to Ibrox
to face champions Rangers and the chance to stretch their lead over a side which
included famous names like Bobby Shearer, Eric Caldow, Davie Wilson, Jim Baxter
and Ralph Brand. The previous season, Rangers had scored 88 goals and were formidable at home. The build-up was overshadowed by fears over Gillie's fitness. He
had sustained a knock to his knee in the win over Celtic and there were significant
doubts over whether he would play. The Glasgow Herald reports that "it took all the
persuasive attention of Sammy Kean" to get Gilzean fit for Ibrox.

"Sammy got on very well with the players, whereas Shankly had to be that bit
more aloof," said Gilzean. "You need the in-between guy and Sammy was that, him
and Lawrie Smith, the physio. They both got on really well with the players. Sammy
was a great character, the joker in the pack. There was never any tension before a
match because Sammy would unwind you. He would tell you about the days when
he was a defender at Hibs and we would say, 'But Sammy, Hibs never had a defence,
they only had a forward line, and that was why they really never won much.' Sammy
was a great character and that is what football clubs are all about. It is not just the
players on the park, you have to have the right backroom staff."

Scottish football history might well have been a little less enriched but for Kean's
soothing words and Smith's healing hands.

Rangers 1 Dundee 5 – Ibrox, November 11, 1961
    *The game goes ahead despite the dense fog which has descended over
Ibrox. There are many empty seats in the stadium after news spreads that the*

game is off, but the confirmation those waiting outside are looking for comes just half an hour before kick-off when the referee declares the game will go ahead [...] Someone cracks to the rakishly dressed Jim Baxter, "get into your working clothes."

Dundee, of all the teams in the Scottish League, probably are the most sombrely dressed. As they take to the field in their dark blue shirts they are barely distinguishable, but they soon begin to dazzle.

There is a big let-off for Rangers when Penman chases Gilzean's long pass from the centre-circle and lays the ball off to Smith. The winger's 20-yard shot flashes past Ritchie, but strikes the base of the post, the Rangers goalkeeper gathers right on the line.

In 13 minutes, it's Rangers' turn to go close when Seith sells Liney short and Christie nips in. He drives past Liney. His effort grazes the post.

Roar after roar comes as Ibrox senses a goal, but the closest Rangers come is when Christie hits a Scott cross on to the top of the net.

The fog starts to return. Within three minutes of the second half, Dundee are two up. Repeat – two goals up. Both come from similar moves. The first – Caldow stumbles, Smith pokes the ball to Cousin, who glides for 20 yards before a perfect pass to Penman. He slings over a beauty and there is Gilzean at full tilt to glance the ball beyond Ritchie.

The second – A minute later the ball is cleared to Cousin, who lopes through the middle and slips to Penman. His precise ball is into the path of the incoming Gilzean who nicks it past Ritchie.

Caldow is making all kinds of mistakes in his battle with Smith and Dundee exploit the uncertainty on the left flank, never neglecting to bring Gilzean into the plan. Smith's corner from the right 16 minutes from time is to the front post, where Gilzean has made a run, and he coolly flicks his and his side's third goal. It's no wonder Gilzean races to Smith, leaping in the air and waving his arms above his head before embracing the winger. Smith is having a devastating half.

Dundee are playing like champions, with skill, guts and punch. Rangers have been fazed by the transformation in Gilzean and Penman. [After Brand pulls one back in the 84th minute] Dundee pour forward and Smith taunts several defenders with his feints before pushing the ball inside to Seith, who gives it to Penman. The impish inside flicks the ball between his legs for Gilzean. He shapes to take the ball with his left and then drags it with his right to kid Shearer and gives Ritchie no chance with a skidding 15-yarder into the goal. Penman completes Rangers' agony when he is on hand to pick up Baxter's short back pass.

Dundee have never played so well. The chief torturers were Smith, Gilzean and Penman; there was no answer to their movement. Today's result could determine the direction of the championship flag.

– The Sporting Post

It was Dundee's finest result since back-to-back League Cup final victories in 1952 and 1953 – maybe their best since before the war. The Hampden wins had been met with fireworks, whistles and bugles at Dundee West Station, whereas the 5-1 at Ibrox had been received with general disbelief across Scotland, not least because the game had gone ahead. Pat Liney said he did not see any of the Dundee goals: "I kept hearing the roars and thinking, 'Well, it hasn't gone past me, so it must be at the other end.' I had to keep asking Hammy what the score was."

Bob Seith says his wife asked him when he got back to the house if the radio had got the score wrong, thinking it was 5-1 to Rangers. And there were those inside the ground who couldn't believe their eyes. "At the game I was sitting beside Hugh Robertson's father and Willie Waddell's sister, and she was groaning away every time a goal went in," says Ian Mackenzie.

It would have been easy for Dundee to think the title was theirs as early as November, but this was merely one win, though in many ways it was much more.

"I can see it yet – Jim Baxter, Ralph Brand, Ron McKinnon, Alex Scott and all – disbelief all over their faces as they made for the tunnel. It was almost laughable," said Gillie years later in his ghost-written series in the Sporting Post. "When last had this happened at Ibrox? And as it also gave us a five-point lead in the league table it was a real blow to the Light Blues. Give them their due – as soon as they had changed and realisation was complete, they came round to our dressing room and handed out congratulations."

Willie Gilzean was one of many to miss his son's four-goal haul, the first by a visiting player at Ibrox since Willie Martin for Clyde 23 years earlier, because of the fog. "Right away we heard the Ibrox phone had jammed all morning with people asking what was happening. I heard manager Scot Symon telling Mr Shankly he'd just had a phone call from a restaurant in town. A bus party had turned back from Ibrox, had stopped to have a meal before going on – and then decided on a last-gasp call to the ground. And I heard later they made it – just 15 minutes after the kick-off.

"They were lucky. Luckier than my father, who had decided to call the whole thing off when he heard the fog forecast in the morning. And he'd hardly missed a game up till then. I'm sorry for any Dundee fans who missed the game. Our team seldom moved better. For most of the time we had Rangers on the run."

Gilzean said Shankly had taken positive steps to change the course of the game with the sides goalless at the break. "It was during the interval in the dressing room that Mr Shankly took Andy Penman aside. What was said I don't know but [...] Jim Baxter hardly got a look at the ball after that.

"I finished with four out of the five. But really, it was too easy. I just happened to be there to put the ball home at the end of some great moves."

Gilzean's humility is a recurring theme, yet it appears to be accompanied by a quiet confidence rather than self-abasement. The explanation need not be multi-faceted; football is a simple game and he happens to be good at it. There is no need for fuss. Many years later his recollections of that foggy day at Ibrox were recaptured by Jim Hendry and his modesty remained. "It was obviously going to be a hard test for us, because Rangers seemed to be our main rivals for the title, but we had a con-fidence about us and we felt we were as good if not better than any side in the league. We had a run of really good victories behind us and that day at Ibrox we just took Rangers apart. Honestly, it could have been seven or eight. I scored four that day and it is easy to say it was down to me but forwards always get the glory and defensively we played very, very well too."

Thousands turned back on the road to Glasgow that foggy day and even some of those who made it into the city gave up with just a few miles to go. Gilzean's childhood friend Ron Ross was among the lucky ones: "Billy Forbes still owes me 30 shillings for the train to Glasgow. I don't think I'll be getting it back, though. He took it to the grave with him. Billy and I got on the Aberdeen-Glasgow train at nine in the morning, so we didn't know anything about the mist. And I remember we went for a drink before the game. I would have been 20 or 21 at the time, and to see a former classmate scoring four times against Rangers was just fantastic."

Gillie wasn't part of the official party which returned to Dundee. "I went straight back home to Coupar Angus from Ibrox and found all sorts of people wanting to shake my hand and say how glad they were and that sort of thing. When I went for a walk the next day, too, it started all over again. Players who lived in Dundee got it even stronger. Waiting for them at the West Station were around 500 fans – many of the people who had been to Ibrox without seeing the game. Somebody said they didn't know whether to greet or cheer."

Gillie's goals were the defining moment of his Dundee career. There were other performances which ranked alongside the one at Ibrox, but none more fondly recalled than that day in the fog. Perhaps because so few got to witness it, the feat became part of the mythology of football fans, becoming ever more incredible with each distorted retelling. Or perhaps it is because the goals really were that good and that those that have seen them since have made up their own minds whether it was striking as an art form or whether Gilzean just "happened to be there to put the ball home".

The goals are on YouTube. The football appears slow, passing moves rarely go above three and the picture is stained by the fog. But one thing is crystal clear: the viewer is observing a youngster having fun. Gilzean lopes about the pitch with a carefree air – whether it's desperately clearing the ball as Rangers seek a consolation at 3-0 to Dundee or celebrating the last of his four goals in that game with all the enthusiasm of a nine-year-old playing shooty-in. In rare moments when he meanders into shot as Dundee defend resolutely, he looks like he could be out for a walk around town; at others his lithe, rhythmic glide is vaguely reminiscent of a wedding guest approaching the dancefloor as his shoulders and hips rock from side to side.

But the most striking thing is the simplicity of his finishing. Gilzean takes just five touches to score four goals. The first three, all from the right, are dispatched with an innate reckoning; the last is more complicated and yet Gillie flicks the ball contemptuously beyond Bobby Shearer before drilling low into the corner.

The following week, Dundee hosted Raith Rovers at Dens Park. The Fifers had produced a shock by beating second-placed Kilmarnock the previous week for their first win of the campaign but following that seminal result at Ibrox, few expected anything other than a rudimentary victory. They got there in the end, but not without an almighty scare along the way.

Dundee 5 Raith Rovers 4 – Dens Park. November 18, 1961
> *A wintry haze cloaks Dens Park. Manager Bob Shankly fields his Ibrox invincibles, Raith are also unchanged from the XI that sprung a surprise against Kilmarnock. [...] The home team start off playing the silky football now expected of them. Raith refuse to yield. In fact, Liney is the busier keeper in the opening minutes and almost concedes when Ure gives him a fright with a header back which is short.*
>
> *[...] Veteran Andy Leigh has a shock in store for the league leaders. He picks up the ball in his own half, moves forward unchallenged and from 35 yards out unleashes a corker. Liney is landing on the ground when the ball rebounds off the inside of the stanchion. It's 1-0 to Raith, 20 minutes gone.*
>
> *Only a fine Cunningham save stops Wishart from equalising in 29 minutes. Cunningham, playing against his former colleagues, stretches cat-like*

to save, sparking a goalmouth melee. The whole Dundee front five are looking for a chance, but Raith stand firm. Cunningham denies Cousin's first-timer, and Gilzean's header from Robertson's centre slips over.

Half-time: Dundee 0 Raith Rovers 1

[…] Second half

[…] Several nifty moves are foiled because the tightly packed Raith defence refuse to be tricked into anything foolish. It does not last. Gilzean is 25 yards out but takes a quick glance to see that everyone is covered and tries a speculative ground shot. The whole Raith defence leaves it for Cunningham to pick up, but to their amazement the giant keeper goes the other way and the ball eludes his grasp as it trundles over the line. 50 minutes gone.

This is bad enough but when Cunningham gifts another goal to Gilzean within two minutes, Raith are stunned. The keeper bends to gather the inside man's shot and lets the ball dribble between his legs.

The game is far from over. Clinton equalises on 58 minutes after Liney completely misjudges a free. Then Lourie leaves Liney helpless with a ferocious shot, and in 63 minutes it is 4-2 when Adamson hammers home the lesson.

Dundee are really up against it. Raith's goals are giving them some indication of how Rangers felt a week ago. Wishart blasts the game open with a flashing drive in 69 minutes. The left-half takes Penman's pass and Cunningham fails to spot his rising shot. Then Wilson twice clears off the line for Raith. Penman slides the ball past Cunningham but the back is covering and clears to safety. Next, Gilzean's powerful header is nodded away by the same player. The excitement is too much for one spectator, who is carried away by ambulance men.

Dens has rarely witnessed such drama. In a storming finale, Seith blasts home the equaliser from 35 yards past the bemused Cunningham with four minutes left, and just a minute later Cousin runs through the middle and passes to Gilzean. He is buffeted about and there are calls for a penalty, but Gilzean stays in control long enough to slip the ball to the incoming Smith and he shoots into the net.

[…] Summing up – It is difficult to find words to adequately describe this magnificent match. For the second week running Dundee had the look of champions, but poor Raith must be bewildered tonight.

Some advice: if you have a weak heart stay clear of Dundee matches.

– The Sporting Post

In the weeks that followed, Dundee consolidated their lead at the top. Celtic replaced Rangers as the team on their tail after the latter endured December defeats away to Jock Stein's Dunfermline and at home to Aberdeen. Dundee suffered minor blips of their own, drawing with Stirling Albion (2-2 at Dens Park) and 1-1 against St Mirren at Love Street. The game against Stirling was noteworthy for two reasons; Gillie had a goal marked off for pushing, and broke his jaw.

Nursing his injury, he, Andy Penman and Hugh Robertson travelled with the Scotland Under-23 side for an international against their Welsh counterparts at the Racecourse Ground in Wrexham on December 5. On a difficult, snow-covered pitch, Gillie had an off game for the second time in as many internationals; his sole mention in The Glasgow Herald match report claimed that "neither Penman nor Gilzean had even an averagely good match; both persisted in trying to play the ball through the centre instead of swinging it to the wings, where the foot was at least better than it was in the middle of the field."

The match ended 0-0 without further impression from Gilzean. He was clearly feeling the effects of his jaw injury in the bone-chilling conditions and would not play again until the start of January. In Dundee's first game without their leading scorer, on December 16, they did not miss him, rattling five past Airdrie with Gordon Smith lining up at centre-forward and George McGeachie coming into the starting XI. However, a week later against St Mirren they lacked his ruthlessness, drawing 1-1 with a struggling side, so it was with some relief that their home match against St Johnstone on December 30 was called off due to snow. It allowed Gillie a further week to recover from his broken jaw and he was declared fit for the visit of Falkirk.

There had been further cold weather over the New Year period and Gilzean, mindful of his travails in snowy Wrexham, opted to change his footwear for the game. Bobby Waddell recalls that Adidas, the German sportswear company, had provided the club with two sample pairs of their iconic Samba shoes. Waddell says that he and Gillie were the first to nab the two pairs of trainers, so they got to keep them. Alan's jaw was now healed and his decision to wear the shoes proved to be a judicious one.

He scored twice, the trainers giving him the edge in a race for the ball with Jimmy Boag which he lifted over the Falkirk goalkeeper's head for the first, and the second coming after a delicate flick with his head following Wishart's vicious shot.

Pat Liney said that from then on, when the ground was hard, Gillie would wear trainers. "Dundee played in South Africa in 1957 just before I signed. They wore rubber soles in Africa and the club brought a load back with them, but they were awkward and uncomfortable things so we tended not to wear them. Alan would wear sandshoes, they were like what are called trainers today. I remember one game at Dens when it was frosty. We were playing Rangers and their players couldn't keep their feet. It gave Alan an advantage. He was just like a ballerina and everyone else was like Ron Harris going into a tackle."

The hero was full of balletic grace; often he would leap so high that he was above the goalkeeper's outstretched arm to flick the ball into the net. When the ball came into his realm there was only one man getting it. Gilzean could change direction in the air, make a split-second decision … did he head for goal or was there another player in close proximity who might benefit better from a knockdown?

"You could see him changing his mind in the air," Ian Ure told me. "It was almost as if he was weighing up the possibilities."

There wasn't a goal scored on a green or school playground in Dundee – and beyond – that wasn't sent on its way by Alan Gilzean in various guises. He was the talk of the jute factories and the pubs and the subject of man-to-man conversations in tenement houses.

Norrie Price, the Dundee FC historian, says that on trips to his grandparents in Arbroath he would play headers and volleys on the green behind the house with the boy next door. "My friend Alan Yule had just got a new dog and hadn't got a name for it. It was a black and white mongrel but it had a lovely nature. We were playing on the green this one day and the dog jumped in and started nodding the ball up in the air with his nose. From that day on, he called the dog Gillie."

As the pitches started to degrade, Dundee's performances started to lose some of their fluidity, and with it came a downturn in results. Ure told Jim Hendry, in Dundee Greats, "there is no doubt in my mind that the good grounds in the early part of the season suited our game to perfection."

In their next nine games in the league and Scottish Cup, Dundee won four, drew one and lost four. While not utterly damning statistics, they were enough to provoke a psychological crisis in the dressing room. "We definitely started to believe we were top notchers and the feeling about was that we would only have to coast through the rest of the season. Unfortunately, all these wee things got to us psychologically – you try that wee half-ounce less and before you know what's happening, things are slipping," Ure added.

The Scottish Cup first round defeat at St Mirren had been particularly galling since the players had fancied themselves for an extended run in the competition. Worse still for Gilzean was a worrying lack of goals. His opener in the 2-1 win over St Johnstone at Dens Park at the end of January might have been his 19th league goal of the season – and 22nd in all competitions – but it was also his last for some considerable time. Notwithstanding a bout of flu which robbed him of three games, it was over two months before Gillie found the target again, during which time Dundee surrendered ownership of top spot to Rangers and very nearly the title.

In between those two goals, Dundee lost their first home game of the season, 3-1 to Motherwell, failed to score for the first time in a 3-0 defeat to Partick Thistle and lost their third in a row when succumbing to Celtic at Parkhead at the start of March. A fourth defeat followed four days later, at Dunfermline. Rangers had a three-point lead over Shankly's side at the top and, while Dundee held a game in hand, the momentum built up by their flying start had dissipated.

The once-enraptured Dens Park support had turned on their team, too. Gilzean told Kenny Ross that he would get the crowd going in games by shouting little things like "Here comes the Hammy magic" or "Watch out for the Hammy magic" when Alec Hamilton would set off on one of his marauding runs, but during the slump one fan directed his ire at the right-back. "This supporter started to shout back to Hammy, 'Where's the effin' magic now Hammy, eh?' and gave him stick every time he went to take a throw-in at that side. Hammy didn't like it very much and, despite the fact that this guy was 6ft 5in or something, and a big bruiser, [Hammy] shouted back, 'Meet me at the players' entrance afterwards and we'll sort it then.'

"When we were getting changed in the dressing room afterwards, Hammy came over to me and said, 'Gillie, do me a favour and come out with me in case that guy's there. I doubt he will be, but you never know, especially as we lost.' Sure enough, when we got outside the big bruiser was there and Hammy, who couldn't fight for toffee, didn't know what to say. The bruiser said: 'Hamilton. Me and you. Gussie Park. Now, and we'll sort it.' To get rid of the guy, Hammy told him he was only joking and had to give him a fiver to go and get himself a drink, and a fiver in those days would have got the lad a few drinks. Hammy thought he was invincible, however!"

Dundee's slump placed great emphasis on the visit of a Rangers side intent on revenge for the 5-1 mauling at Ibrox. It was barely believable that, five months on from that momentous day, Dundee now trailed Rangers. Again there were doubts about Gillie's fitness. He turned up for training on the Tuesday despite feeling the effects of flu, but his temperature started to rise once he began to take part. Bob Shankly sent him home to Coupar Angus and he spent the rest of the day in bed. This time there was no late reprieve. Bobby Waddell took Gillie's place in the starting line-up for the evening kick-off, but Rangers were also missing their talisman, Jim Baxter, who had been ordered to play for the Army against the Navy in an inter-services fixture at Wolverhampton on the same night. In a tense match, during which both teams had their chances, Rangers played with virtually 10 men after their centre-half, Doug Baillie, had sustained an injury early on but limped through proceedings on the left wing. While the points were shared, the real winners were Dundee. They had prevented Rangers from extending their lead to five points and restored confidence in the process. Gillie, though, was to play no part as the revival took hold. His flu was proving persistent and he was missing from the team which beat Raith Rovers 3-2 three days later and from that which beat Hibernian 1-0 the following week, when Bobby Waddell scored the only goal.

I'm sitting in Dundee City Library sifting through a mountain of old leather-bound volumes of the Sporting Post, when I become aware of an elderly gentleman staring at me. It's a well-appointed library with wide oak tables and open-plan working areas. In the next room a class of students are practising a Scottish dirge on their recorders, changed days from the time when librarians would have fixed a steely gaze on people for rustling pages too loudly. The elderly gent is closer now. I feel like I know his face but can't quite place it. "Are you James?" he asks with a half-smile on his lips.

"Yeah, are you, erm, Bobby?" The context of the meeting throws me.

"Yes, pleased to meet you. Sorry to disturb you. I know we said to meet outside, but I was early so I thought I would come and look for you." He has a sympathetic, round face. His eyebrows curl into points at their furthest ends, giving him a slightly grumpy look – a facial trait that has afflicted me personally for many years. He grins and says, "Take your time." I can't wait, though.

"Him and Hammy used to chase nurses," says Bobby Waddell, with something approaching a knowing grin, "but then he started seeing a girl who was in the police in Dundee, so he started to keep more of a low profile."

I had heard nothing of this side of Gillie's reputation until this point. We go for lunch in a pub once run by Peter and Jimmy Marr, the former owners of Dundee FC. Bobby is hesitant, almost reticent in his recollections of Gillie. "He once tried to buy Dundee, you know? It was at a time when the club was going really cheap and Gillie was up for one of the first club reunions. I overheard him asking Angus Cook, the chairman, to name his price for the club. I don't know whether he was being serious, but he certainly looked like he was."

Innocently, I ask Bobby for his favourite story about Gillie. He smiles diffidently "I can't tell you," he says. "There must be one?" I ask. "No, I can't," he grins.

Dundee are playing Queen of the South in a top-of-the-table match in the First Division at Dens Park that day. "I don't sit in with the home fans," Bobby had told me on the phone before we met. "You cannae see the game in the same way, ken?"

It is something of a surreal experience to find myself among the visiting fans with a member of Dundee's league-winning squad, on a chill November afternoon.

Bobby was a peripheral member of Shankly's team, but played his part in their championship win and is well-loved around these parts. He is a regular visitor to Dundee, East Fife or Junior games. "I get on the bus on a Saturday and just decide where I'm going to go then. If you hadn't phoned me I probably would have sat in the house, though," he says, as the temperature slowly tumbles and the rain threatens to start for the umpteenth time that afternoon.

Watching the game unfold, Bobby deconstructs the tactics, shaking his head every so often when a pass goes awry. "It's completely different to when I was play-ing," he says. "We let the ball do all the work with 30- or 40-yard passes to wingers who were stuck to the wing all day."

Just at that, the Queen of the South goalkeeper prepares to take a goal-kick. All bar two outfield players surround or occupy the centre-circle. "Look at that," says Bobby, "there's no room today. In my day, the wingers stood on the touchline, and that gave more room for the midfielders to make runs through the gaps and it made it easier for strikers. It was much more open back then, there were lots of goals. Now the strikers are arriving much later in the box and it makes it more difficult for them to get shots in, or wide players to get the ball in."

Soon after, Dundee win a corner. When the delivery comes in every blue-shirted player makes a run to the near post. Bobby shakes his head in disbelief. "If just one player had stood on the back post, he had an empty net."

Dundee make more of a go of it in the second half, but it is little surprise when the referee blows for full-time with the game scoreless. "No width," says Bobby again as we join the disappointed throngs heading away from Dens Park.

On the drive home I'm struck by a thought: how many goals would Gillie have scored in today's Dundee team and playing those same tactics? The beauty of the Shankly team was its simplicity. Everyone had a role to play; it was a machine. Gillie and Alan Cousin were listed as inside-left and centre-forward, but those descriptions were limited by the terminology of the day. Gilzean would be in the middle as often as Cousin; inside-left was the default position, but he was not constrained by it.

His touch was instant. He moved the ball quickly. And he scored goals – lots of them. This was his job in the machine. It is why those who played with him back then express surprise at the flamboyant, hip-swaying visionary he became at Spurs. The truth is, as Bobby Waddell admits, "he always had it, he must have."

Bobby and Alan might have been team-mates at Spurs had fate not intervened. "I played for St Andrews United boys team. We went on this unbeaten run stretching over 50 games and I scored a lot of goals. Every team in Scotland wanted to sign me at one point, and Bill Nicholson wrote to me asking me and this other boy who played inside-right to join Tottenham. One Sunday, we were due to meet him and someone from Spurs in a hotel in St Andrews at two o'clock. So we sat there waiting, two o'clock came and went and we kept waiting past three, then four and finally at five someone from the hotel said that word had come through from Carlisle that Mr Nicholson had taken appendicitis and would not be able to travel the rest of the way. I got another letter soon after – they're still in the house – but by that time I had made up my mind to join Dundee. I would have signed for Spurs that day, though."

Did he ever think about what might have been? "No, there's point thinking about what might have happened. It didn't happen and that's that. I wasn't good enough for England anyway. I found that out when I signed for Blackpool."

Gilzean scored five in five on his return. The first came in Dundee's very next match, the winner against a spirited but doomed Stirling Albion side. The 3-2 victory on March 31 allowed Dundee to reclaim top spot, with Rangers playing in the Scottish Cup semi-finals. It was an advantage they held until midweek, before the Glasgow side overcame St Johnstone to snatch it back. A week later, in the 2-1 win over Airdrie on April 7, Gille's performance was criticised by The Glasgow Herald, which claimed he and Alan Cousin "have changed for the worst more than most; each nowadays seems reluctant to steer a straight course through the centre – the form of attacks with which they wreaked such havoc in the past". The criticism of his general play would continue in his next game against Dundee United two days later, but at least the goals had returned.

Dundee United 1 Dundee 2 – Tannadice. April 9, 1962

   It's D for derby day in Dundee, bringing one of the most important-ever clashes between the city's senior sides. Anything less than two points will dash Dundee's championship hopes.

   […] Five minutes from kick-off the ground is bulging. Police supervise the marshalling of fans on top of the rubble piled up on the north terracing. Both teams get a great ovation which drowns out three pipe bands.

   […] United go ahead in 15 minutes with a surprise goal. Briggs, gathering from a throw-in, loses control and pushes the ball to Gilzean. Alan fails to gather cleanly and is caught in possession by the left-back and falls under Briggs' robust tackle. As the ball breaks to Irvine the Dundee rearguard are waiting for a foul. Jim is in no doubt and smacks a well-placed daisy cutter to Liney's

right-hand corner. Pat gets a hand to it but can't stop it. The Dark Blues and their fans are stunned.

[…] It's all United. For long spells everyone except Ugolini is in Dundee's half. But 90 seconds from the whistle Gilzean crashes home a spectacular equaliser from fully 35 yards. The unsighted Ugolini dives far too late to get near Alan's swerving shot. The goal comes right out of the blue from a melee on the left touchline. Gilzean leaps up and down waving his arms excitedly as his team-mates rush across to shower him with congratulations.

Reflections – Gilzean's great pick-me-up for Dundee at the very best psychological moment might give the Dark Blues a second half urgency which has been sadly lacking.

Second half

[…] Cousin, operating on the right, forces a corner. Smith floats it over and Gilzean meets it hard with his head, but it's far too high.

Then tragedy. Gillespie and Irvine lash at the spinning ball, Hamilton pushes it out of the way and stops a full blooded kick with his right foot. Gillespie anxiously bends over the right-back as he falls writhing to the turf. But Alec manages to continue after attention. He is limping badly.

– Dundee Evening Telegraph and Post

The rest of the second half failed to make the Evening Telegraph's deadline. Since this was an Easter Monday game there was no Sporting Post to fill in the blank, no idea of how the '2' beside Dundee's name might have got there. Those who missed the match would have had to rely on intricately described action replays from those who were there. For a description of Gillie's second, the winner, they might just as easily have reread the description of his first.

The Glasgow Herald reported "the winning goal, again scored by Gilzean, came only three minutes from full time when the inside-left beat Smith – for the first time – and drove a rising shot past Ugolini from 30 yards."

The Herald report is peppered with references that betray a bias about where it would have preferred the league trophy to go. Gilzean is described as "leaden-footed" and the inside forwards (Gilzean and Penman) as "lethargic". Dundee were "fortunate" having been "generally outmanoeuvred" by a United side who "spent long spells in the middle of the Dundee half".

The insinuation here is well hidden: Gilzean was often perceived as being lazy, but ask him and he would contend that his job was to score goals, not to track back and do the leg work. Like all good predators, it allowed him to conserve his energy for when he really needed it. Craig Brown says: "We wore white shorts at Dundee and after the game we would come into the dressing room and everyone's shorts would be filthy and muddy, but his would be immaculate. He was not the kind of striker who put himself about. He was a gentleman's striker. He wasn't rushing into tackles and chasing up ball. He had this zip about him and although he was not the hardest worker a lot of people said that's why he had that extra zip."

While the Herald report failed to spot the nuances of Gilzean's game, the Evening Telegraph report is more considered, if marred somewhat by the absence of the final 30 minutes. Two other points of interest from the Herald report are that the attendance is estimated at 50,000 compared to the more conservative 20,000 in the Evening Telegraph.

Flicking through year upon year of papers in a Dundee library crystallises an image of the society Gillie was living in, and in many ways it was little different to that of today: houses were burgled, women were attacked, the elderly were assaulted, and there were immigration problems. In one case straight out of Tales of the Unexpected a man is drugged by his wife, thrown through a trapdoor in his kitchen and left there to die. The woman is later charged with his murder. "What has been will be again, what has been done will be done again; there is nothing new under the sun." Except, perhaps, the way in which it is reported by newspapers.

Gillie's own memories of that day do not fit with those newspaper descriptions. "The first [goal] was definitely thanks to United keeper Rolando Ugolini. My speculative shot bounced as it approached the goal and he dived over the top of it. The second from about 25 yards out, screamed right into the top corner and the win was crucial. It was a huge step for us."

Dundee's next opponents were St Mirren almost a fortnight later. Sandwiched in between, an international match between Scotland and England at Hampden Park and the Scottish Cup final in which Rangers defeated St Mirren 2-0 at the same venue. Alec Hamilton suffered no ill-effects from the heavy challenge sustained in the Dundee derby and played in the 2-0 win over England five days later.

Gilzean's candidacy for a place in that line-up had been put forward in the Sporting Post as early as February 1962 following two goals in a dismal game between Scotland and the Scottish League. There was particular interest in getting the team right, because England had thumped Scotland 9-3 at Wembley the previous April.

"Gilzean can be so good with his head that he could outjump those Sassenachs and give us sweet revenge for that humble pie at Wembley," wrote Rambler. "He has scored most of his goals from inside-forward for Dundee. Last season he netted 19 from inside-left, four from inside-right and nine as centre. This season 18 of his 22 have been from inside-left. He started off as a centre of great promise. This would not really be a case of playing a man out of position. Gilzean and Cousin switch so much during a game one is probably in the middle as long as the other.

"The selectors have two chances to give Gilzean the centre berth before the big game. Next Friday, the under-23 side is selected for the Pittodrie game with England and there's the league 'national on March 27."

Gilzean did play in that under-23 game. The Scots went down 4-2, a certain Jimmy Greaves scoring twice. Gilzean failed to score, but made an impression by setting up a goal for John Hughes. Alas, it was not the impression made by Greaves. Gilzean was mightily impressed by the diminutive striker who had just returned to English football with Tottenham after a torrid time in Italy with AC Milan. Little could he have known then that this was a young man with whom he would strike up a great understanding on the football pitch and a great friendship off it.

The second match referred to by Rambler – the annual Scottish League game against Scotland – came in the middle of that bout of flu, and Gillie missed out.

St Mirren arrived at Dens Park licking their wounds from the Scottish Cup final defeat and desperate for points to avoid relegation but they knew Dundee had not beaten them in their previous two meetings in league and cup. Games against St Mirren had the threat of menace for Gilzean in the shape of Bobby 'Red' Campbell. Speaking to the Sporting Post in 1964, he said: "We've had some rare tussles. I remember one game against the Saints when 'Red' had the laugh. My lace had become undone. I noticed but hadn't time to do anything about it as the ball was coming in my direction. I collected the ball with no bother and moved ahead. I had passed 'Red' Campbell when I was suddenly jerked to half pace before losing both my balance and the ball. 'Red' had noticed my lace undone and had jumped on it as I moved past him. There was a smile on his face as I picked myself up. 'Ever seen that one before?' he said." Gilzean would, no doubt, have noted with interest and a modicum of relief Campbell's enforced absence from the team-sheet.

There was an early scare when George McLean hit a post but all was going to plan by the time Alan Cousin gave Dundee the lead just three minutes before half-time. The warm glow inside the stadium intensified when word filtered through from Pittodrie that Aberdeen were beating Rangers 1-0. If results remained the same Dundee would return to the top of the table needing just a draw from their remaining game with St Johnstone to clinch the club's first league title.

The scores remained the same until well into the second half; Dundee were heading towards a memorable victory and a step closer to the First Division title. And then disaster struck when the referee Willie Syme awarded a penalty against Gordon

Smith for handball with 12 minutes remaining. The Dundee players protested long and hard at the decision, most of all Smith, prompting Syme to consult with his linesman over the decision. Smith's dispute was so vocal and such was his standing as a player that Syme felt uncertain that he was correct in awarding the penalty. "I have refereed Mr Smith for 15 years and in all that time I have never known him to query a decision," Syme later told a journalist in the car on the journey back to Glasgow.

Jim Clunie, the St Mirren captain, stepped up to take the kick and lashed the ball towards the top-right corner. Pat Liney started to go to his left, but changed direction and pushed the ball to safety. Within four minutes of that save, Andy Penman scored Dundee's second of the night and the points were safe. When word went out over the Tannoy that Aberdeen had beaten Rangers, the crowd invaded the pitch.

Liney was the hero and Gilzean reflects that his contribution was a significant, if not fully appreciated, one. "There is no doubt Pat was very unlucky to be discarded after winning the championship medal," he told Jim Hendry. "I put his plight in the same category as a guy at Spurs, a centre-forward called Les Allen who scored over 20 goals when Tottenham won the double. And the next season he was in the reserves because the club brought Jimmy Greaves back from Italy. I feel very sad for Les Allen as I do for Pat Liney. Through no fault of his own a player becomes second choice but that gets back to management; that's what being a manager is all about – making tough decisions. You have to be ruthless, and who is to say that Shankly was right or wrong when he replaced Pat Liney?"

Gillie was supremely confident heading into the biggest week of his life as a professional footballer. So confident that he gratefully accepted a £10 wager from Ian Ure that he would not score twice against St Johnstone. Gillie could not see how Dundee could lose if they played to the best of their abilities. There might have been a diffidence about him, but it was allied to a quiet certainty and clarity in his thinking. "My state of mind that day was that if we matched them for effort we would get chances, and I was one of the men in the team the rest of the lads relied on to convert these chances into goals. And I reckoned over the 90 minutes, the way Dundee were playing at that time, I would get maybe three or four chances in any given game and I would back myself to score two out of four any time."

The record books do not state that Gilzean ended the day £10 better off, but he did. His two, and one from Andy Penman, guaranteed the title for Dundee and relegated St Johnstone. For all his joy at winning his first major honour, Gilzean, as a local boy, felt rueful at the fate dealt to the club his father had supported.

"There were a lot of St Johnstone supporters who took a long time to forgive

Alan for what he did that day," says Norrie Currie. Certainly, St Johnstone were in no mood to spend the following season in the Second Division. In his autobiography, Ure's Truly, Ian Ure claims there was an attempt to fix the game. "A message was passed to the players that they could collect £50 each if they made it a draw. The idea was treated with contempt and only served to double our determination."

"I was the local lad and I had, and still have, a lot of friends who are St Johnstone supporters, and the ironic and sad thing that day was that poor Saints were relegated," Gillie told Jim Hendry, in Dundee Greats. "As it turned out, a single point would have done us and Saints would have stayed in the First Division. I felt so sorry for them. Our pleasure was their grief – there was a touch of that for me, too, probably just because of my local connections. Yes, it was a great day on the one hand but sad on the other.

"I was going to travel straight to Perth from Coupar Angus, but I thought I'd best go straight to Dundee because, win, lose or draw, we were going there at night. I recall the Perth road that day was just a mass of traffic and I think Dundee must have had three-quarters of the crowd. On the way through to the match we had plenty of time to think of what might lie ahead."

Approximately 20,000 supporters made the short trip along the River Tay on that scorching hot spring day in 1962, their strength in numbers providing succour to the players sitting in traffic among them. The belief that Dundee were going to win the title seems to have crystallised in Gillie's mind during that journey to the ground.

"We knew on paper we were a better team that St Johnstone, the league table proved that – we were at the top and they were close to the bottom ... our superior skills would take care of the rest."

Nevertheless, there were pre-match jitters. Gilzean recalled some years later that, "Mr Shankly went around trying to calm us all with his 'just play your usual game'. But the butterflies followed us out on to the park. We just couldn't settle down, no matter how Gordon Smith and Bobby Seith tried to calm us by deliberately slowing the pace of the game."

The match report from Dundee's seminal victory at Muirton Park has been ripped out of the leather-bound volume of the Sporting Post that once housed it in Dundee City Library. It would have confirmed Gilzean's belief that Dundee were the better side. Nevertheless, the sweltering conditions, the bone-dry pitch and the nervous tension on the terraces were all contributory factors to a scrappy opening. Dundee soon settled down, though, and with Gordon Smith increasingly getting the better of his man it was only a matter of time before they scored. Inevitably, it was Gilzean, heading past the St Johnstone goalkeeper, Bill Taylor, with the carefree ease that had become expected of him. "I'm told I jumped for joy higher than I've ever jumped for a ball. Somehow we knew we were on the way to the title."

He added a second after half-time, when he ran on to a through ball by Alex Hamilton, stepped past the St Johnstone centre-half, Jim Ferguson, and cracked home his 24th of the league campaign and 27th in all competitions. Andy Penman added another eight minutes later and the title was as good as theirs. When the whistle went, thousands invaded the pitch. The players were carried from it shoulder high.

"The scenes that followed the final whistle were just terrific," added Gillie. "Within seconds the pitch was a mass of wildly excited Dundee fans cheering, clapping us on the back, shaking our hands. Bobby Cox and others were grabbed and hoisted shoulder high to the pavilion. We didn't mind. I don't think anyone could have minded anything at that truly tremendously exciting and wonderful moment."

The players retired to the bath, where they drank champagne before changing. The bus back to Dundee was accompanied by a raucous cavalcade of supporters, and when it entered the city thousands lined the streets. The team was escorted to chairman James Gellatly's house, where they toasted their success before making their way to a city hotel and on to a succession of parties.

Only once previously had a team from the city come close to winning the title – George Anderson's in 1949, when Dundee needed to win at Falkirk to clinch the title and lost 4-1. Now the club could revel in its new-found status as Scotland's best club. They could look forward to a competitive assault on Europe, too. After all, they also possessed the best striker in Scotland.

5

FOREIGN FIELDS

The Royal Hotel sits halfway up a hill in New Street in the former mining town of Dalry in North Ayrshire. It is what Scots call a dreich day; everything looks grey, a snail line of traffic edges its way slowly up the hill. When I arrive at the entrance of the hotel, two locals flash me the kind of look reserved for out-of-towners. Inside is a working man's pub. A dozen regulars sit on stools at the bar watching snooker. Hugh Robertson is upstairs but I'm assured he'll be down any minute. The barmaid pours me a coke and I wait.

When Robertson appears I recognise him instantly. I tell him he hasn't changed a bit and he looks at me quizzically. In reality, he looks like many septuagenarians in his grey slacks and navy sweater and he could easily pass for a patron, but there is that same glint in his eye from the old photos I have seen of him and he still looks like someone who is always thinking of his next joke. Gordon Strachan once said he was the best coach he ever played under and Hugh seems as proud of that as anything he ever did on the football pitch. "One of the boys who drinks in here told me that he had read it in the newspaper and I asked him to keep it for me. I couldn't believe it and neither could some of the boys. They were saying, 'That's the Celtic manager.' "

Strachan and Robertson's paths crossed at Dundee in the mid-70s when the latter finished his playing career at Arbroath and took on a coaching role at his old club. "I was coming up for 10 years at Dundee when they appointed a new manager, Donald Mackay," he says emphasising Mackay's first name. "He wanted his own backroom staff in and he tried everything he could to get me to leave. I was with the first team and he made me reserve team manager. I said fine. Then, after a short while, he told me I would be taking the youth team, and I said fine. Basically, the board wanted me to resign, because if they sacked me they knew I was due a pay-off. I drove a minibus to take the youngsters to games and after a while they came to me and said, 'We're going to have to take the minibus off you,' so I said, 'Fine, here are the keys.' Then eventually they said, 'Okay, Hugh, we're going to pay you off.' They drew up terms for my severance and when I looked them over they were short. I sent the details to my lawyer and they spoke to the club. Finally it was sorted out.

"I decided to write to clubs in Australia, South Africa and Scandinavia not really expecting to hear anything back. But the phone went one day and it was a representative from Herfølge Boldklub offering me a job as their manager." Hugh pronounces the name in Danish. "They were in the Second Division and I took them up in my first season. I was there for seven years and I would have stayed there, but I was paying 50% in tax. I went to the chairman and he told me, 'Mr Robertson there are ways around it. Buy a car.' 'But I have a car,' I replied, 'the one you gave me when I took the job.' 'Buy a house, then,' he said. 'You gave me a house, too. Is there no other way?' And the chairman said, 'Mr Robertson, two of the directors are tax men.'

"When I came back to Scotland I bought this place. The first time I came down to look at it, it was a Sunday lunchtime and it was jumpin', but that was because the other pubs in the town had to close at lunchtime because of the licensing laws."

He pauses for thought and takes the conversation in a different direction. "So, you're writing a book about big Alan?" I tell Hugh that I think Gillie's name has been lost to Scottish football and that I'm trying to help secure his place in the Hall of Fame. He nods approvingly.

For the remainder of his time at Dundee, Gilzean would have his own money wrangles with the club which would culminate in his departure for Tottenham in 1964. At the start of the 1962-63 season Gillie and Robertson were among a coterie of players who rejected Dundee's contract offer of £25-a-week, a basic wage that was bettered only by the Old Firm. The post-maximum wage days were in their infancy and players were anxious to establish exactly what they were worth.

Pat Liney told me there had been concern among some of the other players over the contract demands of their team-mates, but that he was not one of the dissenting voices. "At the end of each season, the manager would tell you how much you were going to get paid for the following season. You either accepted it or left. When Alan, Ian Ure and Alec Hamilton were picked for Scotland, they asked for pay rises and they got them. Some team-mates said it wasn't right that they were getting more, that it was a team game. These were average players in comparison, though. My take on it was that if people like Gillie were able to ensure that I got my win bonus then

I didn't care what they were earning. I knew he was a better player and the better players should get paid more. Today, though, I think it has gone too far and some of the money players earn is outrageous."

The deadlock was broken when Alex Hamilton, Andy Penman and Robertson agreed to new terms and Bobby Seith did likewise the following day. Gilzean and Ure held off for a few days longer, mindful that they were Dundee's most prized assets and, while Ure claimed that the impasse was "simply a matter of pounds, shillings and pence," it was a portent of things to come.

By the end of 1962, Pat Liney's Dundee career was nearing an end. Shankly wanted competition in goal and used his family ties to sign Bert Slater from Liverpool. Within a few months Liney was on his way to his childhood favourites St Mirren. Just as Liney had been an invaluable pair of hands in the title campaign, Slater was to prove equally as effective in the European Cup run.

Hugh and Alan were best pals and room-mates on foreign trips. He remembers Gillie with real affection but admits he has long since lost touch. "I used to see him at reunions with the others but he stopped coming. There was talk that he was ill."

Apropos of nothing, he says: "Alan was at my wedding reception at the Royal Hotel in Cumnock in 1961 and afterwards three or four of the Dundee boys went back to my mother and father's house and had a few drinks. At some point in the night my brother-in-law said to them, 'Right, I bet no-one can score a goal past me.' So they threw down a couple of coats and Gillie and Ian Ure and a couple of the other boys took shots at him. The living room was only from here to the door over there." The door is about four feet away.

His memory of Gilzean's playing abilities remains undiminished. "I still watch football every Sunday. Sunday is my day in here and I watch the first game on Sky in the afternoon right through to the Spanish football in the evening. I think Alan was the best I have ever seen in 50 years of watching and playing football." The more I dig, the more I start to appreciate how well-regarded Gilzean is by his contemporaries. I ask Hugh if he is absolutely convinced of that assessment and his re-evaluation is no less lavish. "He would certainly be in my top five anywhere in the world." He would become one of the most feared strikers in the European Cup in the 1962-63 season.

The campaign started with a tournament in the United States against teams from West Germany, Brazil, Yugoslavia, Mexico and Italy. Gilzean remembers the heat being gruelling; Dundee's first fixture in the New York tournament, against German side Reutlingen, was played out in conditions so draining that Gordon Smith considered retirement. "Gordon was knackered and said to us that he was going to pack it in after this, and we had to persuade him that we were all just as knackered," Gilzean told Kenny Ross. "Even at his age, Gordon was among the fittest players in the squad and we all struggled to cope with the heat and humidity in America."

Shankly viewed the tournament as a useful exercise in allowing his players to measure themselves against foreign opposition, and different tactical set-ups. In a friendly against Saarbrücken, in Detroit, Ian Ure remembers that Dundee could not get the ball and were demolished 5-1. It would be a valuable lesson in retaining possession for their first foray into Europe. In the rest of the tournament, Dundee drew with Hajduk Split and Palermo, beat Guadalajara and lost to FC América.

The opening to the season was dreadful. Drawn in a group with city rivals United, Celtic and Hearts in the League Cup, Shankly's side won just two of their opening six matches. They lost back-to-back matches with Hearts and the Edinburgh club reinforced their superiority over the champions by winning the first league game of the season on August 22, 3-1 at Tynecastle. Notably, Gilzean was absent from four of the seven games in that miserable spell. It was to prove indicative of the season ahead. Having been virtually unstoppable during the previous campaign, Dundee did not win more than two games in a row until May 1963. By then the title was well beyond them, Shankly's side eventually finishing ninth and exiting the Scottish Cup in the quarter-finals at the hands of Rangers.

Despite Dundee's poor domestic form, Gilzean's output increased – 41 goals by season's end was a personal best and would include a seven-goal haul and three hat-tricks – but his league tally reflects the problems the club encountered in attempting to retain their title: 24, with seven in one game against Queen of the South.

Hugh Robertson said that there was a simple explanation for their difficulties. "Visiting teams were a lot more psyched-up the season after we won the league. Europe wasn't really a distraction, but for some reason every time we had a European game we did not play well the Saturday before. Nobody held back or anything, and the Saturday after was all right, but before games we just couldn't turn it on."

In Europe, however, Dundee were a relentless force. They swatted aside some of the continent's finest clubs and very nearly went all the way, finally succumbing in the semi-finals to AC Milan, and a corrupt referee. Spearheading the assault was Gilzean, with nine goals in the tournament. Though that fell short of the biggest tally, José Altafini's 14 for Milan, eight of those came in two games against part-timers Union Luxembourg; Dundee's opponents were not nearly so accommodating.

Their first competitive game in Europe would set the template: an imperious performance and a deluge of goals. Cologne, the champions of West Germany, arrived at Dens Park in early September earmarked as one of the favourites to lift the trophy. They contained 10 West German internationals in their ranks including

Hans Schäfer, the captain and outside-left who won the World Cup in Switzerland in 1954, and Karl-Heinz Schnellinger, named at left-back in the team of the 1962 competition and who would later play in the 1966 final against England. But they would prove no match for Dundee or Gilzean.

Dundee 8 Cologne 1
European Cup, first round, first leg. Dens Park, September 5, 1963
> *The massacre at Dens Park last night was like fiction gone wild. [...] their play even surpassed that great day at Ibrox last season, which up to now had been accepted as Dundee's greatest moment since the war.*
>
> *[...] Dundee made up their minds that attack was the only way to set about the task. And as they did this with such success, the Germans could not retaliate with their master plan. The defenders were completely baffled. Dundee played with the long, swinging ball to the flank. By the time the Germans had marked the inside-forwards it was too late. They were near goal to apply the lethal touch. Cologne were ball artistes but seldom had possession. In the first half they had two shots at goal against Dundee's 15. Dundee, striking like thunder and lightning, did let up after scoring No.8, Alan Gilzean's hat-trick.*
>
> *[...] It was somehow ironical to watch the Dundee team clap Cologne into the pavilion. But this was partly a salute to Cologne's sportsmanship, which was outstanding in the face of such a blitzkrieg.*
>
> *– Dundee Evening Telegraph and Post*

Cologne keeper Fritz Ewert was knocked out in a collision with Alan Cousin, and had a swimming head up to half-time. He thought the score was 2-0 and didn't believe it when told he had lost three other goals. The German press looked for a scapegoat and found Cousin. Zlatko Cajkovski, the Cologne manager, suggested that the result of the second leg might be different, "if, say, the Dundee goalkeeper was injured" and for the return game, three weeks later, local newspapers carried a picture from the first leg in which Cousin appeared to punch Ewert in the face.

In the Sporting Post interviews in 1964, Gilzean says it was deliberately disingenuous on the part of the German media. "The paper was lying around in the hotel lounge and I think I was first to spot the picture. All footballers know how the camera can work remarkable tricks ... but here was a freak shot being used to stir up trouble. Like all continental teams, Cologne had brought a batch of photographers with them to Dens Park – shooting off pictures all through the game. They must have taken home hundreds of shots. One of these was taken from an angle which made it appear that Alan Cousin, jumping for the ball, was deliberately punching Ewert. Most of us just laughed about it and Alan Cousin, the man who never pulls anything in the least shady, took a bit of kidding. 'It's the Greek in you coming out,' said someone to our languages expert from Alloa Academy. But there was nothing funny about it. We were soon to find that out."

It was clear that Cologne were intent on making life as uncomfortable for Dundee as they possibly could when they arrived for the second leg, on September 26. The German team's players had been on a £45 per man win bonus and were irked by not getting it. "There wasn't much of the lift boy who took Hugh Robertson and I up to our [hotel] room," Gilzean told the Sporting Post. "I was just making up my mind that he had a right German-looking neck when he turned round and made that well known cut-throat gesture – with sound effects as he drew his finger across his windpipe. And that was the first indication we had that, ahead of us, lay an amazing, frightening football experience. One that made us realise to what depth continentals would go for victory in big-money competition."

When Dundee arrived for their first training session at the Müngersdorfer Stadium, the game's venue, they were told it was owned by the municipal authorities and closed at five. The only other pitch with floodlights was surfaced with red ash, while Cologne's training ground was being used by one of their minor sides. "I could see Mr Shankly was having a hard job keeping his temper in check as all these yarns were trotted out," Gillie said later. "But there was nothing else for it. We had to make do with a short session the next morning – the morning of the game."

Gilzean's hat-trick in the first leg had marked him as a danger and Cajkovski felt he had the solution in Karl Schnellinger, who had missed the first leg with injury. Acclaimed as the best left-back in the world, that evening he was at right-half. "I felt this hardy lad was there for my special benefit," Gilzean said. "There must have been 40,000 in Müngersdorfer Stadium. What a racket they made. Every second fan seemed to have a sort of hunting horn and plenty of wind to blow it."

Years later, Ian Ure remembered a brutal encounter in a Weekly News interview. "Anything went that night. I admit I should been sent off. One of their forwards aimed a kick at my head that would have killed me if it had connected. I stuck the boot right into his ribs and he went down in a heap. But there was so much going on nobody noticed. Looking back, the funniest thing was big Gillie. The Germans pulled four goals back in between the punch-ups. Alan isn't exactly made for that stuff, and his skill went out the window. Every time he got the ball he would hook it up off the deck and give it an old-fashioned winder as far up the park as he could [...] I can still see him with some fire-eating German thundering at his heels."

Yet Gillie was no mere punchbag. Bob Seith ended up with a booking in the aftermath of yet another over-zealous tackle by Schnellinger which Alan took exception to. As Seith lined up the free-kick, the German defender turned away and, as he did so, Gilzean planted a boot in his backside and ran off. Schnellinger confronted Seith, believing it was he who had delivered the humiliating blow.

That Gilzean lacked bravery is a recurring theme but appears to be unjustified. In his early years he was prone to retaliation when he felt he had been the victim of an injustice, but over time he learned to turn the other cheek. Bobby Moncur, the former Newcastle United captain and hard man, refutes the notion that Gilzean was 'soft', recalling an incident from a Scotland trip in 1969: "We were playing a World Cup game in Germany. Gillie was taking some hammer. Eventually he turned and banjoed centre-half Willi Schulz with a right hand. Schulz dropped like a stuck pig. It was the best right hand I ever saw."

Yet this was uncharacteristic and Moncur noted that Gillie tended to play within the rules. "Playing against Gilzean is something I look forward to. I don't hang back … Gillie won't back off. It's always hard but fair. Schulz must have asked for it, because Alan usually takes his bruises as part of the game."

In Cologne, Gilzean was not the only one to take a pounding. True to Cajkovski's word, Bert Slater was flattened just before the half-hour mark when saving at the feet of Christian Müller. He was carried to a stretcher behind the goal with blood pouring from his head. Cologne's club doctor attempted to lead Slater to a waiting ambulance, but the Dundee goalkeeper refused to get into it. "Bert would have none of it," recalled Gilzean. "Three times he was up off that stretcher. Eventually, he was led to the pavilion by Sammy Kean, still protesting."

Gilzean told the Sporting Post that Slater undoubtedly took a risk in diving at Müller's feet, but that what followed afterwards was malicious. "The tackling was murderous in ferocity. Kicks were made at us when the ball was yards away. Blows were struck without any action from the ref. All the sportsmanship Cologne had shown at Dens was out of the window. Gordon Smith and Ian Ure were the chief victims. I got my share too and was promised a whole lot more. As I expected, Karl Schnellinger stuck to me closer than anyone ever has before. Never at any time did he look in the least bit friendly either." Gilzean added that at one point – no doubt following the kick in his posterior – the German strode towards him angrily shaking his fist and pointing at his chin.

While Slater was being patched up, Andy Penman took his place between the posts. By that stage Dundee were already a goal down and it was 3-0 by half-time. Shankly was anxious to assess Slater's condition at half-time, and felt that if he was in any shape to continue then he must, with Dundee in danger of capitulating. The scene that unfolded was redolent of a Laurel and Hardy movie. "Bob Shankly said to him, 'How many fingers am I holding up, Bert?' recalled Hugh Robertson. "Bob Shankly held up four fingers and Bert said five. I'll never forget that, and straight away Shankly said to Andy Penman, 'Right, you're in goal for the second half.'"

But five minutes after the interval, a bandaged Slater was back, on the wing. Gillie recalled that he was still groggy, but "just five minutes later he was in goal, daring as ever. We lost only one more goal. I'm convinced that we wouldn't have won the tie if Bert hadn't come back. He was an inspiration. Mind you, the Germans never let up because he was injured. Sometimes, when I saw how they went in on him, I shuddered. The crowd lapped it up and screamed their heads off. With this chorus of hate increasing every minute, the game seemed as if it would never finish."

Dundee's problems merely intensified as the final whistle approached. "As the end came near, and it was obvious Cologne wouldn't pull through, the crowd spilled from the terracing on to the track, right up to the touchline. Police and officials ignored this. No one did anything, but mentally, I decided I would dash for it as soon as the final whistle went. Others were thinking the same way, but I was luckier than most. All I got was a kick or two on the shins as we were hemmed in on the way to the pavilion. Bobby Cox and Ian Ure were both struck with folding chairs. Gordon Smith was so badly mauled he had to be helped to the pavilion."

Smith's legs were badly bruised, and there was genuine fear among the players. Fortunately, hundreds of off-duty British Army servicemen had attended the match to support Dundee and they helped defuse the atmosphere. "The soldiers followed, ostensibly to pat us on the backs," Alan Cousin said, smiling at the memory, "but it was, nevertheless, good to see them. There were rumours that Gordon Smith was tripped by a spectator, but I don't know if it was true or just Dundonian banter."

Cologne players threw water on their opponents in the tunnel and Gilzean recalled: "When we got back to the hotel [...] the receptionist turned on us. She'd been at the game. 'You dirty dogs,' she kept shouting."

There was genuine relief when the squad left the following day, but also immense satisfaction. Cologne had been second favourites for the European Cup, and the result imbued a collective belief that had been lacking. As he looks across his bar, Hugh Robertson tells me that he remembers the first game against the Germans better than any other, recalling that when he entered the pitch for the warm-up, Cologne were wearing gleaming new tracksuits and going through well-rehearsed drills, while Dundee, who had swapped their new polo-neck top for the V-necked strip they had won the league in, were a ragged bunch in baggy shirts and ripped tracksuit bottoms.

Any inferiority complex disappeared after the result. "It did our morale a power of good," Gilzean told the Sporting Post. "We felt we could hold our own now with any club [and] that was far from how we felt before Cologne came to Dens Park."

The draw for the second round pitted Dundee with the Portuguese champions Sporting Lisbon. Shankly's side stretched their unbeaten run to seven and moved within four points of leaders Hearts in the league with a 1-0 home win over Kilmarnock, a game in which Gilzean scored the only goal. A Sporting Lisbon representative was an interested spectator, impressed with Gilzean, Gordon Smith and Bobby Cox.

Again, Dundee were underdogs. Sporting Clube de Portugal were an institution, with one of the finest stadiums in Europe and a plethora of international talent from Brazil and Portugal. Dundee's experience in Lisbon, though, would differ greatly from their experiences in Germany. Sporting fans followed them in hordes, asking for club badges to add to their collections, and such was one fan's determination to get a trinket that he offered Alec Stuart, the Dundee reserve, an overcoat in exchange. "The Portuguese people went out of their way to help us," said Gilzean. "They gave us a practice ground to ourselves – and a bus to get around in. And the game was one of the cleanest I have ever played in."

There was no compromise on effort, however, as both teams served up a thrilling match played at lightning speed. Dundee withstood incessant attacks by their hosts until the 89th minute but conceded when the referee ruled that a shot Bert Slater had punched on to the bar had crossed the line when it bounced to the ground. "We came away only one goal down [...] and we felt pretty good," said Gilzean.

Ronnie Scott, the veteran Sunday Post journalist, was a 14-year-old boy during the European Cup run and attended every home game. He remembers not being able to watch or listen to the Sporting Lisbon game because it was not broadcast. "I had a newspaper round and did not know the result until I picked up my papers at seven the next morning," says Scott. "Imagine that – I was a Dundee fanatic and had to wait until the next day to find out the score. When I looked at the paper and saw that they had got beaten 1-0 I thought, 'That's the bubble burst.' "

But Gillie and Dundee had good reason to feel optimistic having dispensed with Cologne in such a convincing manner.

Dundee 4 Sporting Lisbon 1

European Cup second round, second leg. Dens Park, October 31 1962

Dundee supporters must surely have been delighted with the work of
Smith, their master planner and the architect of last night's victory. And he
was fortunate in his choice of executives, particularly Gilzean, who ranged

*and roved with deadly effect collecting three goals in the process. [...] The
first came after 14 minutes. A Smith cross cunningly flighted to the oncoming
Gilzean let the inside-left shoot into the goal as desperate defenders closed on
him. Just on half-time, from another Smith cross, Cousin out-leaped defenders
and headed home from close range. With Dundee now clearly in control Smith
slipped a short one to Gilzean, who evaded two tackles and raced on to score on
the run. When the fourth came, Penman had slewed to the wing and crossed
low to Gilzean, who hooked through almost on the line. Sporting Club fought
valiantly to the end. After 62 minutes they scored through Figueiredo, but by
then Dundee were masters.*
    – The Glasgow Herald

There was a tangible sense of optimism in the aftermath. Backed by a vociferous
support, the players knew they could match anyone – and they had a phenomenon in
attack. "What happened after the second leg against Sporting was that people started
to believe we could go all the way, that we had a team capable of beating the best, and
that we had a player who was virtually unstoppable," adds Scott.

"Gilzean was simply unplayable against Cologne. They couldn't live with him.
Cologne seemed ill-prepared that night and had underestimated Dundee; Gilzean
took full advantage. I don't think Alan Gilzean has ever received the credit he deserves,
and that's because he never pushed himself into the limelight. He was certainly one of
the best players I have ever seen. He was very skilful and a very good passer of the ball.
He would drop deep and ping these great balls down the flanks to open up the game,
and then he would be there in the box to get on the end of the cross."

The final was scheduled for Wembley and Scott says that one of his schoolfriends
was so confident Dundee would go all the way that he booked a bus ticket to London.
"He lost his money on that one, sadly."

Gilzean should have been Dundee's icon during that European run. Every great
team has a face, and in that year's European Cup Benfica's face was Eusébio, Milan's
was Altafini and Dundee's was Gilzean. It seems strange, then, to find him on the
periphery in match reports from the time. Isn't there an old cliché in football that it's
the strikers who get all the glory? Again, it seems his reticence to project himself into
the spotlight helps explain why his feats were treated with an air of banality.

Mention Gilzean's name to those who witnessed that European run and there is a
religious fervour in their voices. Only true greatness produces undying devotion, and
it makes sense that the self-effacing Gilzean, untainted by the delusions of grandeur
that afflict many footballers today, should be the subject of it. It was just what he did;

what he had always done, since those days as a free spirit running around the scouting hut at Craighall. If he hadn't been playing for Dundee, it would have been Coupar Angus Juniors, or Alyth, or whoever would give him a game.

The late Tommy Gallacher, another Dundee football legend and latterly Dundee Courier reporter, saw the same devotion in the eyes of those who turned up at Tannadice in 1972 to watch Gilzean play in a testimonial for Dennis Gillespie, the Dundee United player. This eulogy in Gilzean's own testimonial programme, in 1974, gives some indication of the esteem in which he was and, still is, held in Dundee.

A crowd of 11,000, one of the biggest gates of the season, turned up at Tannadice for the game and there is no doubt that the player the crowd wanted to see most was Alan Gilzean. Chants of 'Gillie' rang round Tannadice Street in increasing volume before the game and during it, and you could sense the expectancy among the crowd every time he touched the ball. The Spurs favourite did not let his fans down. The old touches were there. The clever flicks with the head. The concealed pass and the ability always to be in the right place at the right time [...] They remember Gilzean as a star well before the London crowds were able to appreciate it. They remember him scoring four goals against Rangers at Ibrox, as great an individual performance as ever seen on the famous Glasgow ground. They recall his scoring nine goals, including two hat-tricks, against Cologne and Sporting Lisbon [...] Despite his association with Spurs, Alan Gilzean will always be linked with Dundee as one of the greatest players ever to represent the club. The goals, the honours, the acclaim [...] have not changed Alan Gilzean one little bit.

Next up for Dundee were Anderlecht. The Belgian champions had already dispensed with a Real Madrid side who had won the tournament five times previously and contained Alfredo di Stéfano, Paco Gento and Ferenc Puskás, in the preliminary round. Chief among their ranks was Paul van Himst, the Belgian player of the year and, at just 19, the holder of 16 caps for his country. Van Himst was just one of nine internationalists, with Belgium team-mate Joseph Jurion the main goal threat. Gilzean remembers that "Anderlecht were a delightful team. Technically, probably the best we met in the competition."

The quarter-final first leg was staged in Brussels. The intervening months had not been beneficial to Dundee's title defence. In December, they defeated Queen of the South, St Mirren and Raith Rovers, yet trailed Rangers by nine points. Against Queen of the South, Dundee scored 10 goals, Gilzean's seven equalling Bert Juliussen's club record for a single game set 15 years earlier and falling one short of Jimmy McGrory's Scottish record, achieved playing for Celtic in 1928. We have already examined the circumstances behind Gilzean's record haul and the embarrassment he felt in reaching it. Notwithstanding the injury to George Farm, the Queens goalkeeper, and Gilzean's part in it, it was evidence of a lethal predator at the top of his game.

If Dundee's league position indicated that there was little or no chance of catching Rangers, Gilzean was in no mood to surrender. He told supporters on the train home from Kirkcaldy after the win over Raith that the Ibrox club could still be caught. But all of Dundee's brio from the earlier European games had dissipated.

As winter gave way to spring, the title challenge fell apart and there was a very real danger that their European Cup bid would go the same way. They lost their next two in the league, against Aberdeen and Clyde, and their only competitive games between January 12 and their March 6 meeting with Anderlecht in Brussels came in the Scottish Cup, against Highland League Inverness Caledonian and Second Division Montrose, after the worst winter in years wiped out the league programme. Dundee's indifferent league form prompted talk of a 'Gilzean complex', that they were becoming too reliant on their influential inside-left, who was becoming more and more of a marked man. Shankly, though, stuck rigidly to the tactics and formation that had brought him so much success in the past. Scottish league teams might have become wise to Dundee's strengths and weakness, but they were still an unknown quantity in Europe, and a mediocre league season would be a small price if it meant capturing the biggest prize of all.

Anderlecht 1 Dundee 4

European Cup quarter-final. Heysel Stadium. March 6, 1963

> *Anderlecht, the pride of Belgian soccer up to last night, have quickly found a scapegoat for the terrific European Cup turn-up in Brussels. Most of their Flemish players have no English, but they all seemed to pronounce the word 'luck,' with a gesture towards the joy-crazy Dundee camp. They said in no uncertain fashion that it was their Hungarian goalkeeper Fazekas who brought them this disgrace of a 4-1 home defeat.*

> *Inside-left Joseph Jurion, the man of 40 international caps, told me, "If we had a goalkeeper like Slater, it would have been so different. Fazekas was very bad. Surely he must be dropped for our next game in Dundee."*

> *[...] Here we saw the European team that had not conceded a goal on home soil, the team that held Real in Spain then beat them at the Heysel Stadium, being baffled to the last by a superbly fit Scottish team who played*

a defensive game with admirable coolness and brilliant football. Don't let there be any mistake about it – Dundee had their share of luck. But there was absolutely nothing fortunate in the way they scored their four goals.

Ian Ure put himself right into the world-class ratings on his brilliant performance. Bert Slater was fabulous too. There was Bobby Cox playing the captain's role and saving three scoring shots on the line. And in attack Alan Gilzean, always a menace in the breakaway, cracked home two magnificent goals, and could easily have collected his third hat-trick in this competition.

[...] All the Dundee players were presented with inscribed cigarette lighters. Bobby Cox won an extra prize when his name was drawn out of the hat in a raffle for the match ball, which was signed by all the players. A late arrival at the banquet was Alan Gilzean, who had been to hospital with an ankle injury. No one knew he had even been injured, but in the first 20 minutes he suffered a deep gash on his right ankle. He didn't complain at half-time, although he felt the blood seeping through his stocking. The wound required six stitches. The Belgians were amazed when they heard the extent of the injury for he had never flinched at any time.

[...] The explosion of thunder-crackers could still be heard round the ground when Dundee scored in 65 seconds. The crowd was struck dumb when they saw Gilzean beat Fazekas with a powerful shot from just inside the box with Ure, Robertson, Seith, Penman, Smith and Cousin all involved in a mesmerising build up.

[...] Then Gilzean scored No.2 in the 18th minute and it was a magnificent goal. Cousin's cross from the left was touched sideways by Robertson, Gilzean ran on to it and gave the Hungarian keeper no chance from 20 yards.

[...] Dundee struck again after the interval when Gilzean headed down for Cousin to score from six yards. Anderlecht began to tire in the mud underfoot and Dundee had two further chances to score before Gordon Smith made it four in the 71st minute. Gilzean jumped with Fazekas and the ball broke for Smith, who had an open goal.

[...] Dundee are really making their name. As someone said, "Maybe now even the people in England will realise Britain is still in the European Cup."

– Dundee Evening Telegraph and Post

Alan Cousin told me that Dundee were treated like heroes by the Anderlecht supporters afterwards, and he remembers reading the Belgian newspapers the following day for their reaction. " 'You were dominated' was the headline and then, beneath it, 'but you scored four times'. A crowd followed us about when we left the hotel to walk around the city. Someone spotted Ian Ure and said, 'Ah, defenseur formidable.' Bert Slater was absolutely wonderful that night and I remember someone saying to Bert afterwards, 'what a goalkeeper you are' [mimicked in French]. I think it was Gillie who said, quick as you like, 'Aye, he plays like that every week.'

Jurion, so critical of his own goalkeeper, was full of praise for Dundee. "I can't see us having any chance of reaching the semi-finals now, but the only hope is that Dundee change their tactics, become an offensive side when playing at home, and maybe then we will have more chance to score some goals. The trouble was that this time we faced a team who had a plan of pure defence on a 7-3-1 system." The '1' scored two and made two, all on a gammy leg.

The return at Dens Park was meant to be a mere formality, but Anderlecht dictated play and scored after half an hour. Gilzean missed the previous Saturday's defeat to Airdrie with that injured ankle, but had the stitches removed for the visit of the Belgians. His presence ensured that two Anderlecht defenders shadowed him throughout, and he was unable to add to his tally, but late goals from Cousin and Smith ensured their passage into the semi-finals 6-2 on aggregate.

Gillie recalls the experiences in Portugal and Belgium with fondness: "Those European nights were very special, and that performance in Anderlecht was very special indeed. We had played some great stuff and the Belgians knew they had witnessed a fantastic performance from Dundee; at the end of the game the Belgian crowd gave us a standing ovation and clapped us off the pitch."

After the Cologne trip, it was something of a surprise when they were treated with such affection in their following fixtures ... until the semi-final. "These games, and all that surrounded them, helped make us forget about Cologne," said Gilzean. "And then we were drawn against Milan in the semi-final – and into more trouble. Even before the first game at Milan got started, we had to mark time for about an hour while a boys' game was played. Then, just as we were stripping, there was a knock on the dressing room door. Mr Shankly answered it. There stood a man speaking fast in Italian and obviously demanding admission. But the fellow couldn't get through at all, despite all the gesticulating. Things were getting pretty hot when Mr Shankly put a stop to it all by simply shutting the door on the voluble Italian who, we heard afterwards, wanted to stage an identity parade with passport picture checks and all that sort of thing."

Hugh Robertson says that during the Milan trip the players had indulged in one particularly humorous act of tomfoolery: "We were at this cafe with tables and chairs outside. There was this motorbike outside the cafe and Bert Slater was into his motorbikes. He was always talking about them and what he could do on them. So Alan said to Bert, 'Go on Punchy, let's see what you can do, ride up to the end of the tables and chairs and weave in and out of them on the way back.' Punchy said to Alan, 'Whose bike is it though?' Alan said, 'I don't know, but if you do it quickly no-one will know.' So Bert started up the motorbike and rode down to the end of the cafe, and as he was coming towards us, the chairman James Gellatly stood up with his big cine camera filming it. But as Bert was coming back he must have hit the accelerator accidentally, because the bike started revving and he couldn't stop it. He ended up crashing into Gellatly, who was knocked flying and his camera came landing down on top of him. The chairman was not happy but of course we were all in stitches."

This might explain the over-officious Italian's determination to speak to the players or, more probably, it was a stunt designed to cause maximum disruption to Dundee's preparations. If so, it worked. Dundee were without their captain, Bobby Cox, who had torn his cartilage and was replaced by the inexperienced Alec Stuart. Without the influential Cox, Dundee struggled in the vast bowl of the San Siro in front of 90,000 partisans. Gilzean remembered the sights and sounds of the stadium clearly some years later, of the fans hemmed in by netting which surrounded the terracing, trumpets blaring, sirens and the occasional thunder flash. There was a feral atmosphere and the sensory overload seemed to add to Dundee's problems.

It did not help that the Spanish referee, Vicente Antonio Caballero, seemed hell-bent on making things as difficult as possible for Dundee. Gilzean was repeatedly singled out for brutal treatment by the Peruvian defender Víctor Benítez, but Caballero turned a blind eye. In contrast, Gilzean says, every tackle made by a Dundee player brought some kind of censure from the Spaniard. "I've never seen anything like what he did. Right from the start, he blew for a foul any time a Dundee man went for the ball. I'm not overstating it," Gilzean reflected in the Sporting Post. "The least physical contact was a cert for a whistle against us. With the crowd following the lead and howling at us, the effect was so upsetting that before long we were almost afraid to tackle. Ian Ure, in particular, got a raw deal. High balls which, nine times out of 10, Ian would cut out, became a nightmare. He was scared to go in for them, particularly when they were landing in the penalty area."

Nereo Rocco, the Milan coach, had singled out 5ft 7in Alex Hamilton as a player his tall left-winger, Paolo Barison, could exploit. Ure was being drawn out of position to compensate for the right-back's deficiencies in the air. A succession of missiles were launched to the near post and, with Barison easily outjumping Hamilton, and Ure fearful of conceding a penalty, Milan exploited the situation to maximum advantage. Milan scored all of their goals from crosses and, despite the sides entering the interval level courtesy of an Alan Cousin equaliser, there was an inevitability about a Milan victory. Norrie Price, in Up wi' the Bonnets, notes that some weeks after the tie, Caballero "was found to have accepted extravagant gifts from the Italian club prior to the game, and subsequently he was banned on various other charges of bribery".

Bribery in Italian football was part of the fabric of the sport in that country. Christos Michas, a Greek referee, would be convicted of match-fixing a decade later. The most high-profile game under scrutiny? The 1973 European Cup Winners' Cup final between Leeds and AC Milan. Michas disallowed a valid Leeds goal that night, turned down three penalty appeals, sent off Norman Hunter, the Leeds defender, and awarded a dubious free-kick from which Milan scored the game's only goal. He was later banned for life by UEFA, but Milan kept the trophy.

Caballero seemed as blatant, but his antics against Dundee were less well trumpeted. Ross writes: "The ball appeared to have gone out of play before one goal, and a Milan player was standing on the goal-line, offside for the second. Indeed, the linesman raised his flag, but was overruled."

Milan added two further goals before the end of the game to make the final score 5-1 and leave Dundee feeling "a downcast lot" according to Gillie, who recalled that they then had to attend a reception that went on until 1.30am. Gillie remembers one of the Milan players wanting to leave the function at 12.45am and approaching the coach, Nereo Rocco, to ask if he could go home. At that, Rocco launched into a verbal tirade and started pushing and shoving his player.

Jimmy Greaves experienced Rocco's methods at first hand during his days at Milan. The Italian coach would clutch a long stick whilst conducting training and would prod players he felt were under-performing, or who stepped out of line. He was overweight and would sit in the shade on hot days, sipping cold drinks and barking orders as the players were put through their paces in scorching temperatures.

It is interesting that the experiences of Greaves, and of Denis Law, would shape Gilzean's decision when his own opportunity to move to Italy arrived, 18 months later. But, most probably, he had formed his own opinion of the country long before he sought the counsel of Law or read about Greaves' problems in the newspapers.

The return leg at Dens Park on May 1 was no more friendly and equally controversial. Dundee were much improved but could engineer few chances, with the Italians defending deeply and tackling brutally. Nonetheless, Gilzean broke the deadlock just before half-time, when he got his head on the end of a Gordon Smith cross. Again, though, the Italians got the benefit of key refereeing decisions. Andy Penman had a goal disallowed for offside and Gordon Smith should have won a penalty when he was punched in the box, but the Belgian referee Lucien van Nufell ignored Dundee's protests. One photograph shows Gilzean appealing wildly to the bespectacled Van Nufell, who appears to be admonishing the striker. Gilzean's anger rose steadily during the game. Once again, he was on the receiving end of some hefty challenges from Benítez. The first time Gilzean got the ball, the Peruvian gave him a surreptitious kick which Van Nufell failed to spot. On the next occasion, Benítez allowed him to pass and then took his legs from under him.

"It was another night when things happened that should never happen on a football field. I decided to have no more of it," said Gilzean. "I'd get in first. From then on we were narking away at each other. Not that we were the only ones. Some of the tackling was as bad as anything in Cologne, with Gordon Smith getting the worst."

Things died down after half-time, but near the end, and clearly frustrated at the way in which Dundee's European Cup run was coming to an end, Gilzean lashed out at Benítez and the defender went sprawling. Van Nufell ran towards Gilzean, turned him around to see the back of his shirt and then said: "Number 10. My decision is out. Out, out, out." Gilzean's team-mates surrounded the referee to protest, but to no avail. The European run in which he had played such a significant part was at an end, and in most ignominious circumstances. It was the first time he had been sent off in a game and his most humiliating experience as a footballer until that point. "For me, it was a particularly sad end to our European Cup bid," he said.

Before I leave the Royal Hotel in Dalry, Hugh Robertson has one final story he'd like to retell about his old room-mate. "One of his favourite routines was with Bert Slater. Bert would act like he was a boxer and Gillie would pretend to interview him. He would stand beside him with a pretend microphone and ask, 'Are you a boxer?' and Bert would say, 'What do you think I am, a cocker spaniel?' in this American accent. Of course, the rest of us were all rolling about laughing at this. They had it off to a tee and they would vary the patter, but that's the one that I remember." He's smiling as he finishes off. There's a hint of sparkle left in those rheumy eyes yet.

His smile on that day was the first thing that came back to me upon hearing the news that Hugh Robertson had died peacefully in his armchair at home on March 12, 2010. It was a bitter blow for Dundee supporters, coming as it did just over two weeks after the death of Bobby Cox, the captain of the league-winning team.

§

It is a spring afternoon not long after I have spoken to Craig Brown when I put a call in to Bobby Wishart, the one former football colleague that Gillie still keeps in touch with. It is an Edinburgh number and I imagine a phone ringing somewhere in a lavish house, for no other reason than because I know that Bobby Wishart is a retired insurance salesman and might have saved a few bob over the years. A woman who I presume to be his wife answers the phone in a matronly manner. "We don't have a Bobby here," she admonishes me, "we do have a Robert, though. He wears a hearing aid and can't really hear on the phone very well. What's it in connection with?" I tell her and she adds, "I'll see if he wants to speak to you."

Bobby Wishart's voice sounds weak and distant, but I'm unsure as to whether his frailty is real or pretend. His opening gambit wrong-foots me. "I think he played for Dundee and I think he played for Scotland a few times," he says. "But I can't really remember anything else about him." I have the impression that I'm having the mickey taken out of me.

"I thought you were still in touch with Alan? You spoke to Alan Pattullo of The Scotsman a few months ago," I reply, certain that he's trying to protect Gillie. "I know Alan is quite private, but I think he deserves his place in the Scottish Football Association Hall of Fame. I spoke to one of the judges on the committee, and he seems to think that the reason Alan isn't in it is because he has kept such a low profile since he retired." The reply brings yet more mischief. "Sorry, I can't really hear you very well. I've got a hearing aid."

That night, I send off my nomination to the SFA Hall of Fame. I've figured that if there are names such as Ian St John and Davie Cooper there, then Gilzean should take his rightful place. There is a section on the website for submitting nominations. Into a matchbox-sized space entitled: "Reasons for nominating this individual" I manage to squeeze the following:

"22 caps, 12 goals. Five senior medals. Legend at both clubs he played for. Over 250 career goals. Hugely influential figure in Dundee's league win in 1962 and run to European Cup semi-final in 1963. Held Scottish football's goalscoring record with 52 goals in one season. His record was eventuall [sic] taken by Henrik Larsson, a Hall of Fame inductee."

The missing 'y' is a typo. Let's hope his 'eventuall' nomination is not affected by the standard of my spelling.

6

EH MIND O' GILLIE

He saw nothing perfidious in his decision to leave. Hadn't he always given his best? Hadn't he watched Ian Ure, a contemporary from the Willie Thornton years, leave for Arsenal the previous summer for a significant transfer fee? He was approaching his 26th birthday, he had heard the stories of untold riches in England, he was ambitious and, most significantly, he felt wanted. There were the inevitable criticisms but he had heard them before: he was lazy, he did not defend, all he did was score goals. But was that not his job? He was being asked to play as a forward. He had scored 55 for club and country in the season just ended. How many would he have got if he'd spent the time chasing back?

Dundee wanted to keep him, but there was a marked difference between those wanting to retain him on their terms and setting his own. Of course there would be regret; he had enjoyed some wonderful times at Dens Park and there might be further glories around the corner, but he could not foresee them. The board had sold Jimmy Gabriel to Everton in 1960 and Ure to Arsenal. Most of the money had gone on new floodlights and ground improvements and not enough on improving the team.

No, he had to move to better himself and football could be a fickle game. He had not forgotten how Dundee would not let Doug Cowie train with his former team-mates when his time to move had come. There could be no room for sentimentality.

And then there was Scotland. He had made his debut the previous November and added a cap later that month, then another two in April and May. But there was always that doubt. Everyone knew about the Old Firm bias. He played for a provincial club, and if he moved to Glasgow he would be little better off financially. Dundee paid wages on a par with Rangers and Celtic, and it was clear that this was going to be his only big move. He had to be certain it was the right one. He was planning to marry Irene and start a family. The move would make life more comfortable, it would enhance his international prospects. He would give Dundee their place, though, and present them with his terms.

The George Eastham transfer saga changed football irrevocably. Where once footballers were slaves to their clubs, Eastham's switch from Newcastle United to Arsenal enabled them to throw off the shackles of the retain and transfer system. Eastham was Bosman lite. The players were not conferred absolute rights but they had a much greater say in what they were paid and who they signed for.

Dundee had tried to enforce their hold over Ure in 1963 but John Bloom, a washing machine magnate and Arsenal-supporting millionaire, offered Ure – who had tried unsuccessfully to claim unemployment benefit – a job as a sales rep. Within days, Ure was on his way to London. Gilzean's own move would be much more protracted and reflected Shankly's dogged determination to hold on to his star turn. Strapping centre-halves were expendable. Fifty-two-goals-a-season strikers were not.

Gilzean's decision to leave Dundee hints at something more conventional; a slight glimmer of vanity that is otherwise missing, an intrinsic desire to match himself against the best. There can be no recognition of one's place in the grand scheme of things without a fundamental understanding of one's talent. Gillie knew his worth.

He had conversations with his Scotland team-mates. His room-mate on international trips was John White, the Tottenham inside-right. White told Gillie he was on £85 a week at White Hart Lane, nearly three times what Alan was on. "You play international football and you realise what other people are earning and obviously the first one of that great Dundee side who thought he could do better was big Ian," he told Jim Hendry. "He obviously said to himself, 'I have had two or three great years and now I must cash in.' The club can only pay players what they are bringing through the turnstiles. Nowadays there are sponsorship deals and commercial earnings, but not then, and that meant unfortunately Bob Shankly was just coming to the stage when he couldn't offer us any more.

"Eventually, you would come to the conclusion that you have to move and unfortunately that was the break up of a great Dundee team. At that time there were no long-term contracts, you signed on every year. I came to the end of my contract and I had talks with Shanks to see if he could come up with terms that would suit me."

Viewed from a distance of almost half a century, Gilzean's demands seem primitive in comparison with the earnings of today's players. He submitted a list of terms that he felt had to be met were he to consider re-signing for Dundee. In reality, he had already resolved to leave. His terms included a pay increase, greater insurance cover, benefit guarantees and the provision of a house. Bob Shankly and the board refused to meet his demands and offered the same contract that he had been on the previous season. This was an insult to a player who scored 55 goals for club and country and prompted Gilzean to set a deadline on the decision over his future. On June 15, 1964, the Daily Express reporter Mike Langley phoned Gillie at the family home in Coupar Angus. Gilzean said: "I've turned down the club's terms and it's checkmate. I will leave all decisions until June 30 when my contract ends. Until then I am not asking for a transfer or saying anything about coming to England."

But it was clear from the Daily Express report that Gilzean was intent on Tottenham. He was aware of the London club's interest through the late Jim 'Scoop' Rodger, the legendary Daily Express reporter. Scoop acted as a conduit between ambitious Scottish footballers and English clubs. He helped facilitate some of the biggest deals between Scotland and England and his contacts book was extensive. In effect he was one of the first agents and, crucially for Gilzean, he had the ear of Bill Nicholson, the Tottenham Hotspur manager. Nicholson was a regular visitor to Scottish football grounds, having had great success with the signings of Bill Brown, the former Dundee goalkeeper, Dave Mackay, of Hearts, and John White, from Falkirk.

"I had always said that in England there are the big five, the two Liverpool teams, Manchester United, Spurs and Arsenal; they were the big clubs and I wanted one of them. Scoop was very friendly with Bill Nick and he always told me Spurs were keen – he fixed it for me to go."

There was little likelihood of Gilzean joining Arsenal. At the height of the transfer speculation, in early November, Dundee lost 7-2 in a friendly with the London club at Dens Park, a game watched by Bobby Kerr, Wolverhampton Wanderers' Scottish scout. Gilzean had been singularly unimpressive and Billy Wright, the Arsenal manager, said as much in his column in the Daily Express: "I was dreadfully disappointed by the performance of Alan Gilzean, Dundee's Scottish international centre-forward, whose name has been closely linked with several English clubs this year," wrote Wright. "I would say he is vastly overrated judging on this display. He certainly did not look a player worth £100,000 – a figure which has been widely quoted."

Not that any of this mattered to Gilzean. The presence of Scotland international colleagues Mackay, White and that of Brown, his former Dundee team-mate, had given Spurs a head start. The fact that Bobby Smith had recently left Tottenham was to prove equally advantageous for Gillie.

When asked about the London club's putative interest, James Gellatly, the Dundee chairman, told the Daily Express: "There has been no inquiry or offer from

Tottenham." As Langley notes, these were "almost exactly the words he used about Arsenal last year shortly before selling centre half Ian Ure for £62,500."

The reputed price tag for Gilzean was £80,000. Dundee would eventually budge on the amount, not least because by then they had weakened their hand by purchasing Gilzean's replacement, Alex Harley for £10,000 from Birmingham City, before a deal had been struck for their biggest asset. The theory went that if Harley, who had scored 100 goals in 153 games in England and Scotland, cost £10,000, then Gilzean was worth a comparable fee. But prolific as Harley was, he was not Gilzean.

By June 28, Gilzean had made up his mind to move on. He handed in a transfer request which was rejected immediately by Bob Shankly, but it was only a matter of time. Recalling the moment he decided to leave in Jim Hendry's book, Dundee Greats, he says he knew in his "heart of hearts that I had to go because I thought at the time the team was beginning to break up and, if you recall the history of Dundee, they don't win things on a regular basis every two or three years. There were always long spells in between winning trophies, from the Scottish Cup win back in 1910 to the Billy Steel era in the early 1950s, to the championship side of 1962 and you say to yourself, 'God Almighty, it might be a long, long time before it happens again.' "

Two days after the transfer request, Gillie's contract expired, and when the club stopped paying him his wages he applied for unemployment benefit, as Ure had a year earlier. On Thursday October 22, 1964, Gilzean's 26th birthday, he appeared before a Ministry of Pensions and National Insurance appeals tribunal in a test case to establish whether footballers were entitled to unemployment benefit. Ure's transfer to Arsenal had been completed two days before his own tribunal.

Gilzean was represented by Johnny Hughes, secretary of the Players' Union, who argued that when the Unemployment Act had been drawn up, claims by professional footballers had not been accounted for. When Gilzean's contract expired at the end of June, the retain and transfer system dictated that Dundee were allowed to hold on to the player without having to pay him. "In normal circumstances or business, people can give a week or month's notice," said Hughes. "But the professional footballer is tied by the retention system." Hughes added that the retention system interfered with Gilzean's right to use his skills to his best advantage and that it was odd that he could claim sickness or injury benefit but not unemployment benefit.

The Ministry said that the terms offered to Gilzean were no less favourable than those offered to similar people in his line of work and that he had not presented a strong case for why he had refused to accept terms. Hughes argued that Gilzean could earn up to three or four times his Dundee wage in England. His appeal was thrown out, with Gilzean threatening to take the matter to the Ministry's Commissioner.

The dispute rumbled on over the summer, with Gilzean, aware that the club had made approximately £120,000 from the Ure transfer and various cup runs, refusing to sign terms. Clubs interested in Gilzean watched from afar. And, then, just over three weeks after he handed in his transfer request, John White, his friend from Scotland international trips, died on Crews Hill golf course in Middlesex on July 21. The 26-year-old had been crouching under a large oak tree at the side of the first fairway, his bag by his side, when he was struck by lightning and killed instantly.

Albert Burr, a 55-year-old club steward, told the following day's Daily Mirror: "Nobody saw Mr White arrive. There was a terrific downpour with a clap of thunder and a bright streak of lightning. Nobody realised it had struck the tree which is within sight of the clubhouse, or that anybody had been hit."

Dave Mackay says that the day before White had invited him and Cliff Jones to play, but they had declined, saying that the sky was black and White was mad to contemplate a game. "It was the last time I saw him," Mackay revealed in an interview for an official Tottenham DVD in 2009. "It took me a long time to get over that."

Bill Nicholson broke down and wept on hearing the news of White's death. He was asked by police to identify the body and was unable to keep his usual, steely composure. The death of the good-mannered, freckle-faced Scot robbed his wife Sandra of a husband, a young family of a father and football of one of its greatest players.

Not only was White's death a devastating blow to Nicholson on a personal level, he had been robbed of one of his best players. In 1964, the double-winning team he had built so carefully was in decline. Danny Blanchflower had retired, Bobby Smith had moved on and Mackay was still overcoming the effects of a second broken leg. In March 1964, Nicholson paid Fulham £72,500 for their England international midfielder, Alan Mullery. A few months on, and anxious to fill the gap left by White, he approached the same club with an offer for Johnny Haynes, but he opted to remain at Fulham and Nicholson turned his attention elsewhere.

Prior to departing for a short holiday in England, Gilzean wrote to Dundee requesting that he be allowed to play while the club awaited offers. Shankly told the press that it would take £100,000 to buy his player and he would resist every effort to let him leave. Still it rumbled on, Gilzean training on his own, playing golf with friends, and going on long drives to fill his days, until eventually there came a break in the impasse when Dundee announced that they would be prepared to listen to offers for him if he re-signed for the club. Mindful that his selection for the international match against Northern Ireland on November 25 was in jeopardy, it was all the incentive that Gilzean needed to return to training, and he agreed to a two-month deal. On October 13, he joined his team-mates at Dundee's training ground, Caird

Park, for the first time since the previous season. It was essentially on the proviso that he would be allowed to leave. On October 24, he returned to the starting line-up for the league game against Hearts. Shankly was only too willing to accommodate his talismanic striker, having watched his side struggle for any kind of consistency at the start of the 1964-65 season without him.

Jim Hendry gives a flavour of the tension around Dens Park during the stale-mate, suggesting that young boys sat at school desks praying that no-one would come in for Gillie; that he would tire of not playing, return to Dundee and play out the rest of a long and glorious career with the club. Despite the fans' impatience to see Gillie donning the navy shirt again, his first game back proved to be somewhat anti-climactic, a 2-1 defeat by Hearts. A week later, though, Gilzean scored both goals as St Mirren were beaten 2-0 and, while he did not score again until his hat-trick against St Johnstone on December 5, Dundee did not lose a match with him in the side.

By then the saga was nearing its end. Wolverhampton Wanderers, who had watched Gilzean a year earlier, had entered the frame in the summer of 1964. Sunderland and Italy's Torino were among the frontrunners. Tottenham, at this point, maintained a watching brief. The Torino vice-president, Giovanni Traversa, was expected to fly to London to meet the club's roving agent, Gigi Peronace, with a mandate to spend whatever it would take to bring Gilzean back to Italy. However, when Peronace spoke to the Dundee press he revealed that Orfeo Pianelli, the club's president, would be replacing Traversa in the negotiations. If this was an indication of the Italians' desire to sign Gilzean, they were equally determined they would not pay over the odds.

Torino had been quoted a price of £80,000 by Dundee initially, but the signing of Harley and a lack of direct interest in Gilzean forced them to reappraise their valu-ation. Just days before Gilzean was due to play for a Scotland XI in John White's tes-timonial match at White Hart Lane, Torino broke the stalemate by cabling Dundee, requesting permission to approach the player.

Peronace was a smooth-talking salesman and had persuaded British-based play-ers such as Tony Marchi, John Charles, Denis Law and Joe Baker to move to Italy. Speaking from his London hotel, he told the Evening Telegraph: "I have just had a phone call from Signore Pianelli. He will arrive in London on Wednesday. Contact will then be made with Dundee and we would be prepared to start out for Dundee on Wednesday evening or Thursday morning to see what are our chances of get-ting Gilzean. He is the player we have absolutely set our sights on. If we do not get him for Turin, then we can pack up and go home. We are not interested in any other British player. We know what we are prepared to pay. We do not wish to become involved in any auction with other clubs. But nothing more can be done until Signore Pianelli arrives."

Torino's efforts, though, would ultimately founder. The British press had reported that the one snag was the presence of Gerry Hitchens, the former England and Aston Villa centre-forward, among the playing personnel at Torino and said that Italian football rules stated that any team wishing to sign a foreigner must transfer one out of the country. This was not the case in 1964. Each club was allowed two overseas players. It was an entirely different reason that would deny Torino.

Time had been against them from the start. When Peronace and Traversa watched Gilzean score twice as a Scotland XI thrashed Spurs 6-2 in John White's testimonial, they liked what they saw, but with 10 days to go until the deadline elapsed for signing new players, and with no takers for Hitchens, they walked away from the deal and signed Italian international striker Sergio Brighenti from Modena. Gilzean, in any case, had no interest in moving to Italy. By mid-November, Sunderland thought they had concluded a deal when Dundee accepted a bid of £60,000, only for Gillie to turn down the move, thus clearing the way for Spurs.

There were conspiratorial claims that Gilzean's participation in White's testimonial had been orchestrated by the SFA and Dundee in order to parade him in front of Spurs. However, it would take another series of protracted negotiations before his move to White Hart Lane would materialise. Later, Bill Nicholson recalled the intense haggling that went on first with Dundee and then Gilzean. "From the moment I asked Bob Shankly, the Dundee manager, for a price, the talks dragged on for three weeks and three times I had to raise my offer. We were in competition with Sunderland, who had offered Gillie more money, and the Italian club Torino, although Gillie told me afterwards he was not interested in going to Italy. Denis Law and Jimmy Greaves had been playing for Italian clubs and Law warned him off."

Gilzean confided in friends that the terms offered by Sunderland had been "out of this world" and when he met with Nicholson on the banks of the River Tay after Dundee had accepted Spurs' bid of £72,500, he wanted to ensure he got the same deal. "When I met Gillie in his car beside the Tay, he told me he was keen to come to White Hart Lane, but Sunderland had offered him £20 for a win and £10 for a draw," explained Nicholson. " 'They can't do that,' I said. 'It's illegal. In the regulations it says a club can only pay £4 for a win and £2 for a draw.'

"I must have convinced him I was telling the truth, because he rejected Sunderland's offer and accepted my lower one. A few weeks later I met the late Alan Hardaker, secretary of the Football League, and asked him what clubs were allowed to offer players after the maximum wage restriction was lifted.

" 'Can they offer money for points?' I asked. 'Yes, they can, providing it's written in the contract,' he replied.

"I was staggered. 'But what about the regulations about £4 for a win and £2 for a draw?' I said. 'What's the point of having regulations if you don't stick to them?' 'It's a play on words,' answered Hardaker. 'Under the new system, you can pay them what you like.' I told him it might be a good idea if the Football League passed that information on to the clubs.

"I saw Gillie about it a few days later. 'I'm afraid I misled you,' I said. 'I've seen Alan Hardaker and he tells me Sunderland were within their rights to offer you £20-a-win.' 'I knew I was right,' answered Gillie. Typically of him, he didn't submit a wage claim, but I made sure his contract was improved. The following season we introduced bonuses on a sliding scale."

Bob Shankly would not recall the affair with nearly as much affection. He had viewed Gilzean as crucial to his plans of building another great team. He could just about bear the loss of Ure, who by 1963 was one of the finest defenders in Britain, but Gillie meant the difference between winning games and losing them. Teams win with great goalscorers, they don't lose with great defenders. In the aftermath of his departure, Shankly snapped when reporters asked him about the saga. "I'm sick of the word transfer. I've had six months of the business. I've been hindered in my proper job for Dundee. Now let's get back to the real job."

Shankly was clearly not that tired of the word, however. Just days after the sale of Gilzean, he bought Charlie Cooke for £30,000 from Aberdeen. Cooke, in his short spell with the club, would wow the Dundee crowd as Gillie had done, before following him south to Chelsea. However, the manner of the departure clearly irked Shankly long after the event. "The whole thing left a bitter taste in my mouth, but I try not to let that cloud my memory of the man," Shankly told the Weekly News almost 10 years later. "I have followed his career since he joined Tottenham but I have never actually seen him play since he left Dundee. Nor have we spoken a single word since that day. It's not a question of holding a grudge – we simply haven't met."

I could not help shake the feeling that something about Shankly's protestations suggested otherwise. It was a question I asked Ian Ure, Bob Seith, Pat Liney and Hugh Robertson, but none could recall there being any sense of ill-feeling over his departure or, specifically, any direct falling-out between Shankly and Gilzean.

The 1963-64 season had provided the record-breaking backdrop to Gilzean's departure. His 52 goals that season included a club record of 33 in the league. He scored more goals than games he played in in the league, League Cup and Scottish Cup. He would add another three for Scotland, having made his debut in the 6-1 win over Norway in a friendly on November 7. He did not score that day at Hampden but he did set up the first of Denis Law's four goals with a trademark downward header from a John White cross. His overall performance drew praise from the press men, too. "Gilzean had a fine game. He seldom wasted a ball and there were more shots last night from a Scottish centre-forward than have been seen for some time; he saw a shot and a header hit posts." His display cemented his place in the starting line-up for the British Championship match against Wales a fortnight later.

Watching Gilzean against Norway was Jock Richardson, Tottenham Hotspur's Scotland scout. When Richardson died, his son sent Spurs historian Andy Porter a series of notebooks filled with scouting reports. One sheet, franked with the number 12, contains the observations on Gilzean Bill Nicholson pored over.

Nicholson would watch Gillie 13 times before signing him. Whether that was an indication of his assiduous approach or something else is noteworthy. The Tottenham manager was looking for a foil for his prodigious goalscorer Jimmy Greaves, a role previously filled by the robust Bobby Smith who was nearing the end of his career and had moved to Brighton. Smith was a brutish presence in attack and Greaves had enjoyed a fruitful partnership with him, thriving off the psychological advantage the aggressive Smith brought to the attack. Gilzean was the antithesis of the old-style centre-forward. He was much less physical than Smith, and Nicholson had concerns about whether he would be making a mistake in opting for a more subtle partner. Football was changing, however. Ralph L Finn writes, in London's Cup Final: "There are not many of that brand of footballers left in Britain today. Since Nat Lofthouse retired, centre-forwards have tended to be of slimmer build and less effective. Nicholson failed in his search for a Smith-type player, but he did the next best thing, that of buying the best available player of the opposite kind!"

Richardson wrote in his scouting report:

Gilzean, Dundee FC, CF, 6ft 1 inch, 7/11/63, Scotland v Norway
  Watching the international match at Hampden I was particularly impressed by the play of the Scottish centre-forward, Alan Gilzean. He worried the Norwegian defence into making quite a few mistakes and he had many shots from all angles at the opposing team's goal. He was very unlucky not to score and besides having fast, good ball control, his heading of cross balls is very good. In my opinion he has earned his place in the Scottish team for a few seasons [...] If he plays for his club Dundee as he did on Thursday no wonder he is the chief goalscorer. He always seems to be in the game. He is

also very hard to knock off the ball and carries a hefty shoulder. A player I can recommend. – 11/11/63 Jock Richardson

§

Richardson's prediction that Gilzean had earned his place in the Scottish team for several seasons to come proved inaccurate. Between November 1963 and November 1965 he appeared in 10 of his country's 15 internationals, scoring six goals. In the next four years, he would feature just five times, scoring five goals. Of a possible 33 international matches he played in just 15 and found the net on 11 occasions. He was the victim of Scotland's high turnover of managers during the decade. Jock Stein, John Prentice, Bobby Brown and Malcolm MacDonald all took charge during the 1960s and each had his own ideas. Neither Prentice nor MacDonald selected Gilzean. Only Stein saw what the others did not, but he was denied Gillie's services when Tottenham withdrew him from the squad for a crucial World Cup qualifier against Italy in 1965. Brown, who became Scotland's first full-time manager in 1967, continued the trend set by Prentice and MacDonald until the European Championship qualifier against Wales that same year. Gilzean scored twice.

During Gillie's period in the wilderness, Jim McCalliog, Willie Wallace, Joe McBride, Alex Young and Jim Scott were among those preferred in the forward line. Between them they mustered just one goal in the nine games for which Gilzean was overlooked. While Brown may have masterminded the victory over world champions England in his first game in charge, his win ratio of 32.14% is among the worst of Scottish national team managers, and it is tempting to conclude that his numbers might have been better had he included Gilzean. In the 12 games in which Gillie featured, Scotland won six times, drew once and lost four.

What makes his absence more baffling is that he was generally regarded as a good influence around the squad. Bobby Brown thought so much of his good humour and humility that he used him to encourage the younger players, notably Tony Green of Blackpool. Speaking in 1973, he said: "Many times I paired him off with a youngster as a room-mate. Tony Green was a typical example. When [he was] first called into the pool, Tony was so shy he'd hardly speak a word. He waited for the big names to approach him. Seeing the way Alan conducted himself, Tony soon realised football is the same game whatever the level involved. From that point he opened out."

There were plenty of laughs to be had when Gilzean was on Scotland duty, too. On one trip, Willie Johnston, the Rangers winger, remembers purchasing a diamond ring for his fiancée from a dodgy backstreet shop after the owner convinced him that it was an expensive jewel by cutting several sheets of glass in half before his very eyes. Over a cup of coffee back at the team hotel, he showed the ring to Gillie, who took one look at it, smiled and said: "You've been done, Willie." At that Johnston took the ring and proceeded to scratch it heavily along the glass coffee table he was sitting at, whereupon the diamond disintegrated.

The next day, the Scotland players were waiting on their coach when Gillie was the last to board carrying a huge transistor radio which, according to Johnston's autobiography, Sent Off At Gunpoint, was the size of an average suitcase.

"'Can you get Radio Scotland on that?' shouted one of the players.

'You can get anything on this, son!' replied Alan as he sat down. He then pulled out the aerial which almost touched the roof of the coach, before turning the radio on. Nothing! Not even a peep! Eventually he opened the back of the radio to check the batteries only to find that inside there was absolutely nothing at all. Willie smiled and shouted 'Alan, you've been done, son.'"

Gilzean's goal return began to tail off from 1969. He scored just once in his last seven international matches – against Wales in that same year – and it became easier to leave him out. Tommy Docherty did not select him during his short reign between 1971 and 1972, nor did his successor, Willie Ormond, this at a time when Tottenham were enjoying a period of relative success and Gillie finished joint third in the polling for the Football Writers' footballer of the year award for 1972-73.

Gilzean's 22nd and last cap came in 1971 against Portugal in a 2-0 defeat in European Championship qualification. Come November, Docherty replaced Brown and Gilzean did not get another look in. Docherty had considered him, but said he got the impression that Spurs were nursing him. "I was looking for players who would be in line for the World Cup in 1974, so I didn't call on him."

He should have had at least one more cap but, having been selected to lead the line against England in a European Championship qualifier in 1968, he sustained a hamstring injury in training and his place was taken by John Hughes, the Celtic striker. Mike England, the Tottenham and Wales centre-half of the 1960s and 1970s, suggests that injuries real or imagined might help explain Gilzean's low cap count: "Bill Nicholson would say we were injured and would pull us out of friendly internationals. He would tell me I couldn't play for Wales and then the Welsh FA would get a phone call to say I wasn't fit. If Alan only won 22 caps that might be part of the reason, but I still think he should have won 30 or 40."

Gilzean's continual omission, and that of other talented players based in England, was a source of great consternation to team-mates and contemporaries. A popular theory in the 1950s and early 1960s was that the Scotland team should comprise only players based in the country. It seems faintly ludicrous that any country could afford to overlook some of its best players simply because the individuals in question felt they could better themselves by moving. English-based players were portrayed as mercenaries; they were no longer the men supporters queued to see every week but rather, according to a 1963 article in World Sports magazine, "a stranger who condescends to come home occasionally to play at Hampden". They were known as 'Anglos', signifying a pejorative status among the pure, uncontaminated Scots.

John White suffered directly at the hands of such malevolence. White, along with Dave Mackay and Bill Brown, was part of the Tottenham team that thrashed Rangers 5-2 in the first leg of their European Cup Winners' Cup tie at White Hart Lane on their way to winning the trophy in 1963. Ten days later, White was named in the Scotland team to play Northern Ireland at Hampden. Resentment was still smouldering when the Scots took on the Irish and White had an indifferent game, though Scotland won 5-1. He was booed and barracked by his own supporters every time he touched the ball. Any doubt that the Spurs players were being targeted disappeared when, during the second leg of the European Cup Winners' Cup tie, Mackay was booed as he retrieved a ball from the track during the warm-up.

Where once Gilzean had been the victim of the bias against provincial clubs like Dundee, the same fate would befall him at Tottenham. "No question," said Mackay. "He suffered like Denis Law and others. There was a strong anti-Anglo feeling. Whenever Scotland got a bad result the fingers would point straight at the boys from the south. The old 'tartan team' idea would get an airing. When you look at some of the players who have worn a Scottish jersey when Gilzean, Law and others were out, it was ridiculous. Alan was proving his ability week-in, week-out against top-class opposition, yet he would be left out. Instead, some guy who was playing only four or five hard games a season would be put in and expected to beat the world."

There were rumours that Law and Gilzean did not get on, that they could not play together, but neither of the protagonists give any credence to either claim, nor do the numbers stand up. Of the nine games in which Gillie and Law were paired in attack, Scotland won four and lost two; Gillie scored six times, Law five.

"Gillie is a friend," said Law in a 1973 interview with The Weekly Post. "As for our not blending, I would think he was ideal for me. I like to play it quick and sharp, and Alan has this great ability to play one-touch stuff. There's nobody better to give you that half-yard extra space. Had he played for Scotland more often they would have been a better team. He also has the sort of wacky good humour that keeps up morale. You get to know to check the salt and pepper pots. I'm not the only guy who has found the lid slackened and got the lot in his soup."

In the same interview, Gillie answers the charge that the two men were not best matched. "Perhaps he and I did go for the same ball sometimes, but so do I and Martin Chivers. When you have twin strikers, there are bound to be the odd chances which you both flash at."

Ironically, given Gilzean's desire to leave Dundee to further his career, his apogee with Scotland arrived at the start of his international career. He may have made a further 17 appearances for his country following his move to White Hart Lane, but it is winning goal on a grey and wet afternoon against England, in April 1964, for which he is best remembered.

Scotland 1 England 0 – Hampden Park, April 11 1964

Scotland went to Hampden Park on Saturday and achieved what they set out to do. They beat England for the third successive year, in the end comprehensively, and the first such run of victories for Scotland since 1882 was a matter of congratulation. Neither side, however, gave an exhilarating performance and the match left little feeling of elation.

[…] In the first half Banks' groping fingers touched a Gilzean header on to the inside of a post and the ball broke out instead of in. In the second half Scotland twice had strong grounds for being awarded penalty kicks when Armfield brought down Gilzean and Moore obstructed Law. But the only reward came to Scotland 12 minutes from time, when Gilzean headed home the winning goal direct from Wilson's corner kick. […] White, denied the space and time which he needs, was of less value than he can be, particularly in his service to Henderson. This latter failure was especially unfortunate, for it was on the shoulders of Henderson and Gilzean that the chief burden of attack fell. Of course, they buckled down nobly to their task but how much more effective they might have been if their colleague had seen to it that the lines of supply to them were more continuously kept open. It was an obvious move, for Gilzean's artful flicks and passes often had opponents going the wrong way.

– The Glasgow Herald

Raymond Jacobs' match report sheds light on a facet of Gilzean's game which perhaps goes some way to explaining why Scotland managers viewed him with suspicion. His ability to think quickly was a given, but sometimes he thought too quickly, and if he wasn't being serviced properly then he could sometimes be lost to games. Gilzean was never bitter about winning so few caps: "So much depends on whether the team manager fancies your style of play," he said in 1973. "I have always regarded a Scottish cap as a bonus. It's great to play for your country, but they don't pay your wages. It's your club you have to keep happy."

His biggest disappointment during his international career involved Scotland's failure to reach the World Cup finals in 1970, after losing a qualifier 3-2 against West Germany in Hamburg in October 1969, a match in which he scored to level the game at 2-2. A draw would have left Scotland requiring a win over Austria in Vienna a few days later to secure their passage to Mexico.

Gillie had some illuminating explanations for why the nation had underachieved for so long. They were the same problems the Scots would face for years to come. "[West Germany] were the luckiest blokes alive that night, and they know it. We pulverised them, and still lost. How, I just don't know. For me, that was the greatest Scottish performance. For just one night they forgot their 'England Complex'. Scotland international performances have suffered terribly because they regard the England game as the only game to win. If England lose, they clinically examine how they lost just another game. If Scotland lose it's a national disaster."

Flicking through some of the old cuttings which Bill Hutcheon, the editor of the Dundee Courier, provided for me at the start of my search for Gilzean, I reacquaint myself with a couple of reports which I had almost forgotten about. After his goal against England, Gilzean was in demand. In the Courier and Advertiser, he reflected: "I knew I had to go to the ball before [Maurice] Norman and [Gordon] Banks and headed it quite well, but I wasn't sure about the direction. I came down off balance, facing away from goal, and from the terrific roar I knew it must be in. But even when I turned and saw the ball lying in the net I could hardly believe it."

There was even time to talk to his mother Barbara, who was preparing to move house while waiting for Alan to return home from his international exertions. "We're flitting to just around the corner," she said. "What a weekend this has been. The phone has never stopped ringing with people wanting to speak to Alan and offer him congratulations and best wishes."

Two months later, Coupar Angus town council honoured its famous son in a ceremony which the Provost John Davidson described as "unique in the annals of the town". Gillie, who attended the ceremony with his father, mother and Irene, was presented with a gold wristwatch which had been purchased using subscriptions from people in the town and all over the surrounding area.

In an article in the Dundee Courier and Advertiser dated Friday June 12, 1964, Provost Davidson is reported to have told those gathered that he had been in the Borders recently and when he told people that he came from Coupar Angus they had remarked "that's where Alan Gilzean is from". The article continues: "In a speech of thanks Alan said that school football had been 'his best subject'. But many times he had doubted if the football was worth the trouble he had got into because of it. But he had got over the rows he got for trampling on gardens and playing in his best clothes and had joined Coupar Angus Boys' Club after school."

A week later and Gillie, again accompanied by Irene, was presented with a handsome trophy cabinet by his former school, Coupar Angus Junior Secondary School, which clearly had forgotten all about the trouble caused by its sometimes errant former pupil. In turn, Alan presented the school with the dark blue Scotland jersey he had worn on his debut. Again the Courier and Advertiser were first with the story, noting that "out in the playground afterwards Alan was besieged by young autograph hunters, many of whom were young ladies". Today, the jersey is housed in a cabinet at Coupar Angus Primary. The young girl that I met in the street outside the Gilzean family home in Stuart Crescent remembered that, but not his name.

§

The 1963-64 season was franked by goals. By the end of September he had 13. A month later it was 20, including four against his boyhood idols, Hibernian. In a five-match midwinter stretch Dundee scored 31 goals, Gilzean taking his total to 38. His 39th and then 40th, equalling then surpassing Alex Stott's 15-year record of goals in one season for Dundee, came in a 6-1 win against Forfar in the Scottish Cup. Stott, who had travelled up from Coatbridge for the game as the guest of Dundee, said quietly "that's it" as Gillie's second went in, before adding: "I'm glad he made it. I'd have been most disappointed to have come all this way and not seen him do it."

Gilzean's feat was all the more impressive because he had been involved in a road accident earlier the previous month which left him with a long scratch down his face and, more crucially, a bashed leg. Not even that could stop him. Standing in Dundee City Library I mentioned this prodigious spree to Bobby Waddell, but he said somewhat dismissively that all the goals had come in the cup. "Not all," I replied. "Look at this game in the league against St Mirren when Dundee scored nine". "Ah, that game. The goalie was found guilty of betting against his own team. I'll never forget it," Bobby chuckled, one eyebrow raised as he looked at me side on. "On one occasion he threw the ball straight at my feet. I sidefooted it back into the empty net."

A year after the 9-2 thrashing, that goalkeeper, Dick Beattie, was jailed for taking payments to throw games. One picture from the game shows him punching the ball into his own goal but as Norrie Price notes in Up Wi' The Bonnets, "although it was Dundee's 5-1 home win over Saints in 1963 which featured in the prosecution evidence, Beattie again made some spectacular blunders in the 9-2 game, though there was no denying the deadliness of Gilzean."

His hat-trick against St Mirren that February was his fifth of the season, taking his tally to 43. And still the goals kept coming. There was one against Motherwell in the Scottish Cup quarter-final replay in March; a double in the semi-final against Kilmarnock at Ibrox. By now, he was going by the nickname 'King', the same one that would be adopted by Tottenham fans years later, and his display in that semi was regal. "Gilzean was brilliant," reported The People on March 29. "Apart from his two goals he directed the smooth-moving Dens Park attack with passes that made it look so simple." The Sunday Post said his performance was "in the five-star class".

Goals 47 and 48 arrived in league games against Kilmarnock and Celtic. He reached the half-century with two against Partick Thistle, a week before the Scottish Cup final versus Rangers.

The cup final was to prove an anti-climax for Dundee, and Gilzean in particular. Carrying an ankle injury for much of the second half, he was blunt and ineffective. The Glasgow Herald noted that "it was particularly disappointing that Gilzean was so astonishingly reluctant to bring the full weight of his firepower to bear". Kenny Cameron scored Dundee's goal, cancelling out Jimmy Millar's opener and Dundee were just two minutes from a replay, thanks mainly to the goalkeeping of Bert Slater, when Rangers struck twice in quick succession through Millar and Ralph Brand to complete a clean sweep of trophies. The one consolation was that Dundee were guaranteed a place in Europe, but their efforts in the European Cup Winners' Cup would be doomed to failure the following season. Drawn against Real Zaragoza in the first round and shorn of Gilzean, who had not been registered for the competition because of his transfer dispute, they lost gamely 4-3 on aggregate.

Cameron, whose goal in the final was a delightfully taken effort Gilzean would have been proud of, hooking the ball over the keeper after a neat take on the run, scored 123 league goals in a 17-year career. He says that Gilzean was the supreme penalty box striker, and in his early days looking on from the sidelines he would examine his game closely: "The thing that I learned from him was watching his movement in the box. He wasn't always on the move – just when the ball came into the box. He wasn't there too early and he always got in front of the defender. I would notice that he would get across players in the air. Those were the key things mainly: movement in the box and his timing of runs."

What made Gillie's formidable presence in the area more impressive is the recognition that he was not a lumbering giant. At 5ft 11in (Jock Richardson was two inches out) he was above average height, but not freakishly tall. Richardson would have watched a gangling striker that day against Norway; he could look ungainly, with one shoulder higher than the other, but it was an entirely superficial matter.

Jim Crumley, the nature writer, summarises the impact of Gilzean on Dundee much more eloquently and poetically than this author ever could in a chapter of hero worship in his acclaimed book, The Road and The Miles. Recounting a part-fictional conversation with his 'faither' in a favourite old pub, Crumley details in delightful Dundee dialect the Gilzean phenomenon.

His faither is going through a familiar routine, guiding his son around the pub, looking at old photos of Gillie. The barman, who has heard it all before, rolls his eyes. At one particular picture, faither and son stop. Gillie is jumping off the ground, his feet together, head and shoulders in perfect alignment.

"Nijinsky in studs," faither says to son.

Faither talks about the Dundee of the 1950s and how they played good football but were never taken seriously. There was, as the old man says, "the cred-i-bull-ity gap" between what they had seen and what came after.

"Ken hoo the snaa iself drahs doon the braes like curtains hingin aff the hulls? An the very quiet wakes you an the room's no as dark as it should be? Ye step oot intae the Ferry streets a the pliss is ah whusht an when ye wahk among athin that's familiar … but athin's cheenged. Ye try an reconvene the ahld familiar street in yer heid, just as it was yesterday wi'oo the snaa. An' fur the meenit, ye cannae?"

"Well, son, that's what it was like when Gillie came."

"He was a goalsmith, son and he made 24-carat goals. Week after week, gemme efter gemme, and of course it rubbed aff on abdy else. Won the league. Beat the best in Europe. Europe, son! This man put the name of this town – Dundee – on the lips o fitba-playin Europe, and wherever they trehd to pronounce it – Germany, France, Belgium, Portugal, Italy – ah they plisses – it was synonymous wi cless. Whu cless we had, son. Whu cless. He did it. Gillie – he was the spark.

"Defences owre ah Scotland, owre ah Europe, trehd tae snuff him oot. Couldnae. Ye cannae snuff oot the sheen o gold, ken? They trehd to hold him doon, kick him doon, knock him doon, pull him doon, and on the rare occasions that beh one cheatin way or other they got him doon, they couldnae keep him doon. Nae mair than they could keep him oot the net.

"Goals. Gillie made goals like Hoagy Carmichael made songs, son.

Stardust. He made goals like the Picts carved stanes. Exquisite! Couldnae keep him of coorse … 1964 awa tae Spurs like Buhll Broon afore him. Well, we didna grudge him that. Ye couldnae grudge Gillie nothin."

"It's over: Gilzean joins Spurs", proclaimed the Dundee Evening Telegraph's back-page headline. 'It' referred to the six-month transfer saga. It could just as easily have meant the end of an era. Norrie Price, the Dundee FC historian, recalls that when he heard the news it felt like learning of a death. "It felt like a life. I didn't want to think about him. I tried to erase Gillie from my mind, but I had an uncle who lived in London and he would go to watch Spurs and he would come up home to Arbroath and tell me how well he was doing. It was heartbreaking."

The £72,500 fee set a new record between Scottish and English clubs and took the bill for Nicholson's rebuilding of Spurs to almost £500,000. The Daily Mirror reported that Gillie was due to travel by sleeper to London on Thursday December 17 and had managed to catch up with Irene, who had been directing traffic in Dundee just a few yards down the road from Dens Park as her fiancé was signing his Spurs contract. "Alan phoned me with the news. I'm relieved it's all over," she said.

Rather than reflect on his time at Dundee, Gilzean, like Irene, could express only relief at the end of the protracted process. In a first-person piece with the Daily Express he explained his reasons for choosing Tottenham: "I'm a Spurs player at last", he said, "and I couldn't be more delighted with the world. For months now – long before I tabled my request for a transfer back in June – I've wanted to play in English league soccer. London was my goal, and when I first heard that Spurs wanted me, I knew within myself that White Hart Lane was where I wanted to go. But a soccer player's life is short and sometimes not altogether sweet. It is always up to the player to get the best financial deal out of any transfer. That is the only reason why everyone must be sick by now of the name of Alan Gilzean in the papers. Every day it hit me and, like everyone else, I am heartily sickened that the negotiations have dragged on for almost nine months. But, at the age of 25 [sic] I have only five or six top years left in the game and it is up to me to try to get the most out of football while I am on top. Once you hit the slide then the days of the big money are gone.

"Time … that more than anything else was what I wanted. My head was buzzing with facts and figures. Torino made me a terrific offer. The money went into five figures and any player in his right senses must think at least twice about such a prize dividend. Once again, time was the enemy. When I thought about Denis Law and Jimmy Greaves and what they went through in Italy, it made me wonder whether I would be doing the right thing by signing for an Italian club. In the end I decided that, for Alan Gilzean, Italy was out. My soccer career would finish in Britain. That's where first Sunderland, then Spurs stepped into the picture. Both offers were tremendous but London was always in my mind. Spurs manager Bill Nicholson travelled north and in a Dundee hotel we sat down to talks. Once again it wasn't simple. When everything appeared boiled down, the old question of finance popped up. Contracts were ironed out and re-ironed. Negotiations were on and then appeared off. And at times I thought everything and all my hopes would fly out of the window. But just two weeks ago we had our final meeting and for the past 14 days my fingers have been crossed that everything would be okay. Now I have got my wish, I am a Spurs player, bound for London, and the financial terms are excellent. What more could I ask for?

"Dundee can only hit the big time occasionally. With Spurs I can look for something big every season. Yes, for Alan Gilzean the future is rosy."

7

BRIGHT LIGHTS, BIG CITY

Clickety clack, clickety clack. The Glasgow to London overnight train rumbles through the sleepy countryside. In the refreshment carriage, Friday night commuters unwind with a beer or a glass of wine. An elderly woman in expensive clothes has had one too many. She wobbles as she makes her way towards the sleeping berths, the undulations of the track forcing her to check her step. Finally, she slumps in a seat beside me, looks up and says "sorry" to no-one in particular. Within seconds she is sleeping. Three young women opposite giggle, a couple to my right exchange knowing looks. Eventually she awakens, and makes her way shakily out of the carriage. It's approaching 11 o'clock and over the next hour the automatic doors open and close at regular intervals, the refreshment carriage slowly decanting and refilling. The well-to-do pensioner, however, does not return. Clickety clack, clickety clack.

Back in the claustrophobic, violently blue cabin, I arrange and rearrange my possessions. I check my tickets for the nth time, and re-read the emails exchanged with John Fennelly, the Tottenham Hotspur press officer.

Cliff said that he was meeting you in the main foyer at 10.30am so just go through the main gates and in the main double doors. Ask for Cliff at reception and they will track him down for you. He will then introduce you to the others.

'Cliff' is Cliff Jones, the tremendously gifted winger who illuminated White Hart Lane for many years and was a member of Tottenham's great double-winning side of the early 1960s. Jones, from the famous Welsh footballing family, joined the club in 1958 from Swansea Town and made over 300 appearances for the club, scoring well over 100 goals. His father, Ivor, played for Swansea and Wales, uncle Bryn also played for his country, Wolverhampton Wanderers and Arsenal and a cousin, Ken, played for Scunthorpe United. Cliff had been at the club for over six years when Gillie arrived in December 1964. A few weeks prior to our scheduled meeting, I phoned him at his Hertfordshire home. I missed him at first and spoke to his wife, who informed me that her husband was playing golf and asked if he could phone me back. A few hours later, and much to my surprise, the phone rang and it was Cliff.

"We called him the Scottish soldier," he told me in his rich Welsh accent. "We were playing a pre-season tournament in Amsterdam, it was like a five-a-side competition and there was this military tattoo on at the same time. One day we were sitting outside at a bar and this Scottish regiment was marching back to camp. They must have recognised Gillie because they shouted over, 'Gilzean, it's Gilzean.' The next thing we know, Gillie's over talking to them and then he's marching off to the barracks with the boys with the sergeant's sash draped over his shoulder. It was another 24 hours before we saw him again."

There was one other brief memory: "When he scored that goal against England in 1964, his whole village chipped in to buy him a gold watch. He treasured that watch. He was respected and loved by so many people."

I check everything again and then switch off the light. Clickety clack, clickety clack, the train lumbers on. Insomnia comes quickly in this cramped berth. Clickety clack, clickety clack. I think about Gillie and what he must have thought about as he made this journey almost 45 years earlier. He was, by then, a seasoned traveller, but there was bound to have been the odd butterfly as he made the solitary trip. There were new team-mates to meet, a new manager to impress, a first training session to get through. At least Bill Brown was there. He'd played with Bill at Dundee. He was a good lad, Bill. He came from Carnoustie. He'd had his ear torn quite badly playing at Dens once. Norrie Davidson, the tiny Aberdeen striker, had jumped to head the ball with his mouth open and as he came back down his teeth had closed around Bill's ear. It was hanging by a few strands when he eventually stood up. He went off straight away, had it stitched up at the DRI and played the rest of the second half. That was typical Bill. He would need all that east coast resolve if he was going to get his way back into the Spurs team, would Bill. This kid Jennings was getting good reviews at Spurs. They were in a bit of transition, but there was the chance for him to stamp his place in the team with Smith and White no longer there. No, he would be fine at White Hart Lane. He'd been impressed by it a few weeks earlier in John White's memorial game and he'd scored twice. 'What a ground,' he'd thought. At Dundee, the doors opened out on to the street, but at Spurs there was a gated entrance with Tottenham Hotspur Football Club in huge letters on the side of the stand. They got over 50,000 for the big games, five times as many as Dens and, even though they were going through a rough patch, there were still some great players there. He'd seen some of them at first hand just a few weeks earlier in John White's match. Jimmy Greaves, Alan Mullery, Cliff Jones and Dave Mackay were all top-class performers and would walk into any side in the country. But there was a gap up front and if he could fill the centre-forward slot then it would help his Scotland ambitions no end.

Clickety clack, clickety clack. Knock, knock, knock. "One hour to Euston," says the hostess as she hands me a tray containing a breakfast of sorts. I think of the interviews I've lined up with Cliff and "the others", Alan Mullery and Phil Beal, as I chew on a rubbery bacon and cheese roll.

I have a quick bird bath, a shave and change into my best suit. I spend considerably longer packing and repacking a case that is crammed with a laptop, two voice recorders, reference books, notepads and pens which spill out as I add clothes and the rest of my belongings. Eventually, I make my way off the train and alight upon the nearest bus stop on Euston Road. I try to imagine that I am following in Gilzean's footsteps, but give up when I pass my first McDonalds. The No.30 takes me into the heart of Arsenal country in Islington where I have booked a room. I have, though, taken out indemnity from potential loss of face by choosing an apartment on Tottenham Road, which is a Pat Jennings kickout from White Hart Lane.

I have arranged to meet Phil, Cliff and Alan inside the front doors of White Hart Lane at 10.30, but such is my unfamiliarity with the transport links and geography that I arrive on Tottenham High Road a full 45 minutes early.

It's a bitterly cold autumn day and I decide to kill time in the club shop. The youthful assistant at the front door greets me with a friendly "Good morning, sir." He can hardly be more than 16. After 10 minutes of loitering among keyrings and mugs, I happen upon something of genuine interest: Martin Chivers' new autobiography, Big Chiv. I finger the pages sweatily. The pit of my stomach is tightening at the thought of interviewing three former Spurs legends and, once in a while, I have to take a deep breath. Leafing through Big Chiv is containing my nerves and, like last-minute swotting for an exam, arming me with a little bit of extra Gillie information.

I turn to a chapter titled The Glory, Glory Years and there are some surprising revelations. It comes as a bit of a jolt as, just days earlier, Chivers had declined an interview request when I had told him I was writing an account of Gillie's life.

The Gillie of Martin Chivers' book is a different one from the man described by his Dundee team-mates. He is portrayed as a heavy drinker and someone who "lived hard and played hard". Chivers speculates that although Gillie "drank all the time, at home or away on tours … and probably got pissed more nights than not, that man proved himself time and time again on the football field. He never let anyone down. How could you not get on with such a character? Everyone loved him. He also loved the ladies and they loved him."

There is the story about the supporter who phones Bill Nicholson to complain that he had seen Alan Gilzean leaving a club at two o'clock in the morning. The Spurs players wryly pointed out that he was going into the club.

Then there is the one about the players finding Gillie in his car outside White Hart Lane, still drunk from the night before. The boys smuggle him into the pack on the training run around the playing track, but Gillie won't stop chattering and after a couple of laps he trips and lands in the wooden box used for storing the half-time numbers. He looks like he is in his coffin. "Quick, nail it up now," shouts one wag.

The best is left to last. Tottenham are on an end-of-season tour to Japan and six of the players are invited to a sumo wrestler's house for a meal. Vast quantities of sake are consumed, whereupon Gillie takes a shine to a young geisha, whom he fails to realise is the sumo wrestler's wife. Fortunately, the host is too polite to protest at Gillie's close attentions. The next day on the bus to training Gillie nurses a plastic bag, clearly worse for wear. Later, during the training session, he grabs a bag of balls, drags them behind one of the goals and promptly falls asleep among them.

These snapshots of Gillie were of a person I had barely seen before. The quiet lad from Coupar Angus is transformed. I scan my memory for a description of this person in my conversations with former Dundee team-mates to that point and ascribe his metamorphosis to London life. The hints had been there but they were no more than that. In any case, so what? Gillie was a footballer who liked a drink and had an eye for the ladies. As revelations went, it was up there with discovering that George Best did likewise. Other notable passages included Gillie's pathological dislike for Bob Wilson, the Arsenal goalkeeper, and Bill Nick's decision to pair a young and impressionable Steve Perryman with the much older, more worldly Gilzean.

This was not the first time I had been taken aback by something I had read about Gillie and it brought back memories of when the search had first begun, and that Hunter Davies article in the New Statesman which speculated about his perception of football as merely a job. Again, I was struck by the limitations of placing labels on people, of pinning them down to an over-simplified set of character traits.

As I made my way out of the shop, copy of Big Chiv tucked in my bag, I spied another possible source of information: a DVD of the 50 Greatest Spurs. I knew Gillie was included in this somewhere, but I wasn't sure where, and so I made my second purchase of the morning. I took one final deep breath and exhaled slowly, walked out of the shop and out on to the High Road, turned right at Bill Nicholson Way and through the gates of White Hart Lane.

There is nothing arcane behind the doors of modern football stadia. Their reception areas, offices and corridors are like those of hotel chains. There are glass-fronted entrances, uplighters and downlighters, colour-coordinated walls. But there are details that hint at something else, like crush barriers, security personnel and backroom staff in club ties; or, say, a 50-cap ex-international strolling about.

A glamorous receptionist smiles, tells me to take a seat and points towards a modern, black settee. A BBC cookery programme is on a television overhead. I had expected continuous loops of Spurs goals, interviews with legends, or black-and-white film capturing the double-winning team in its beautiful, ruthless glory. Instead, I'm watching someone fry a haddock.

There are concessions, though: a ceiling-to-floor-length photograph of the open-top bus which carried that double-winning team up the High Road, and a replica of the FA Cup in a glass case.

The first player to arrive is Phil Beal. Phil was breaking into the Spurs team when Gillie arrived. He signed schoolboy forms when he was 15 and made his debut in 1963. He sports a friendly smile and, while he is a bit thicker around the stomach and face, he is instantly recognisable as the man who patrolled the Tottenham backline with a quiet authority and distinction during the late 1960s and early 1970s.

We shake hands and make small talk. Phil asks how I want to do the interviews, "one at a time or altogether?" "Altogether," I say, not really sure which is best, just grateful that I've made contact with at least one of the men I had come to see.

Phil introduces me to a shaven-headed chap called Nick and tells him that I'm writing a book about Alan Gilzean. "Alan Brazil was talking about your book on Talksport yesterday," Nick tells me. This is a surprise since, as far as I was concerned, the book idea was not in the public domain. "Yeah, Alan Brazil said he had been speaking to Gillie," he adds. "Where is he, these days?"

I tell him Weston-super-Mare, as far as I know. A clutch of former Spurs players arrive all at once. The club pays a stipend to these old pros in return for appearances in hospitality lounges, where they talk about their time with the club and mingle with expectant supporters, eager to hear their tales of the glory, glory years. For fans, it's the equivalent of opening night at a major blockbuster, for the players an endless rerun of the same movie. Bobby Smith, the double-winning centre-forward, is next to arrive, then comes Martin Peters, the World Cup winner, and Ralph Coates, the player whom Bill Nicholson admitted was purchased from Burnley because she was his wife Darkie's favourite. I had been trying to contact Ralph for weeks. I stop and ask him if it's okay to give him a phone. "Yeah, sure, phone any time after six."

I recognise Cliff Jones instantly. He is bespectacled and sports a full moustache but, those cosmetic differences aside, he looks more or less exactly like he did as a player. Again, we shake hands, before ascending a modern staircase to one of the hospitality lounges. Alan Mullery is running late and will have to wait for another time. I have been granted half an hour and we are already 15 minutes in when we sit down around a low table overlooking Bill Nicholson Way. Supporters are gathering outside the ground waiting for a glimpse of today's superstars while I am inside speaking to Jones, widely regarded as the greatest left winger in the world at the start of the 1960s and Beal, a defender who won three trophies with Spurs and was considered unlucky to have been playing at the same time as Bobby Moore was captaining England. I could chat all day about their own careers, but we're here to talk about one man.

Cliff Jones I always thought Gillie was an interesting character, a fantastic player; there's no doubt about that. He was possibly one of the best front players that Tottenham have had in as much as that you could play the ball up to him anywhere; he had great control. Another thing that I don't think people often recognise is the fact that he was such a terrific trainer and, although he had quite an interesting lifestyle, it never interfered with his training or his game of football and he was just, I thought, a terrific professional.

Phil Beal My first memory of Gillie is that he was a good socialiser. I mean, Gillie liked a drink but, on the other hand he was a good trainer. I think he had to be because of the social life he used to live. There were loads of times he used to come in and sit next to me in the dressing room and I used to say to him, 'Cor, Gillie you been out again last night?' The smell of alcohol used to be on his breath but he would go out there and he would train harder than those who hadn't been out there for three or four nights. So Gillie used to live hard, but he used to train hard as well.

CJ His social life never interfered with his training and with his football life and he always gave 100% when he was on the field.

PB I think Bill Nicholson would have put his foot down if he thought it was going to affect his play.

CJ Absolutely, yeah.

PB And I think, because it didn't affect his play and it didn't affect his training then Bill Nick would have turned a blind eye to the things that he did outside of football. Not just because it was Gillie, but anybody – if it had affected their training and their playing, I think he would have put his foot down. I remember once before a game Gillie and I were first to arrive and sitting in the dressing room he let out this huge burp. I asked him 'Cor Gillie, are you all right?' and he said 'Aye, I had a big fry for my breakfast.' That just wouldn't happen nowadays.

James Morgan Bill Nick once said that he needed to be led, but if you showed Gillie a set of bagpipes he would follow them anywhere. What did he mean?

PB I think it's the Scottish tradition that was in Gillie. I remember when we used to play Arsenal down here. Alan Gilzean really had a dislike to Bob Wilson in goal, because Bob Wilson had some sort of Scottish relation somewhere along the line which enabled him to play for Scotland and Gillie took a disliking to that. He used to say, 'How can Bob Wilson play for Scotland when he's not Scottish?' I think what 'follow the bagpipes' boils down to, he was being true-and-true Scottish.

CJ He was a very patriotic Scottish man and the thing he treasured more than anything was that watch that was presented to him by the village after he scored the winning goal against England at Hampden Park. That remained with Gilzean as his great moment in football. I would think that was the pinnacle, knowing Gillie, yeah. And the night in Amsterdam with the Black Watch.

JM Was there any inkling as to where he might have been?

CJ Probably he wouldn't know himself. But he'd had a good time, that was certain. I suppose we can say [he was private] because nobody knows where he is, do they?

PB Well, we think we know he is in Weston-super-Mare. I think it's a real shame that since he's left Tottenham no-one's ever seen him. Not just for those who played with him but for the supporters. They would love to see Alan Gilzean back.

CJ But I think because of that, it has become a bit of a cult status thing with him.

JM Can you describe his relationship with Jimmy Greaves?

CJ It was just an instinct between them. He [Alan] had a great touch and awareness and you could play the ball up to Gilzean any way. The head, the chest, the feet and he had just great control. When that happened, Greavsie knew there was going to be something on for him and it's the reason they were called the G-Men.

PB They had a great friendship as well. That was the big thing between the two of them, on the pitch as well …

The rest of Phil's answer is left hanging in the air as Alan Mullery makes his entrance, shakes my hand and sits down. Mullery is a ball of energy and, as someone who has spent many years in broadcasting with Sky Sports, he rarely pauses for breath, ad-libbing and wisecracking as he reels off anecdotes. Two fascinating snippets of information about Mullery stuck out from my research: one was that he was a devout Christian, the other that he had contemplated suicide with his wife in the midst of financial hardship in the 1980s. Listening to him chattering enthusiastically now, it is hard to believe he was ever so low. And he swears like a trooper.

Alan Mullery I think anyone that socialised with Gillie – well, you didn't see them very often. There was only Dave Mackay that could keep up and nobody else. You know, Bill Nicholson watched him at least a dozen times, Gillie. Who was the fella, Jim, that used to be in Scotland? He was a scout. Great big fat fella with glasses.

JM Was it Jim Rodger, who was a journalist?

PB Yeah, that's him.

AM Every pre-season, we'd play Rangers down here and then we'd go up there the following year. Jim Rodger was always there at the airport, at the hotel, talking to Bill, and Bill had sent him to watch Alan Gilzean I don't know how many times. I remember he always used to sit at the front of the coach. I was a terrible traveller, so I would sit up at the front and used to hear their conversations. Jim Rodger thought Gillie was great, but wanted Bill to watch him. Bill watched him 12 times. Can you imagine the skill and ability that Alan Gilzean had, you only had to watch him once and you'd buy him, wouldn't you? But Bill watched him 12 times.

PB That was what Bill was like. Bill would go and watch a player over and over again before he would make a decision.

AM He used to employ people to do that. Jim Rodger would get a fee for that …

CJ But you've got to see it for yourself.

AM He would go and watch until he was absolutely certain that he could fit into the side. I'm sure it happened to Cliffy when he was down at Swansea, and I know it happened to me at Fulham. Not Phil, because he came through the ranks.

PB Well, he watched me. I did a training session down here as a youngster. Then I had to play in three games before he would sign me as a schoolboy.

AM Bill couldn't pick out a fella instantly. He would watch the traits that a fella had. But Gillie had so many. He had fantastic skill. If you remember Berbatov here a couple of years ago, a couple of times the ball would come over his shoulder and he pulled it out of the air and you'd turn round and say, 'it's Gillie'. As soon as I saw Berbatov, he reminded me of Gillie. Now, for Bill to go and watch him 12 times before he bought him, whether it was his character outside the game or whatever I don't know, but his skill I would say was second to none. There was something about him that got him to go over and over to watch this fella who had outstanding ability. What was it that him and Jimmy Greaves had? It was a relationship. As soon as they went on the field they reacted in the way you would if you'd been living with your wife for 50 years, you know? You know exactly what she is going to do. It was like that with Greavsie and Gillie.

Some months later I would discover that, during a game against Peterborough in the FA Cup in 1968, Greaves missed the chance to score an open goal because he was too busy talking to Gilzean to notice that the ball was trickling across the unguarded goalmouth. At that point, I knew exactly what Alan Mullery meant.

PB They used to love each other if one of them scored a goal. There was no bitterness or anything, there was no, 'you didn't give it back to me', or, 'you took it on and scored a goal'. When each other scored a goal, they went crazy with each other.

AM It's not very often you get that. If you looked at Bobby Smith, who is here today, Bobby Smith was what you would call a very greedy centre-forward, because he loved scoring goals himself and was brilliant at it. If you look at Gary Lineker, selfish, absolutely selfish. He played for this club and didn't think of anyone else when he was in front of goal. If you look at Clive Allen, leading goalscorer here one season, got over 50 goals. He was one of the greediest centre-forwards you've ever seen in your life, never thought about other people when he had the chance of scoring. But Alan Gilzean and Jimmy Greaves weren't like that.

JM His record was phenomenal at Dundee, 169 goals in 190 games, but when he came here he was a different player. Was that a sign of his adaptability?

AM He fitted in immediately. I should think after his first game, he fitted in. The crowd took to him. It took me nearly a bloody year, him it was straight away.

CJ Wasn't [the transfer] clinched with the John White testimonial match when Gillie played in it? He was outstanding in that, Bill saw him and I think that was it.

AM I've always thought about this. To watch him play, in that game alone he was fantastic. Why did Bill go and watch him 12 times [the testimonial was No.13]?

JM Martin Chivers mentions a story about a sumo wrestler and his wife …

AM I remember him. He was a great big fella. He came in the door and he had to turn sideways to get in. And Gillie ended up wanting to fight him. Took him on, didn't he? He'd been on the sake and this fella took his robes off. Gillie said, 'I'll fuckin' beat him.' 'Naw, don't be daft,' we said, but we were egging him on at the same time, saying, 'Get 'im, get 'im. Get his gear off.' Gillie said, 'I'll run at him with me head and butt him in the guts'. We were in this flat and there were a few people standing around and there was sake and this and that. This guy was the most gentle fella, he must have been about 7ft tall, this geezer and Gillie says, 'I'm going to fuckin' knock him over.' And he stands back about 15 yards and he's gearing up for the run up. This guy's just standing there, and then Gillie runs at the fella and butts him. He bounces off and almost knocks himself out.

And he was on the floor and this fella just went, 'huh, huh, huh' and started laughing at him. We pissed ourselves laughing at him and then he got up and got back on the beers. It was amazing. She was a very pretty girl, the fella's wife.

Mullery acts out the scenario, stretching his arms to show how wide the wrestler was, charging towards me to mimic Gillie, and holding his face as he pretends to have been hit. It is an infectious performance, which has Phil, Cliff and myself guffawing.

JM Hunter Davies says that Gillie just saw football as a job.

AM Gillie never went to watch matches, he was a bit like Greavsie. Jimmy never went to watch matches and there again, they were very similar. There were other things to do for Gillie. Where we would love to watch other teams play, or players we were going to be playing against. If I didn't have a game I'd go to a match.

PB He wasn't interested in football.

CJ I still think there was a love of the game for Gillie. He did love the game, I have to say that. Just the playing side. The same as Greavsie.

PB Very rarely after training sessions would Gillie stay behind though. I think he liked his own company.

AM I think that's been proved now since he's been missing for all these years. I mean, the times he's been invited back and refused. I suppose he's become a hermit.

CJ I know he's a bit of a private person and he had his own circle of friends. But it never involved players, did it?

AM No, not at all.

PB Any invitations to go anywhere with your wives, Gillie wouldn't go. He had no interest in going. He had his own friends outside of football.

AM He only had one friend at Christmas. That was Dave Mackay wasn't it? They used to go to various dos and have a few pints together.

CJ New Year's Eve. Hogmanay. Och aye.

PB He used to mix when we would go away, you know? Like when we played away, or when we went on pre-season tours? Gillie always used to mix then, but apart from that, when he was here, at home, he didn't mix socially with the lads.

JM Was that at odds with how he was on the pitch, where he was flamboyant?

AM It's a bit like actors. I always remember sitting with Eric Morecambe and his wife one night at a do. Around the table was James Hunt, and there was a guy, what was his name, he was on television with a girl, Gareth … Gareth Hunt was his name. Fine looking fella. Eric Morecambe literally wasn't the Eric Morecambe you saw on television. I remember a woman came up to him and asked him for his autograph and he turned to this woman and said, 'Do you mind? I'm eating.' Every time someone came up to him, they wanted him to be the Eric Morecambe that was on television and he was never like that.

I went to Luton Town one day and he was sitting in the dressing room having a cigar, all on his own. I was at Brighton at the time, and he walked into the dressing room and he sat down and said, 'Right lads, I want you to go out there and kick fuck out of them' … and then he stopped. 'Oh, you're not Luton, are you?' and he walked out again. We were all pissing ourselves laughing, but he wasn't like that. Off the stage, he wasn't a comedian and he wasn't a funny person.

For Gillie, that might have been where being a player was like being like an actor. He could have been on his stage with 60,000-odd people here, or playing for Scotland, but after that he didn't want to be that person, he wanted to be someone else. I remember him coming on as sub one day for Scotland versus England and I was standing about 10 yards from the line. As he come on, I said, 'Good luck, Gillie,' and he said, 'Fuck off!' [Laughing] Next thing I know, he's fucking doing me and I thought, 'I'm going to go and see him on Monday!' [All laughing]

CJ It's always been Alan Gilzean. He's always had his private life.

AM If I met him now I would imagine he would be as nice as pie and reminisce.

JM Do you think Gillie became more streetwise when he came to Spurs?

AM The nice thing about it at the time was that we already had Scottish players here.

PB I don't think he could afford to be any different and I don't think he would have felt he was a cut above everybody or below anybody else, he would have put himself on a par with the rest of us.

CJ I think he was the same as any of us players. We all had our circle of friends, we all had our families and Gillie was no different from any of us.

AM I would think it would be more difficult to fit in now than years ago, because what you had years ago was English, Irish, Scottish, Welsh people. Now with all the foreign players there are little cliques, whereas there were never any cliques here.

CJ We had a close relationship as a team.

AM I think Bill bred that.

PB Bill wouldn't have wanted there to be cliques, he would get rid of them. That's why the club was successful, because if there are no cliques everybody is together.

JM We've talked about his strengths as a player, but what were his weaknesses?

There is a long pause. It's the one question footballers don't like to answer. There is an unspoken bond among players – one can call another anything he likes, on the pitch or in the dressing room, but never, or rarely, to the press. Cliff answers first.

CJ We've all got weaknesses somewhere along the line.

AM I can't think of any weaknesses, as a footballer, that he had.

CJ No, no.

AM Some people say he might have lacked a bit of pace but he wasn't slow. I think if you were to nitpick it might be his pace.

CJ That's the only thing you could level at him.

AM If he'd had Greavsie's pace then that might have been different, but that was the make-up of the two as a pair. Greavsie over 15 yards was – whoof! – as sharp as could be, whereas Gillie could control the ball, he could keep people off the ball, his heading ability and touch play were outstanding. I don't think he needed pace.

PB I don't think he was the type of player who, if there was a full-back, he would take him on and put a cross in.

JM You've already touched on Gillie's capacity for a drink …

AM He was as fit as a flea.

CJ It never affected his training or his playing.

I'm not fishing, merely trying to tease out an anecdote or two, but I sense it's unlikely to be forthcoming and, instead follow a different line.

JM Cliff, you played on the wing, did you watch for anything in particular, say if he made a run to the front post or peeled off to the back post before crossing?

CJ I never used to pass the ball.

AM Cliff was one of those greedy bastards we were talking about earlier. He never used to pass the ball to anybody.

PB I have never seen anybody today that can flick on a ball from the near post from a corner or free-kick like Gillie used to. His touch was superb for a little flick-on, a little touch. We used to practise and practise, but for Gillie it came naturally. There was never a time when you thought, 'Oh, he's got too much on that one,' or, 'Oh, he's put it over the bar.' It was just perfect.

AM I think everybody profited from him, whether it be Greavsie, Martin Chivers, Martin Peters or any of us. To have him in your side was an asset. Sometimes you get liabilities, those who play some games and are out of this world and other times they are absolutely rubbish. His consistency, that's what made him the player that he was. I can't think of any games were he didn't put in the full shift. I can't think of any games where he didn't show that skill and ability.

He was just a joy to watch and play with. He could jump and stay there. If you look back to the 1970 World Cup final, Brazil against Italy, look at the first goal. Pelé scores from a cross from the left-hand side. He's up there and he's hanging. They had this wonderful knack of being able to jump and stay there while other people were coming down.

JM Did you practise your heading, Cliff?

CJ Mainly natural ability and I was encouraged to do it. I could see the defender and I could see the ball and I've got to be favourite if I'm prepared to put myself there. I was different from Gillie. Gillie used to do it from a standing jump where I used to be running at the ball.

AM Also, in those days we used to have balls hanging from the ceiling in the gymnasium just over there and we used to get up and practise jumping. You could raise them to certain heights and Cliff and Gillie could get up higher than anybody.

I am aware that the interview has overrun by 10 minutes or so but it quickly comes to a juddering halt when the three legends are shuffled off by the Tottenham commercial manager. They are late for a meeting ahead of a busy day in corporate hospitality but, before they depart, all three are anxious to learn whether I have enough. They all say to phone them if I need anything else. I make my way back downstairs, through the double doors at the entrance and off towards the media room. For a brief spell inside the hallowed walls of the club I had supported for most of my life, I felt part of the fabric. Departing through those double doors denudes me of any misapprehension.

Inside the media canteen, Stan Collymore, Jonathan Pearce and a host of other faces from the world of broadcasting and print journalism have their heads buried in laptops, getting in some last-minute cramming for the game ahead.

I have arranged to meet Andy Porter, the Tottenham club historian. He hands me a folder stuffed with pictures of Gillie's time at Spurs. One of them, in which Gillie is seen leaning against a post as he awaits a corner kick, seems to encapsulate everything about his time at Tottenham. Next, Andy offers me a photocopied sheet: Jock Richardson's scouting report. We chat for half an hour before Andy has to leave. "I'll see you in the press box when the game starts," he says.

Craig Brown is tucking into his lunch, fork in one hand, plate in the other. He was one of the first people I spoke to when the search for Gillie began and is as accommodating now as he was then. He's locked in conversation with Ron Jones, the BBC radio commentator, when I approach him.

"Ron, this is James Morgan, he's writing a book about Alan Gilzean."

Within minutes, Craig and I are discussing his Dundee days. "Do you know Hugh Robertson's father was the mayor, or something like that, of Auchinleck? Aye, the place came to a standstill the day wee Shug got married," he says, before moving on to talk about Steve Archibald, another Scot who played at White Hart Lane.

"Have you spoken to John Duncan?" Craig asks. "I've got a number for him. He replaced Gilzean at Dundee and then he came here the season he left."

Tottenham are at home to Stoke City today. Thirty-nine years earlier Gillie scored one of the goals in a 3-0 win, but such trifling matters are insignificant to those sat around me. This is a special anniversary. It is five years and one day since the death of Bill Nicholson. A five-minute video on the jumbo screens is shown before kick-off. Former players recount his greatest feats: the double in 1961; the FA Cup a year later; a Cup Winners' Cup; another FA Cup; two League Cups and a UEFA Cup. One man is missing from the interviews and the old footage; I presume Gillie's failure to make the cut is just an oversight. As I'm pondering this, a thought occurs: it is October 24, and I have forgotten that Gillie's birthday has been and gone in recent days. He is listed online as either October 22 or October 23. I make a mental note to clarify this confusion.

There is little confusion in Stoke's defence, relentless Tottenham unable to find a way through. Peter Crouch has two Gilzean-esque headers cleared off the line, and when Stoke break late on their winning goal has a sense of preordination about it.

When Gillie arrived at Tottenham in December 1964, the club was in a state of flux. Dave Mackay was injured, John White was dead, Danny Blanchflower's career had been effectively ended by injury against Rangers in a European Cup Winners' Cup match in 1962. The Irishman made just 15 appearances over the 1962-63 season and then called it a day. Bobby Smith had also gone, leaving a void in attack that Bill Nicholson hoped his new £72,500 striker would fill. The Tottenham manager's rebuilding project was so expensive that the match with Everton on December 19 – Gillie's debut – was billed by the press as football's first million-pound match. Other key arrivals during the previous 12 months had been the centre-half Laurie Brown from Arsenal (£40,000), right-half Alan Mullery from Fulham (£72,500), right-winger Jimmy Robertson from St Mirren (£25,000), left-back Cyril Knowles from Middlesbrough (£40,000) and goalkeeper Pat Jennings from Watford (£25,000). Tottenham, the Bank of England club, had spent £280,000 and, when added to the capture of Greaves from AC Milan (£99,999) and others, theirs was a first team with a market value approaching half a million pounds.

Spurs were in seventh when Everton arrived, eight points behind the leaders Manchester United and with 10 wins and one draw in 11 home games. Their consistency at home was matched only by their inconsistency away, where they had accrued just four points, all from draws. Despite Nicholson's vast spending, attendances were down. On December 4, 1964 the Tottenham Weekly Herald reported that "a mere

396,000 fans have passed through the turnstiles." It was the lowest figure in 10 years. Nicholson's decision-making was questioned openly by the press and by fans puzzled over his persistence with Jennings rather than the vastly more experienced Bill Brown, and the refusal to blood talented youngsters from the reserves. The delay in signing Gilzean had irked them all the more. One article speculated that his arrival from Dundee could add 10,000 to the gate. Fanfare, the report's author, was right, up to a point – 24,019 watched Spurs beat Sheffield Wednesday 3-2 in their previous home game, 42,056 would watch Gilzean's debut against Everton, and 56,693 would watch the club's next home game. Although the rise in attendances could be explained by the Christmas holidays, there is another theory. The Spurs crowd had seen something they liked; they had seen Alan Gilzean. Yet, while supporters were hugely impressed by his debut, the Sporting Post match report which Dundee fans would have pored over seeking news of their old hero suggested there was more to come.

Tottenham 2 Everton 2 – White Hart Lane, December 19, 1965

Alan Gilzean, Spurs' £72,500 buy from Dundee, made his debut in England today. Our special London football reporter gives his 10-point weigh-up.

Spurs gave Alan Gilzean an easy start. Manager Billy Nicholson asked him to play an orthodox centre-forward game – to patrol the middle of the field. He was a vital part of Spurs' attack. [...] Gilzean to Spurs was the nearest approach to a centre-forward the Londoners have had since they discarded Bobby Smith. Big and strong, Gilzean was effective in the middle. He took a pass and gave a quick return with head and feet.

In this company he could forget his £72,500 fee. Spurs alone cost £410,000 on the transfer market. Everton, too, are big spenders. Spurs fans considered that Gilzean is the right type of player to get the best out of Jimmy Greaves – nodding and turning balls in the danger area, exploiting the gaps.

Work rate? Well it isn't very high when your job is to patrol the middle. For a player in a straight-up-the-middle centre-forward role Gilzean could not show much inclination to wander and make the occasional excursion to the wing. Gilzean picked a good match to start in England. Everton are rugged and hard. There are no half measures. Alan stood up well and this is the kind of stuff he is going to get every week. In the air Gilzean was adequate up against big, strong England cap Labone. On the floor he had a lot of nice touches. Enough to make Spurs fans realise that he can play inside-forward. Alan had speed enough for the job he was asked to do. On this form the Spurs have not bought a replacement at inside-forward for the late John White. They have a straight old-fashioned centre with obvious touches of class.

Gilzean has too much ability to spend 90 minutes glued around the middle of the penalty area. He should be free to move and create space for himself and chances elsewhere. But perhaps this was one to settle in with.

Bill Nicholson certainly thought so: "Considering he never had a chance to do any training with us, or we to do any training with him, I think it went quite well. Naturally, the sooner we get to know some of the things he does, and he learns some of our methods, it will be quite useful all round," said Nicholson, before explaining his decision to start Gillie at centre-forward. "This was the easiest way to fit him into the team without previous match practice. There are other formations which we can use, but they will take a lot of preparation and practice."

Gilzean's debut was perceived as a qualified success. Spurs fans were notoriously hard to please in the years after the double in 1960-61 and, leaving aside the observation that Gilzean was a new signing and therefore likely to be granted more time to settle in, it is clear the crowd were impressed. The following week's Tottenham Herald headlined with 'Perfect partner for Greaves has arrived' and praised Gilzean for his ability to make the ball glance off him and for his creativity but wondered, like the Sporting Post correspondent, whether centre-forward was his best position.

Nevertheless, that was the position in which Gillie lined up on a bone-hard pitch in his next game, at Nottingham Forest on Boxing Day. He would score the winner in a 2-1 victory, starting and finishing the move which ended with him scooping the ball home with 12 minutes to go, to end Tottenham's long sequence of games – dating back to February 29 – without an away win. It would prove to be the club's first and last of the 1964-65 season. Gilzean would score again versus Forest, two days later in a 4-0 win for his first goal – at least in a Tottenham shirt – at White Hart Lane.

Jimmy Robertson, the young Scot who arrived earlier that year from St Mirren, was the inspiration and set up all four goals, crossing expertly for Gilzean to complete the scoring with, predictably, a flicked header from an outrageously difficult angle, six minutes from the end. The Spurs fans who had claimed the old battle hymn Glory, Glory, Hallelujah as their own during their European Cup nights, sung the loudest they had done all season.

Despite arriving almost halfway through the campaign, Gilzean would score 16 goals in the league and FA Cup, during which time his partnership with Greaves began to flourish. The England striker would score 35 times in 1964-65, 18 of those coming after Gilzean arrived. Statistically speaking, not much appeared to have changed but there was a marked upturn in Tottenham's attacking performances. It was in defence that the problems appeared to lie. A measure of their problems came in the 7-4 win over Wolverhampton Wanderers on March 27. This was Gilzean's best game for Tottenham since his arrival. It was becoming increasingly evident that, as Alan Mullery noted, everyone was benefiting from his benevolence on the football pitch and his unerring ability to pick out team-mates with delicate passes with either foot and, especially, his head. Against Wolves, he had two shots cleared off the line, scored two and created two of Jones' three goals.

But was this not the style espoused by both Nicholson and Blanchflower? Of doing things with a flourish, of beating the opposition, not merely waiting for them to die of boredom? This had been the mantra preached by Blanchflower; it was the motto of the double winners. It was indicative of English football in any case, distinct from, say, Italy, where Nicholson was already noting how "defensive football had ruined the game there". And yet, in winning the double, Spurs kept 15 clean sheets and conceded just once on 16 occasions in 42 matches. This new team had managed 10 clean sheets and 14 single-goal concessions in the same number of games. A key difference was the number of times Spurs lost 1-0 – four in 1964-65 as opposed to none in 1960-61. On such basic principles were league titles won and lost.

It was clear that Nicholson would have to revamp further if Tottenham were to reassert themselves as England's top team. It was also clear that Gilzean's arrival had been a success. He was a popular member of the team, quickly striking up a fabulous rapport with Greaves on and off the pitch. A measure of the early impact the pair made on the public consciousness came when they were both named to play for Stoke City in Stanley Matthews' testimonial against a World Stars XI side containing Lev Yashin, Ferenc Puskás and Alfredo di Stéfano in April 1965. Stoke's side, essentially a English League select, lost 6-4 against some of the finest footballers of the day.

Dave Mackay, who had spent the entire season recovering from a broken leg, was another firm friend. As compatriots, they had been united by a common bond. It helped that they liked what the Scots refer to as 'a good bevvy'. Greaves, though, appeared to hold a special affinity for the quiet yet acerbic Gilzean, who, in many ways, was a mirror-image of himself. "They could conjure goals out of the air when there didn't seem a sniff of a chance," says Mackay. "Jimmy did most of the scoring, but they worked together with all sorts of decoy moves that must have been a nightmare to mark. Almost all their goals, too, came from quick short-range stuff, where you have to be deadly accurate under pressure."

Despite his 17 goals prior to Gillie's arrival, Greaves expressed his relief at the arrival of an established strike partner with which to share the burden. The old married couple analogy that Alan Mullery made came back to me upon the discovery that

Greaves' first wife was called Irene, the same name as Gillie's. "What a difference with Alan Gilzean. We were made for each other," said Greaves. "We had an understanding right from the off and I was never happier than when playing with Gillie by my side. I was as comfortable with him as I had been with big Bobby Smith. I don't think Gillie gets nearly enough credit, perhaps because he is a deep Scot who doesn't try to cultivate an image for himself off the pitch. I would say he is one of the greatest players I have ever seen or played with. He is tremendously talented on the ball, is a master of the flick header and a lot braver and harder than critics seem to think."

An illustration of how quickly the G-Men blended came in an April league win over Blackburn Rovers in which Gillie scored his first hat-trick in Spurs colours, and Greaves got the other two in a 5-2 victory. Earlier that year, they had been irrepressible as Spurs dismantled Ipswich Town in the FA Cup fourth round, also hitting five. Greaves set up Gilzean for the first and scored the second. Gilzean got the third from a Cliff Jones cross, then provided a graceful pull back for Greaves to notch the fourth. Greaves added the fifth from the spot after Jones was fouled.

Greaves added: "[Gillie's] such a good finisher himself, and he'll score plenty, but he's such a fine player that he concentrates on making things happen. To him, it doesn't matter who scores as long as the goals are obtained. If someone else is the final link in the chain it's all right with him. We missed Bobby Smith because he's the traditional type of English centre-forward, making openings by skill and powerful play. I think Gilzean will work up just as effective a partnership in a different way."

Yet the burgeoning partnership was not enough to prevent Spurs from exiting the FA Cup in their next match, on February 20, a limp 1-0 defeat by Chelsea.

It had been a hectic six months for Gillie. He had left Coupar Angus and Dundee, moved into digs in London and then on to a hotel. He married Irene on Monday, March 22, 1965 back in his hometown in the Abbey Church. The 90 guests invited to the reception included former Dundee team-mates Hugh Robertson, Bert Slater and Andy Penman. Ian Mackenzie, his lifelong pal, was Gillie's best man.

Alan and Irene did not go on honeymoon. They were too busy setting up home and by summer they had bought a house in Bush Hill Park, Enfield. In any case, he had to face Wolves on the Saturday. His life had changed considerably and yet there were still those Spurs fans who questioned the signing's wisdom, given the state of Tottenham's half-back line. Mullery had arrived from Fulham the previous year, but with Mackay injured and Blanchflower retired, there was a belief that Bill Nicholson should have invested more heavily in his defence.

It took a 14-year-old boy to put the Gilzean purchase into perspective. A letter to the Tottenham Weekly Herald from a J. Galloway, 37 Summerhill Road, N15 read:

I have chosen Gilzean as my favourite player, because in the short space of time he has played for the Spurs he has proved himself well worthy to be included in the reconstruction of another successful Spurs team. When he first appeared for Spurs in the centre-forward position he was greeted, after a short spell of the game, with shouts saying that he was just a waste of money. Others who realised that he had not yet adjusted to the pace of English soccer awaited the time when he could produce his full skill and ability. It took him some time to adjust his play, but when he had finally settled down in his favourite position of inside-left, he proved to the spectators that he had not been a waste of money, as they had said previously.

He soon brought into effect his mastery of the ball by flicking, with the side of his boot, accurate passes to the oncoming forward when he himself had his back to goal. Many of these such passes led to the scoring of goals. His mastery of the ball is also shown when he and a couple of defenders are chasing the ball and he suddenly backheels the ball accurately to a team-mate while the two defenders are stranded.

Although he has only played for half the season he has scored the second highest amount of goals. Out of these he has scored a hat-trick and many of the goals he has scored have been headers. He is a very good header of the ball and he provides a wonderful partnership with Greaves. He is also very effective in the dribble, where his mastery of the ball helps him greatly.

In defence he can be very useful as he is able to beat many of today's forwards in the air; altogether he is a very good footballer and has proved himself very worthy of a regular place in the Spurs team.

Gilzean admitted that the hefty price tag and anxiety about how he would cope had played on his mind in those first few months. It was his appreciation of their significance that allowed him to do so. "Believe you me, the worry of costing an enormous amount of money could get you down," he told World Sports in April 1965. "I deliberately tried not to think about it and was helped by the fact that players around me in the Spurs side had cost big fees and not been weighed down by them.

"Ian Ure, who played with me at Dundee before moving to Arsenal last season, warned me that it would take a good while to get used to the faster pace. I was fortunate in settling in quickly, and all the players worked to make my transition easier. The pace is faster because of the big-match atmosphere in the games. At Dundee, there were small crowds and no atmosphere except for a few big matches against

Rangers. With Spurs, it's like playing against Rangers every week and I find the tense excitement pulls the best out of me." But things would get worse for Gilzean before they got better.

§

That night, back in my hotel room, I flicked open Big Chiv and looked at a few photographs. There was Martin Chivers on the day he signed for Spurs, a snap of him lying in a hospital bed with his knee in a cast from 1968 and others of him scoring goals in the 1971 League Cup final and 1972 UEFA Cup final. The grand opening of his hotel, his Spurs hall of fame induction, and on the pitch at White Hart Lane for a charity game alongside his two boys, Luke and Nick. Nick Chivers, the Nick who had told me about my book getting a mention on Talksport. Football, it seemed, was a smaller world than I had first imagined.

8

Deja Vu

Twice in the past week, two of the greatest brains in British football, John Motson and David Pleat, have made the same observation – that Dimitar Berbatov, the new taste thrill of White Hart Lane, reminds them of Alan Gilzean. Each hesitated slightly after their aperçu, realising that most listeners might not know who they were talking about.

I have a totally clear memory of Gilly, […] but I hadn't seen the comparison – and still don't. Both elegant, artistic strikers, but Gilly was slimmer with a baldy head. His most distinctive skill was in the air, he could flick the ball on from corners and take free kicks so subtly that you half believed he hadn't touched it, yet he had changed its direction enough to land it in the corner of the net. He was adored by the fans, the first to my knowledge to be hailed in their chants as the "King of White Hart Lane".

I got to know him when writing my book, 'The Glory Game'. I can remember that his wife was a policewoman, that he liked a drink and was dead lazy – getting into his Jag to drive a hundred yards to the newsagent. But what I mainly recall is something I have never come across in a footballer before – he had little interest in football. It was just his job.
  – Hunter Davies, New Statesman, March 26, 2007

"Football's not a job or a career – you're meant to enjoy it. I get paid to enjoy myself."
  – Alan Gilzean, circa 1972

Above: Alan pictured around 1950. When he wasn't playing football, much of his time was occupied with scouting activities, the highlight of which was the jamboree at Sandringham to mark the Queen's coronation in 1953. Pictures courtesy of Ian Mackenzie

Above: The Coupar Angus Boy Scouts team. Gilzean is second from the right on the bottom row; his future best man, Ian Mackenzie, is two from the left.

Below: Pictured on the tee box at Hazlehead Golf Course in Aberdeen. Gilzean enjoyed the game and would later play at Crews Hill in Enfield, the course on which John White was killed.

Pictures courtesy of Ian Mackenzie

Above: The classic Gilzean leap, in a game against St Mirren in April 1962 on the way to winning the title
Picture: DC Thomson

Right: As well as golf, Gillie was a keen cricketer. Here he prepares to take the crease for Coupar Angus, with some young fans keen to see him in action
Picture courtesy of Ian Mackenzie

Champions: The party started, below, after victory over St Johnstone, Gilzean scoring twice to win a £10 bet with Ian Ure that he would do just that. Above, the team display the league trophy back at Dens Park. In both pictures, Gillie hovers in the background, happy to let others take the limelight, a metaphor for his career. He is third from left above and second from right below.
Pictures: DC Thomson

You've won a watch: Gillie towers above England goalkeeper Gordon Banks to score the winning goal at Hampden in April 1964, sealing a hat-trick of wins over the 'Auld Enemy'. Coupar Angus would later present their son with a gold watch to honour the achievement, one of Gilzean's proudest moments. But despite his talent, he would regularly be overlooked for Scotland.

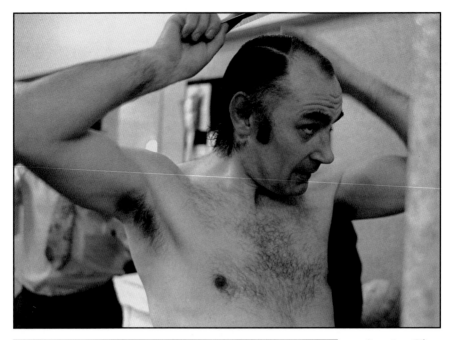

Party time: Gilzean styles what's left of his hair before heading out in 1972. Spurs team-mates recall a player who socialised hard but worked even harder on the training ground the next day. Picture: Frank Herrmann / Offside

The Glory Game: Gilzean and Pat Jennings lift captain Dave Mackay aloft after winning the FA Cup in 1967. Mackay, a fellow Scot, was Gillie's great friend and drinking partner. Picture: Barrats / S&G / EMPICS / PA

Last hurrah: Martin Chivers, Gilzean and Cyril Knowles parade the League Cup around Wembley after beating Norwich in 1973.
Picture: Peter Robinson / EMPICS Sport / PA

Mutual admirers: Bill Nicholson moves to congratulate his favourite striker after the League Cup win as Martin Peters looks on.
Picture: Popperfoto / Getty Images

Rightful place: Gilzean is presented with his Scottish Football Association Hall of Fame award by old Dundee team-mate Craig Brown in 2009. Picture: SNS

The great obsession with pigeon-holing players into types, taking out a stamp and sticking someone else's name on an individual's head in order to make sense of him, actually makes little sense at all. It is part of human nature to compartmentalise; it helps us explain what we cannot fathom. On a more practical level, and in the absence of first-hand experience or even television footage, it gives us a mental picture of that which we have never before seen, but think we have. But in trying to sate our hunger for the truth, we stifle our imagination.

It is why, when a new young player breaks through in Argentina, he is instantly labelled 'the new Diego Maradona', a futile practice. Not only has the game evolved athletically, players' builds have too, and the game has become faster and more skilful, or faster and less skilful, depending on who you speak to. No player is 'like' Maradona. Not even Lionel Messi, the latest 'new Maradona'. Players may share characteristics, like running style or great dribbling ability, but no two people are truly alike.

If genius is part-chaos, how can one player ever be considered the same as any other? Attacking midfielder Esteban Cambiasso was hailed as a 'new Maradona' when he left Argentinos Juniors for Real Madrid in 1995, and eventually buckled under the weight of a city's hopes. In 1998, he returned to Argentina, and by the time he came back to Real Madrid in 2002, something had changed. Such was the profound psychological damage, that these days he is a consummate *defensive* midfielder for Internazionale and Argentina. He became a world-class player in spite of the Maradona comparisons, not because of them.

At 17, Norman Whiteside played in the 1982 World Cup finals and drew favourable comparisons with George Best, whom he replaced as Northern Ireland's youngest ever player. Nationality and talent aside, the only other similarity was that they both started their careers with Manchester United. At 6ft 2in, and possessing the physique of a middleweight boxer, Whiteside would rampage through teams. Best only weighed 10st and bamboozled his way past opponents. (The one common factor was alcohol, and the deleterious effect it had on their United careers).

There is nothing inherently wrong with using comparisons but they should never be taken too literally. In these days of saturation coverage, when commentators search endlessly for the bon mots to make their dialogue come alive, it is inevitable. It is why, twice in the same week in 2007, John Motson, BBC's veteran Match of the Day commentator, and David Pleat, summarising on ITV, likened Dimitar Berbatov, then of Tottenham Hotspur, to a Spurs striker of the past, Alan Gilzean.

Having had the opportunity to watch Berbatov in the flesh, I feel I am in some position to comment on his abilities. On the flip side, my exposure to Gilzean is limited to a few clips on YouTube and grainy archive footage. There's the 5-1 win over

Rangers at Ibrox in 1961 when Gillie scored four; his first, a near-post flicked header from a corner on the right is trademark Gilzean; his second, a nonchalant finish under the goalkeeper after a run from deep to the front post, is brutally simple; his third, from a corner, is like a combination of the two previous goals, a timed run and a flicked finish. The fourth looks uncannily familiar. There is the graceful pirouette and left-foot strike into the bottom corner, and it has a portent of the future in it.

Another clip is from a Match of the Day I recall from childhood. During the 1980s, the BBC showed a series of classic matches from the 60s and 70s. One was Tottenham's 5-1 league victory over Manchester United in 1965. Gilzean scores the first, a stab over the line which is classic Berbatov. Then there is a leggy run and pass to Jimmy Robertson for Tottenham's fifth, which bears more than a passing resemblance to the Bulgarian's velcro-booted style. It's impossible to draw a conclusion, but you see why Pleat and Motson were struck by the similarity.

In the Hunter Davies quote above, some might say the author of The Glory Game is being disingenuous; noting exactly the similarities between the two, splitting hairs on purely cosmetic lines. Though some, like Craig Brown, the former Scotland manager and team-mate of Gilzean's at Dundee, believe that the only comparison is cosmetic: "Gilzean was a far better player than Berbatov is. He had more to offer. He was a talisman, a flashing, flashy player. The only similarity I can see is in size. Gilzean's finishing was better than Berbatov's. He'd cost around £20m today."

There is something quaint in the last observation, given that Berbatov cost Manchester United closer to £30m when he left Tottenham in the summer of 2008, but Brown is certain that Gillie was superior to Berbatov.

As is Ken Jones, the distinguished Daily Mirror sports writer and cousin of Cliff Jones. "Someone said to me once, when Berbatov signed, that it was just like looking at Alan Gilzean. I said, 'What? You must be joking.' There was a period of five years when Gilzean was one of the top strikers in England, he was unplayable. He created the run to the front post for corners before anyone else knew about it."

Berbatov lasted just two seasons at White Hart Lane before demanding a move, while Gilzean was given a testimonial for his long service. Gilzean was 12th on the club's 50 Greatest Players DVD, Berbatov nowhere. Some might argue that Berbatov was not there long enough to be considered, but his two seasons equalled Jürgen Klinsmann's time at the club, and he was 15th. I was pleasantly surprised to find Gilzean ahead of the German and his former strike partner, Teddy Sheringham (14), sitting between Paul Gascoigne (13) and John White (11). Lists like these ignore players who were never captured on film, but they provide a sense of what the player meant to the club, and in Gillie's case what the club meant to the player.

"I'm a Tottenham man at heart and Tottenham was my club; I don't think I could really pull on another team's jersey with the same feeling as I did for Tottenham," Gilzean tells Brian Moore on The Big Match in 1974, the introduction to his profile. "It gets into your blood. Once a Tottenham man, you're always a Tottenham man."

What follows is a Gilzean masterclass: he climbs between two defenders at the back post to head a cross from the left powerfully past Bob Wilson in the Arsenal goal; on an utter muck heap of a pitch against Chelsea, he controls a Pat Jennings kick with his head before slipping in Greaves, despite two defenders pulling at his shirt and the sand underfoot tugging at his ankles; stabbing the ball over the line in that 5-1 win over Manchester United; in a final clip, his neck looks like it might snap as he contorts his body to flick a cross from the right inside the left-hand post.

"The Spurs fans over my 10 years have been fantastic to me, and if I have given them half the thrills they have given me it must be fantastic." For supporters like myself too young to have seen him play, this interview provides a glimpse of what is meant when older fans say modern-day players are not committed to their clubs.

Like Gilzean, Berbatov has been accused of being lazy. Certainly, it was one of the main criticisms that Spurs fans had of him. Yet, he was undeniably sublime at times. He gave two virtuoso performances in how to lead the line in the 2007-08 season: one in a league game against Bolton after Robbie Keane, his strike partner, had been sent off and the other in a League Cup quarter-final away to Manchester City, after the Spurs midfielder Didier Zokora had been dismissed. Tottenham won both games playing with 10 men for large periods. The foundation for the victories was Berbatov's wonderful gift for alleviating pressure on his tiring team-mates.

Facially, Berbatov is not unlike Gilzean. A long nose and a higher than average hairline are the most obvious traits shared by the two and, despite the caveats about comparing players, it is tempting to conclude that Hunter Davies is wrong. I could not shake this quixotic notion that the spirit of Gilzean was alive and well in the form of a moody Bulgarian. Alan Mullery had seen it and so had most of Gillie's former team-mates.

Berbatov has reached two European finals and lost both – tellingly he did not start in Manchester United's loss to Barcelona in 2009 or Bayer Leverkusen's loss to Real Madrid in 2001. He is Bulgaria's all-time leading scorer and has been voted their best player six years in a row. Gilzean spearheaded Dundee's run to the European Cup semi-finals and won the UEFA Cup with Spurs in 1972, scoring the competition's first hat-trick on the way. He scored 12 goals in 22 internationals. But what, really, does this tell us? The only option left is to listen to subjective opinions and, overwhelmingly, the ones I listened to judged Gilzean the better of the two.

Steve Perryman made more appearances than any other in the white shirt of Spurs; he remembers watching Gilzean as an apprentice and being mesmerised by his ability on the ball. "The complimentary seat Spurs gave you was in a stall low on the track and you sat with all the other schoolboys and apprentices," says Steve. "And you were at ground level and you'd think, 'Christ, this is quick. Arsenal-Tottenham, wow!' You just felt the love for Gillie. Someone made a comment one day and said he could sit in the middle of the pitch and have a crap and he'd get applauded. It was that sort of respect for him, he typified what Tottenham was about for those people. He had this extra edge of class that they just loved. You know, like Berbatov? Except Berbatov sort of smacked it back at them, because he went on to other things."

The son of a former professional footballer and a former professional netball player, Berbatov's upbringing in Blagoevrad before, during and after the fall of the Berlin Wall, could not have been more different, one assumes, to Gillie's childhood in 1940s and 50s Coupar Angus. In 2006, he joined Tottenham, and that's when the comparisons started. Some claim he was every inch Gillie's successor. Others say that, while both had grace and sublime touch, Gilzean's better work ethic, consistency and loyalty mark him down as the superior of the two players.

Berbatov is three inches taller than Gillie – but nowhere near as effective in the air. Their strike rates for Tottenham were around 1 in 2 for Berbatov and 1 in 3 for Gilzean. But statistics lie. Gilzean spent the latter part of his career playing somewhat betwixt and between, neither an out-and-out striker, nor a conventional midfielder. Indeed, some might say, the epitome of the modern attacker.

They share a diffidence that some mistake as aloofness and a fierce determination to keep their private lives private. In 1973, Gilzean said: "I love football, and regard myself as lucky that I have had the privilege of playing with so many great players. But after the game my life is my own, and I would hate to be constantly in the public eye." He hinted that was part of the reason for his decision to leave Dundee for London. "After the game, the lads used to go for lagers and, of course, stories used to get back to the manager about the team being out on the booze – particularly if we were in the middle of a bad run. In London, it is far easier to relax because, as the capital city, it is full of celebrities. It takes a lot of pressure off your personal life not being recognised everywhere you go."

In Chris Davies' book, Deadly Dimitar, Ulrich Dorst, the Bayer Leverkusen press officer, says Berbatov "didn't like giving interviews. You virtually had to force him. And when he did, he only talked about football. He never discussed his private life."

His departure from Tottenham would cause the club's former player and manager Terry Venables to remark in The Sun that Berbatov had been a "poisonous presence".

Gilzean's time at Tottenham is recalled only with fondness and warmth by both supporters and former team-mates who, nevertheless, still see striking similarities.

It is one of the first observations Mike England, the centre-half who arrived at Tottenham in 1966, makes when asked to describe Gillie as a player. "He had a hell of a name in football. He was a tremendous player," says England. "He was renowned for his touches and was very like Dimitar Berbatov in his ball control and in the way he looked like he wasn't really putting in the effort."

There was another similarity, too. "He just made it easy for other people and he made it look easy. When, sometimes, someone does something that looks so easy, sometimes the crowd don't appreciate how difficult it really is. He had this magical flick with his head. He used to go up and glance the ball on, and it was very, very clever, the way he played. He used to just get in front of centre-halves, it was very difficult for defenders to play against. He always had the knack of making sure he just got to the ball, which is a skill in itself. You don't get many people with the heading ability that he had. He mastered the art of just flicking it."

Hunter Davies, meanwhile, touched on something else in that New Statesman piece. "Old players get invited back all the time, offered cushy numbers in the hospitality suites, but Gilly, so I'm told, has never been seen once at White Hart Lane," he wrote. "Former colleagues have tried but failed to locate him. The last anyone heard, he was back in Scotland, working in a warehouse."

I knew this to be partially incorrect. Gilzean had been back at Spurs since he retired, according to Andy Porter, the Tottenham club historian. Andy told me that he once saw him sitting in the stand at White Hart Lane during a reserve game when his son, Ian, was at Spurs. "He sat right at the back of the West Stand, buried into his overcoat," Andy said. "No one seemed to notice him, though."

But the general point remained: Gillie had been seen much less often at Spurs than he had at Dundee and, in the months that followed, I would begin to realise that Hunter Davies had been right. Why had he not been back at Tottenham?

§

"Has Gillie given you his blessing?" asks Pat Jennings in a deep County Down accent, which has lost none of its Irishness despite almost half a century in England. I tell him that he knows about the book. "Because I wouldn't want a book written about me, if I hadn't given permission," he adds.

"I can understand that," I say. "I'm writing the book with the best of intentions. It's a book about football. It's about his career as a player. "

"I can give you five minutes," says Pat abruptly.

When I check my recorder at the end of the interview I have managed to eke out another 11 minutes and 41 seconds. He says all the usual things about Gilzean – "great touch, brilliant in the air" – and confirms that Gillie lived in a house in Park Lane in Enfield. "It's just around the corner from here, about a mile down the road," he adds. I toy with the idea of walking to Park Lane and exploring, but I'm not sure of the house number and I'm not altogether certain Pat would remember it. "My memory isn't the best for these things any more," he tells me when I ask him a question about the comparisons between Gilzean's partnership with Jimmy Greaves and that with Martin Chivers.

We're holding this conversation in a Waterstone's in Enfield. Earlier, I stomped around the streets nearby for a good 45 minutes looking for the shop. I didn't know, but I had been blown so far off course that I was just minutes away from Crews Hill Golf Club, where John White had been killed in 1964. Gillie became a member there himself, and was playing off eight by the early 1970s. I was struck by how affluent the area looked. I had tried and failed to imagine myself in Gillie's shoes on my previous visit to London, but this time I could picture him in this setting. It seemed much more real and I could understand why someone would have given up the Perthshire countryside for life here. It was picturesque, there were golf clubs, a lawn tennis club, parks and shops. Enfield town had the world's first cash machine installed at Barclays Bank in 1967. The Waterstone's bookshop is 100 yards from it. The occasion is a signing for Morris Keston's book, Superfan. The legendary Tottenham supporter, who has an entire chapter dedicated to him in The Glory Game, has just published his own book and Jennings is an old friend.

I missed Morris on the day of the Stoke City game. He had been in the media canteen at the same time, but I didn't recognise him. I finally caught up with him by phone, and he told me that he had heard the rumours about Gillie living as "a vagabond". The last contact he had with Gillie was when Cyril Knowles died in 1991 and Gillie sent Morris one of his old Scotland jerseys for auction. It fetched £2,500. "He was very close to Cyril," Morris said when I first spoke to him, in March 2010. "But he kept himself to himself, mostly. Nice, quiet Gillie."

Morris organised Pat's testimonial in 1977, the year Tottenham were relegated. He wasn't involved for Gillie's. The Northern Irishman, his country's most-capped player, stepped aside for Gilzean in 1974. "It was my turn, I'd been there longer, but Gillie asked if he could go first and I said yes, and then in the season I eventually had my testimonial, we were relegated."

"So he owes you a few quid?" I ask Pat, and we both smile. He's mellowed a bit and we both know I've gone over my allotted time. "You would never begrudge Gillie anything. He was such a popular player and such a good player for the team. He was a smashing lad. That was the great thing about that Tottenham team under Bill Nick. It was the togetherness. I mean, you can imagine what the local derbies were like to Gillie, with him living locally. Bill Nick would say there were two games we had to win all year and that was the Arsenal-Tottenham games. Over the years you can imagine how that rivalry was drummed into us. Today, with foreign players, it doesn't mean as much to them as it meant to us. I was with the club for 13 or 14 years, Gillie 10, Greavsie, Mackay – we all spent all those years there and we knew what the rivalry meant."

At regular intervals readers approach Pat looking to chat. A small boy has his photo taken; a woman asks if Pat will sign a book: "Can you put, 'For Nobby,' and can you sign it, 'Happy birthday?' It's for my partner's dad." It is not hard to divine that the taciturn Jennings is not wholly at ease with this kind of thing. It probably helps little that there is an anecdote-hungry hack sitting at his left shoulder. I had not expected any great revelations about Gilzean, but he relaxes just a little bit more.

"He's had loads of requests to come down here and do stuff, and he doesn't want to know. Signing sessions for books or even photographs. I've never heard from him and, like everyone, we'd love to see him. I work in hospitality and even today there have been people asking about him. I mean, he used to live just down the road."

Did anyone not think Gilzean and Berbatov were similar? Pat saw nearly all of the Bulgarian's games for Spurs and was at the club for Gillie's entire career.

"I see the comparison. When you look at them, yeah. The touch, yeah. Gillie was better in the air. For me, Gillie was better. It's swings and roundabouts and you would be picking holes, but Gillie had a fantastic touch as well; Berbatov has an unbelievable touch, but everything worked with Gillie and Jimmy. His control into feet was brilliant, defenders would be in at his back and he would feel them there and the next minute he would be round and turning them, like something you would have seen Kenny Dalglish doing. He had a lovely build for a front player, so he was up there in the first place. He was as good a header as anyone in the country at that time and every team seemed to have a big centre-forward, more so than nowadays. They tend to play it into feet more, but in our day it was much more important to have a big man. It cuts your options if you don't have one and you have wingers."

Pat's lift has arrived and, as he finishes giving his final answer, we stand and shake hands. "Good timing," he says, although I could have done with another half an hour. "If you speak to Gillie, tell him I was asking for him."

Then a Spurs fan makes his way over to the table. "I used to see you drinking in the Bell and Hare every week, and every week I would ask for your autograph," he says. "You would be in there with Alan Gilzean, having a beer." Pat turns towards me and says, "You should speak to this man, he's writing a book about him."

§

The 1965-66 season would prove a lacklustre one in front of goal for Gillie. He scored just 15 in total, having scored 16 from December to May in 1964-65. He reached 13 with a hat-trick in a 4-3 victory over Burnley in the FA Cup fourth round on February 12, but would score just twice in the remaining 14 games, the nadir of which was when the G-Men were dropped for the trip to Sheffield Wednesday on April 9, a game in which Phil Beal, of all people, took Gillie's place at inside-left.

It had promised to be a season of greatness for Tottenham and Gilzean. The club were top after the 3-2 home win over Leeds United on September 8, but by December they were six points adrift of leaders Liverpool, with a game more played. Their problems started when Jimmy Greaves contracted hepatitis B at the end of October and didn't play for three months. An indication of Tottenham's travails without Greaves came with the return game against Manchester United at Old Trafford. Having won 5-1 at White Hart Lane with Greaves in the side, they lost the away game by the same score. Gilzean was ailing without his strike partner. In the home game against United he had been easily the best player on the pitch. In the return, his only noteworthy contribution was a booking following a clash with Nobby Stiles.

Nevertheless, while the season would ultimately peter out, that 5-1 win over the champions held in it an element of something virtuous. The Tottenham Weekly Herald proclaimed Gilzean the "architect of the victory" and the headline "Gilzean & Greaves rout the champs" summed up the speed with which the G-Men had established themselves as the most-feared strike partnership in the country.

Tottenham Hotspur 5 Manchester Utd 1 – White Hart Lane, October 16 1965
Every so often Jimmy Greaves chooses to remind his sometimes doubting critics that he is the world's most lethal footballer near goal. The fact that he chose Saturday – the day the champions were in town – was not only highly appropriate but the memory of his lone-goal dash will stay with the 58,000 crowd for many seasons to come. In those few seconds Jimmy Greaves almost stole the complete show – but he would be the first to admit that the real architect of Tottenham's best performance since winning the European Cup Winners' Cup was the magnificent Alan Gilzean. The elegant Scot, twisting

*and turning with a flick here, there and everywhere was far too much of a
handful for United's defence.*

*In the 25th minute, Neil Johnson's dangerous cross was headed off the back
post by Jimmy Robertson, the ball broke to Gilzean and he tapped it home.
Thirteen minutes later Greaves – who says he can only score goals? – pushed a
perfect pass inside Shay Brennan, United's right back, and Johnson skimming
in from the left whipped the ball past a startled Dunne.*

*Shades of the double side were recalled 15 minutes into the second half
with the killer one-two touch. First Greaves went solo and then two minutes
later a five-man move ended with a reverse pass to Eddie Clayton who shot
hard and accurately into the bottom left-hand corner from 25 yards. This alone
atoned for his glaring miss before half-time.*

*[...] But Tottenham were not done. Four minutes after Charlton's goal,
Gilzean hedged down the left wing closely guarded by three men. With
superb control and timing he manoeuvred clear and when he finally passed to
Robertson, the winger had time to take the ball forward and smash a tremendous shot past the disbelieving Dunne.*

– Tottenham Herald

Eight years later, Paddy Crerand, who had marked Gilzean that day, confirmed
that his compatriot had been one of his most difficult opponents during his career:
"When Alan and Jimmy Greaves were playing for Spurs we used to think a good hard
tackle in the first five minutes would keep them quiet," he told The Weekly News.
"But it never worked that way. You just couldn't get at Gillie. He had so much ability
to touch the ball away first time, and you were a yard short of the tackle when he
made the pass. And he was the worst in the world to mark near goal. You would keep
an eye on him all afternoon. Then suddenly a figure would slip in blindside and you
were dead. 'You so-and-so bandit!' I would shout. And you'd get a grin."

Crerand wasn't the only Manchester United legend impressed with Gilzean.
Denis Law expressed similar admiration in the same interview, and it addressed
another problem I had with that Hunter Davies article, the claim that Gilzean "had
little interest in football. It was just his job".

Law liked Gilzean. Speaking in that same Weekly News interview, he said: "Not
just because of his play. That's quality, of course. What I especially like about Gillie is
the way he can look at football from a bit farther back. It can be all crash, bang out
there but he won't carry any bad feeling when the whistle goes. For him, the game's
over. Win or lose, he'll come into the players' lounge and have a beer and a chat. He

enjoys his game and he knows that one result isn't going to change the world. That's probably why he has lasted so well. The game gives him genuine pleasure."

There were other highlights in that season for Gilzean. He created Greaves' two goals in the 3-2 win over Leeds in September which sent Spurs top. There was a hat-trick for Spurs in a 4-0 win over the Hungarian national XI in a friendly in November, where he played at inside-left and looked much more like himself than he had done at centre-forward. He scored the only goal – yet another header – in a 1-0 win over Sheffield United in mid-December. Clive Toye of the Daily Express claimed he had climbed so high in despatching it that "there was almost snow on his hair". There was the 4-2 home win over Chelsea at the start of that month: two goals and "a remarkable performance of crisp perfection" according to the Weekly Herald. But for all the highs, there were more lows; in that same paragraph was the phrase: "What an enigma is this man Gilzean. His last two matches with Spurs have been atrocious."

It might just as easily have been written about Dimitar Berbatov, 40 years later, as he struggled to justify that £30m price tag at Manchester United.

The 3-2 defeat at home to Sheffield Wednesday seemed to sum up Gilzean's woes. Wednesday had been without an away win all season, or a victory at Tottenham since 1938, and "the biggest disappointment in the Spurs attack was Alan Gilzean. Without Greaves, a great deal depended on Scotland's centre-forward. Alas, he was off colour, appearing ponderous, sluggish and thoroughly out of sorts. In fact, it looked as though it was he who was suffering from jaundice [rather than Greaves]. The final blow came when he headed against the upright and scooped the rebound over the bar in the dying seconds. An equaliser could have saved Spurs face a little."

The entire 1965-66 campaign would prove to be one of disappointments and Gilzean's lot would improve little with the return of Greaves. The England striker was a pale shadow of the player he had been before his illness. His malaise would dog Spurs' season and disrupt his preparations for the forthcoming World Cup finals. He struggled to recapture his form but, such was his importance to England, he was included in Alf Ramsey's squad. He would miss out on a World Cup final appearance after a poor tackle by the defender Joseph Bonnel, in England's final group game against France, opened his shin to the bone and left Greaves requiring 14 stitches.

There was disappointment for Gilzean on the international stage, too. Bill Nicholson pulled him out of the Scotland team for the World Cup qualifier against Italy in Naples on December 7, 1965, a game which the Scots lost 3-0 to end their hopes of qualifying for the World Cup to be held in England the following year. It was particularly galling for the Scots because Jock Stein, the manager, was forced to play three centre-halves in attack during the game, including Ron Yeats, Gillie's old army colleague and nemesis from his Dundee days.

It had been all the more frustrating for Gilzean since he had played well and almost scored a second goal in the 1-0 win over the Italians at Hampden Park a month earlier. Ultimately, though, Scotland's fate had been sealed in October, when they succumbed to a surprising 2-1 defeat at the hands of Poland.Scotland created enough chances to win by a significant scoreline, but they could not improve upon Billy McNeill's 14th-minute goal. Poland absorbed all of the Scots' pressure and while Gilzean and Law were inches away from adding a second, the goal that would have sealed the points would not come. Poland scored twice in the final five minutes and the Scots were jeered off by a 107,000-strong crowd.

Meanwhile, the return of Greaves for the home game against Blackburn, almost three months to the day since his last appearance, against West Bromwich Albion on October 30, lifted everyone's spirits. It also gave Spurs fans another glimpse of Mike England, the defender who was earning rave reviews at Ewood Park.

Tottenham Hotspur 4 Blackburn Rvrs 0 – White Hart Lane, Jan 29, 1966

The return of Jimmy Greaves enlivened what would have been just another run-of-the-mill game and also put another 8,000 on the gate. Deep in the relegation mire, Blackburn impressed in patches. They produced some slick approach work but most of the attacking moves were stereotyped and the man who really caught the eye was man-mountain England at centre-half.

But the opposition was not too troublesome for Tottenham and Jimmy Greaves was allowed to venture back into the game at the shallow end. The whole attack seemed to move with more sharpness and confidence than for some time. Gilzean looked happier, Robertson faster, Clayton more constructive and Frank Saul a real firebrand up front. Was it just a coincidence?

Dave Mackay's free-kick was nodded down to Saul who slammed it home from Gilzean's knock down. Then with Spurs down to 10 men, Saul returned the favour with a square ball to the Scot.

Eight minutes after the interval Greaves was brought down in the box by Newton and Mackay signalled Jimmy to take the kick and with a swing of the boot he was back in the scoring charts.

It was left to Gilzean to complete the scoring. He was first on to Phillip Beal's long one into the Blackburn penalty area and he nipped in to score after a nudging contest between Frank Saul and Blackburn right-back Wilson.

– Tottenham Herald

Everything appeared rosy after a handsome victory but Nicholson was soon being criticised for rushing Greaves back too soon as Tottenham limped to the end of the campaign. The illness had a crippling effect on Greaves' game: the quick-thinking and turn of foot were missing.

The team would ultimately finish eighth in the league and, for the second successive season, would exit the FA Cup in the fifth round, following an ignominious defeat to Second Division Preston North End, who had already overcome a tough Bolton Wanderers side to set up their meeting with Spurs. The 2-1 reverse forced Bill Nicholson to eat humble pie, too. Just days before the tie he told the Weekly Herald: "Bolton were very unlucky to lose the replay but I am glad we will be playing Preston. Bolton are a hard, tough side and would be a difficult team to have to play."

The exit to Preston was made all the more disappointing because Tottenham had secured their passage into the fifth round following a match which most had agreed was the greatest cup tie seen at White Hart Lane since the war. Gilzean had been struggling to make the game. He took a tumble while training in the club gymnasium, and then limped off after sustaining a nasty kick in a practice match at Cheshunt, the club's training ground.

Two goals down to Burnley after four minutes and missing Dave Mackay with flu, even the most optimistic Spurs fans had given up on Wembley for another season.

Tottenham Hotspur 4 Burnley 3 – White Hart Lane, February 18th, 1966

A nerve-jangling, cliff-hanger of a battle left the 50,611 crowd as limp and exhausted as the players themselves. Alan Gilzean took the major honours for his fine hat-trick in Tottenham's pulsating fightback. But there were other heroes. The absence of Dave Mackay gave Frank Saul a chance of showing how wrong Bill Nicholson was to contemplate dropping him from the side. And then there was Cliff Jones. He began the game with his thighs strapped up. Before the interval he had taken such a pounding that his right arm was hanging limp and useless. Praise too for captain of the day Alan Mullery. He kept a cool head and his steadying influence helped ease Spurs back into the game when all seemed lost. Commiserations for Burnley and particularly their centre-forward Irvine, who managed a fine hat-trick and yet still managed to be on the losing side.

It was Irvine who gave Burnley a shock lead after only 40 seconds, the Spurs defence standing mesmerised by a slick move down the right flank. Another four minutes and Irvine again hypnotised Tottenham while he flashed another ball home.

Spurs pounded back gallantly and forced an encouraging series of corners. In the 36th minute Jones jinked his way his way down the left and centred for Gilzean to head home. Here was a glimmer of hope.

Five minutes after the interval, Jimmy Greaves moved over to take another corner-kick. He swung it inwards and Gilzean headed the equaliser. Tottenham's tail was up but 10 minutes later Irvine completed his hat-trick after a period of intense pressure. But Frank Saul, the man who was going to be dropped, provided another equaliser. Mullery pushed the ball to Gilzean, who sent Jones away. The crippled winger's pinpoint centre was confidently taken by Saul and hammered home.

It looked like the teams were all set for Turf Moor for the replay when, with two minutes remaining, the irrepressible Gilzean popped up on the edge of the area and sent the ball flashing inside the right-hand post. The thundering roar which greeted the unbelievable confirmed that it will be a long time before we see such a thriller at Tottenham again.

– Tottenham Herald

However, the defeat at Preston a month later would infuriate the increasingly desperate Nicholson, who was worried about his side's complacency. He had ordered the players to train on Christmas Day in an attempt to keep them away from temptation on the back of the 5-1 defeat to United. He said: "However careful they are, the players are bound to eat more, drink more and be in a smoky atmosphere over the holidays. An hour's training on Christmas morning, followed by a hard workout the next day to sweat it out of their systems, will make all the difference." Two wins in successive days over Sheffield United backed up his argument. But it was a short-term fix. Tottenham would win just four league games over the rest of the season as their remote title challenge slowed and then dissipated altogether.

The defeat by a Francis Lee-inspired Preston prompted an alternative remedy – a screening of the game in front of the players. "We had to suffer all that rubbish for 90 minutes, so I don't see why the players should not suffer too," said Nicholson. "They were rubbish. If my 'A' team could not do better, I would advise them to get out of the game. In fact, I shall ask the 'A' team to make their candid comments after they have seen this film. Where can you start when you have so many failures?"

The Tottenham chairman, Fred Wale, was equally forthright: "I never thought I would see a Tottenham team play with such lack of spirit." The Spurs fans who met the team as they stepped off the train at Euston later that evening belted out a parodied "Glory, glory hallelujah, the Spurs go crawling out."

Desmond Hackett noted in the Daily Express that "Gilzean was noticeable for wearing his shirt outside his shorts but could as easily have worn it over his head."

It was apparent that Tottenham's problems were not all of their attackers' making, though. They would concede 66 goals to add to the 71 they had given up the previous season. It was becoming increasingly apparent that Nicholson would have to spend more of Wale's money if defensive frailties were to be put right.

By April, Bobby Moore was being heavily linked with a move from West Ham. The soon-to-be World Cup-winning captain had expressed a desire to leave Upton Park and when news of the right-half's interest in joining Spurs was made known to Nicholson, he was keen to do business. "We are always interested in good players. The trouble is that the players we want are not usually available. We always keep working away and hope that the situation may change. Here it looks as though there is a useful player who is becoming available."

Spurs hardly helped their case as suitors by losing 4-1 to West Ham at White Hart Lane at the height of the uncertainty over Moore's future. Nevertheless, Moore was desperate to come to Spurs and the plan was to let his contract, which was due to expire in June 1966, run down, thus freeing him to make the switch to White Hart Lane. But Football Association rules stated that if he wanted to represent England at the World Cup finals he had to be under contract to a club. He signed a one-month extension at Upton Park and went on to lift the Jules Rimet trophy a few months later, at which point West Ham offered to double his wages to £150 a week and gave him a new three-year contract.

Allan Harris, the former Chelsea defender who was now at Coventry City, was another mooted new arrival. Nicholson had tried to sign Harris when he had moved to the Midlands club, but had failed despite a lucrative offer. However, the player that seemed most realistic of those available to Spurs was Mike England. The centre-half had just been relegated with Blackburn Rovers and was widely regarded as one of the finest defenders in the country. At 24, he was already the captain of Wales and he had been a member of Blackburn's all-conquering youth team which won the FA Youth Cup in 1959 and the European Youth Cup the following year.

Nicholson, though, would have to be at his persuasive best to ensure the signature. Manchester United were also interested and the transfer was further complicated by Blackburn's demands for a player in exchange. Relegation had infuriated the shareholders at Ewood Park and the club's annual general meeting had been a stormy one in which new signings were demanded.

One Sunday paper speculated that Bill Brown or Alan Gilzean might be offered in exchange for England, but Fanfare, writing in the Weekly Herald, dismissed the notion out of hand, saying that the author might as well have added "the name of Jimmy Greaves to their pin-sticking forecasting".

Gilzean's future was safe for the time being. Indeed, on more than one occasion, Bill Nicholson singled him out for praise, noting of his player's role in Frank Saul's goal in the memorable 4-3 win over Burnley, that "it is a long time since I have seen such a fine pass to a winger. [Cliff] Jones took it magnificently. It was a miracle that no Burnley player managed to get to the centre and Saul ran in beautifully".

However, Nicholson's obvious faith in Gillie did not stop supporters speculating on what the player might be worth if the manager were to embark on another one of his spending sprees. One supporter wrote to the Tottenham Weekly Herald saying "I would sell the pretty but too often ineffective Gilzean and sign either Hateley or the much improved Strong of Liverpool. Both players have expressed a desire to leave their present clubs ... with perhaps £50,000 coming back into the kitty for the sale of Gilzean." The correspondent, a D. Macdonald from Phillip Lane, fails to explain why £22,500 had fallen off the transfer fee that Spurs had paid 18 months previously.

As the season came to an end, Tottenham were due to set off on a tour of North America. First, though, they played a friendly with Sarpsborg, the town in Norway which supplied the club with its Christmas tree each year. Gilzean, who had failed to score away from home in the 1965-66 season, clearly enjoyed the Norwegian scenery, netting twice in a 3-0 win. Tottenham returned to London on the Monday evening and met again the following morning. Bill Nicholson accompanied them on the coach to London airport before seeing them off to Bermuda. Nicholson was not the only missing party. Jimmy Greaves was scheduled to play at the World Cup and Cliff Jones had a recurring knee injury, while Neil Johnson had made way for Terry Venables, who arrived at Spurs from Chelsea near the end of the season.

Nicholson's absence from the trip was deliberate. "I would have loved to have gone on tour, but at the moment I am more interested in next season," he said. "That is my chief concern. I must be on the spot in case any players in whom I am interested come up for transfer." One player did come up for transfer, Mike England. Gilzean stayed at Spurs, as did Bill Brown, and no swaps sweetened the deal. There was no need: Blackburn received £95,000 for England, a British record for a defender.

Gilzean frustrated Tottenham fans in his second season at the club. He looked ineffective and disinterested at times, far removed from a player who would later be widely regarded as a legend. In that one respect, he was exactly like Dimitar Berbatov.

9

The G-Men

Bill Nicholson was worried. Gillie had seen it in his face. He'd even called a meeting in the summer in which he'd said Spurs had to win something at all costs that season, which was most unlike Bill. He was a purist; he wanted football played the right way and to hear him say that it didn't matter about performances demonstrated the pressure he was under. But the fans had shown their displeasure. Some even thought Gillie should be sold. He hadn't played as well as he had done in his first season, but as far as he could see the problem wasn't in attack, it was in defence. The previous season they scored five against Aston Villa, but conceded five. You couldn't sustain that. Dave Mackay had come back, but it was clear he was still recovering from his second leg break. Maybe this new kid from Blackburn Rovers was the answer. He was a fine defender, Gillie had seen that earlier in the year when he'd won everything in the air against him at White Hart Lane. He could play a bit, too. He'd been a midfielder in his early days and he liked the ball at his feet.

Mike England turned his back on football in 1988. He had just been sacked as Wales manager and was experiencing a personal crisis. The death of the Scotland manager, Jock Stein, during a World Cup qualifier three years earlier had affected him so badly that he turned down four job offers after the Welsh FA's decision.

The 1985 match between Scotland and Wales was a thriller. Wales needed to win to secure a play-off against Australia for the 1986 World Cup finals in Mexico, while the Scots needed a point to take their place. Most assumed Stein had suffered the heart attack because of the stress suffered. Scotland appeared to be heading out after a Mark Hughes goal in the 13th minute, but equalised seven minutes from time with a Davie Cooper penalty. Cue pandemonium on the sidelines. England says that Stein had been embroiled in a running argument throughout the game. "A photographer had been bothering him all night and in the end Jock got off the bench and dragged him away," England said. "Jock had asked him to move several times but he refused and in the end Jock physically did it himself. Jock then held his chest and I knew he'd had a heart attack."

Later, it became clear that Stein had not taken the diuretics that helped control an ongoing heart problem, but the image of one of the game's greatest managers dying in front of him haunted England. "It really did affect me for a long time afterwards," he told the Lancashire Telegraph in 2010. "I was sacked after that. I couldn't help feeling, 'How could they sack me after all that?' I was then offered four other jobs in football but I decided against it, I realised there was more to life."

When I phone Mike England at his home in Clywd, north Wales, he sounds every inch the cheery gent depicted in Big Chiv, Martin Chivers' autobiography. Chivers notes that England was one of those men who had a long fuse, but if you lit it you had to stand back. He recalled an away game at Newcastle when a fan threw a cup of hot chocolate that landed on England's mohair suit as the Spurs team prepared to board a train. He flattened the Newcastle supporter, just one of hundreds inside the station, provoking a Benny Hill-style chase of the Spurs team around the platforms.

Like the other Spurs players I have spoken to, he tells me that he hasn't seen Gillie in some time but that he would dearly love to catch up. Mike was invited back to White Hart Lane when Tottenham celebrated its 125th anniversary in 2007. The ground was a spectacular sight, bedecked in white and pale blue, the colour of the first kit the team wore. Two men were conspicuous by their absence as Tottenham and Aston Villa played out a thrilling 4-4 draw, two men who had epitomised an exciting era when 4-4 draws seemed to happen every other week: the G-Men.

"I was very surprised when him and Greavsie weren't there. Everyone was there except Greavsie and Gilzean. It was the likes of Alan Mullery, Cliff Jones and Phil Beal. I was very disappointed that Jimmy and Alan weren't there; I was looking forward to catching up with them. They're in the hall of fame at Spurs, aren't they?"

I inform Mike that they aren't. That they are listed as legends on the club's website, but that's as far as it goes. "I've always wondered why I haven't been included in that," he says with a hint of sadness. "I was there a long time." He has every right to be perplexed. Mike England was considered to be Bill Nicholson's last great signing for Tottenham, joined when the club was starting to emerge from its mid-1960s wilderness years and won four trophies.

It took England until the New Year to settle fully at Tottenham, yet his impact could be gauged almost immediately. Alan Mullery says that the team had a meeting at Cheshunt before the season began, during which Bill Nicholson said that it didn't matter how Tottenham played that year, just so long as the players won a trophy and returned to Europe. It appeared to work, at first. Spurs won eight of their first 11 matches at the start of the 1966-67 season and there was an undeniable feelgood factor around. They scored 23 times and the G-Men were back. Gillie had netted six, Greaves nine when, at the end of September, Spurs sat one point clear at the top.

They produced some wonderful displays in that opening spell. They defeated Leeds United 3-1, during which Terry Venables, who had arrived from Chelsea for £80,000 at the end of the previous season, and England made their White Hart Lane debuts. Mullery, Greaves and Gillie got the goals, although it was noted that Gilzean was "still in dubious form". There were impressive wins against Newcastle (2-0), Arsenal (3-1) and Manchester United (2-1), a game in which Spurs trailed with three minutes remaining but nicked the points when Gilzean equalised with a customary header and then flicked the ball through to Greaves to cap the comeback.

And then, inexplicably, it started to unravel. A 3-1 defeat at bottom-placed Blackpool heralded the start of a six-match run without a win; Tottenham earned a single point from October 15 to November 19. Complacency seemed the only explanation. Tottenham lost at Chelsea, who were fellow title contenders, but then crashed to a 1-0 defeat at home to Aston Villa, just one place above Blackpool. A week later they drew with Blackpool, Gilzean scoring two great goals in the first 20 minutes to give Tottenham a 2-0 lead which they squandered.

Villa and Blackpool would be relegated, but not before Spurs dropped another point in a 2-2 draw in their return game against the Midlanders. Those disappointing results against relegation fodder would cost Tottenham dearly and prove the difference between Spurs 1967 joining the immortals of 1961 as the second side of the 20th century to achieve the double. Such were the small margins between the two.

I'd asked Pat Jennings how close the team had come and how important Mike England had been to the transformation from one season to the next: "The season Gillie arrived we were unbeaten at home but we couldn't win away, and that tells its own story about the team. Mike England was a brilliant centre-half. I would say he was the best centre in England at that time, but that was us. We always bought the best players: Mike, Martin Chivers, Alan Mullery, Gillie, the late Cyril Knowles, Jimmy Greaves. Whenever they became available, we bought them. Then unfortunately, after the League Cup wins and the UEFA Cup, the price of players started to spiral and I think our directors didn't want to be part of that, but then decided too late that if you were going to compete you needed to buy whatever players you needed, and pay whatever needed to be paid. That, unfortunately, was why we got relegated. The team wasn't good enough, and all of a sudden we were down, the great Tottenham Hotspur. That was after Gillie had left, though."

Gilzean was absent for the game which started the slide in 1966-67. He was sent off for swearing at a linesman in a League Cup game against West Ham United and given a 14-day suspension. The Tottenham Weekly Herald reported: "Gilzean, normally a phlegmatic sort of character on the pitch, had his name taken five minutes earlier for arguing and his dismissal followed an incident on the right touchline when referee HG New refused to give Tottenham a free-kick for hands. The Scottish international presumably said something but Mr New would not even tell Bill Nicholson why Gilzean received marching orders."

The ban could not have come at a worse time, ruling Gillie out of a game that had taken two years to plan: the friendly Spurs had agreed to play against Dundee at Dens Park when they had purchased the striker. Gilzean travelled for the match but watched from the stands as his new side beat his old one 3-2 with two goals from Greaves and one from Mackay. Dundee, though, proved plucky opponents with goals from Alex Kinninmonth and Jim McLean, and were unlucky not to equalise.

Indiscipline aside, Gilzean's form was concerning Nicholson. He speculated that his dismissal against West Ham might have been prompted by the pressure he felt under, with supporters unimpressed by recent contributions. "We haven't been too impressed, either," Nicholson told the press in October. "We have kept pressing him and the pressure might have been responsible for him swearing at the linesman."

Then, as quickly as the malaise had swept through the Spurs side, Nicholson found a remedy, or perhaps the patient healed itself. It seems linked to England finding his feet. Tottenham embarked on a 24-game unbeaten run after Christmas, conceding just five goals in the final 16 matches. Gilzean found his form and the G-Men were flying by season's end. "To be fair I think we were still a few points behind Manchester United, but if we had got on the run earlier I think the team was good enough to beat anyone," Pat Jennings told me.

With the league championship seemingly out of reach, attention turned to the FA Cup. Spurs were given a tough draw against Millwall in the third round, but it wasn't so much the opposition that they feared, but the venue. The Den had a reputation as one of the most intimidating grounds in the country. Millwall had been promoted the previous year from the Third Division and fancied their chances.

"We played in front of 42,000 at Millwall on the Saturday at the Den and they had to shut the gates about an hour before kick-off because so many people had turned up to watch the game," Alan Mullery said in Matt Allen's book, *Jimmy Greaves*. "We got a 0-0, which we were pleased with because Millwall is never an easy place to get a result. We took them back to White Hart Lane the following Wednesday and another 60,000 turned up to watch us win 1-0, with Gilly getting us the goal. I think that first game against Millwall was the toughest we had in the competition. If you have ever been there you'll know it used to be a nightmare place to go and get a result."

In the fourth round Spurs were paired with Portsmouth; it was to prove one of those irrepressible days for the G-Men, despite sturdy resistance by the opponents.

Tottenham Hotspur 3 Portsmouth 1 – White Hart Lane, FA Cup 4th round, February 18, 1967

Portsmouth [were] intent on dragging Spurs down to Fratton Park for a replay. At the interval they stood a 50-50 chance of the plan succeeding for Spurs seemed singularly bereft of ideas. [...] Two goals in 90 seconds by Alan Gilzean early in the second half, however, quickly put a new complexion on the game and a sizzler by Jimmy Greaves finally muffled the Pompey chimes.

[...] In the 52nd minute, Cliff Jones was obstructed on the halfway line. Mike England placed the long kick brilliantly just to the left of the Pompey goal for Gilzean to soar in and nod the ball into the net.

Tottenham pounded on the attack again straight from the resumption. The ball was cleared to Robertson who slipped it through to Gilzean to turn into the goal. Gilzean looked offside but referee Mitchell allowed it after checking with the linesman. The result was put beyond doubt 10 minutes later when Gilzean delicately chipped the ball to Greaves. Jimmy burst past two defenders, accelerating all the time before flashing the ball home. – Tottenham Herald

Spurs carried on apace in the league. A 1-0 defeat by Manchester United had all but put paid to their chances of winning the title and a run of three successive draws at the end of February and start of March confirmed their fate. Nevertheless, the team were playing with a brio not seen since the double-winning days. When they met Chelsea at the end of that sequence of draws they played some sublime football, and when they scored after 10 minutes they looked capable of running their London rivals off the pitch. Alas, the scoring ended there for the hosts and, despite a number of chances for Gilzean and Greaves, the match finished 1-1.

Tottenham won every league game bar one – a 0-0 draw against Liverpool at Anfield – until the end of the season, securing third spot. The momentum would take them all the way to the FA Cup final, where they would meet the Chelsea team they had been unable to beat in the league. In the fifth round, Spurs eased past Bristol City thanks to two goals by Greaves and then survived a stringent test at Birmingham in the sixth before demolishing the Midlanders 6-0 in the replay. Terry Venables scored a rare goal and then added a second before Gilzean got on the end of a cross by Jimmy Robertson to make it three. Greaves got two after half-time and Frank Saul completed the rout. The semi-final pitted Spurs against Nottingham Forest who, second in the league and chasing Manchester United for the title, were slight favourites. But they hadn't accounted for Jimmy Greaves and his happy knack of scoring goals against them: he had scored 24 times against Forest before the semi-final.

Tottenham Hotspur 2 Nottingham Forest 1 – Hillsborough, FA Cup semi-final, April 29, 1967

Spurs reached Wembley with a happy blend of controlled soccer, solid defensive play, and two deadly accurate shots from outside the penalty area.

[…] If Forest had had [injured striker] Joe Baker in their forward line it might have been a different story but in the event the Spurs defence – with Mike England dominant – maintained their fine record.

[…] Tottenham's goal in the 32nd minute, however, came out of the blue. Mike England put the ball up to Alan Gilzean, who nodded it down to the feet of Jimmy Greaves. Instead of moving it forward and beating his man Greaves unleashed a terrific left-foot drive that spun into the net like a bullet.

[…] In the 66th minute Terry Hennessey, the Forest wing-half, and by my count the best player afield, made his only mistake of the game. A moment's hesitation led him to be caught in possession by the hard-working Frank Saul who took the ball forward a few yards before blasting home a tremendous shot from fully 20 yards.

Four minutes later [the injured Dave] Mackay was led off by trainer Cecil Poynton to be replaced by Cliff Jones. And so continuity with the double team of 1961 was maintained at Hillsborough six years later. – Tottenham Herald

I sat down to watch highlights of this game on the Pathe News website in anticipation of seeing the G-Men combine to deadly effect for the opening goal. Phil Soar, in his history of Tottenham, described it in much the same way as above, as had Matt Allen in his book on Jimmy Greaves. Indeed, Allen notes that Mike England's free-kick – towards the head of Gilzean and down to the feet of Greaves – had been a regular tactic at Spurs throughout the course of the season … but when I watched the goal it bore little or no resemblance to the one described by Allen and others.

Mike England is in the box for a corner which is taken off his head; Dave Mackay competes for the loose ball, but it is partially cleared again by a Forest defender. Cyril Knowles seizes on the clearance and slips it right to Greaves and the striker hits a first-time shot into the bottom corner in off the post – this last description was the only part of the goal that resembled what I had read. And then it struck me that the author of the original match report had got it wrong. Perhaps the Tottenham Weekly Herald correspondent had simply looked at his notepad at the wrong time and, having witnessed the G-Men go through that routine so often, thought it was fairly safe to assume that if Greaves had scored it, then Gilzean had flicked it down to him from a Mike England free-kick. Either way, it gives an indication of the problems with slavishly adhering to press reports for information, and is yet another example of a factual inaccuracy involving Gilzean repeated as fact thereafter.

One fact beyond contention was that Chelsea reached the final having beaten Leeds United 1-0 at Villa Park. The build-up to the first all-London FA Cup final was all-pervasive. There was a cup final record, which featured the entire Tottenham team signing Spurs Go Marching On and 12 other hits, before anyone had heard of cup final records. Terry Venables took solo on Bye-Bye Blackbird, Jimmy Greaves belted out Strolling and somewhat incongruously Dave Mackay (Edinburgh), Jimmy Robertson (Glasgow) and Gilzean (Coupar Angus) sang I Belong To Glasgow. One company was offering 8mm and 16mm film of the match, at £3.15s.0d for a 200ft standard silent recording, up to 400ft with BBC commentary for £30.15s.0d.

Talk in pubs around the capital centred on one topic: slick Tottenham with their G-Men, or robust Chelsea with their tough defence and emerging winger Charlie Cooke, who had scored the winner against Leeds at Villa Park? The same Charlie Cooke on whom Dundee had spent a chunk of their fee from Spurs for Gilzean.

The players were caught up in the occasion too. A week before the final they were invited to a dinner at the Hilton, organised by the Anglo-American Sporting Club, a boxing club that hosted posh dinners. Both cup final teams were there and they sat at tables opposite each other sizing their opponents up until Terry Venables, who had left Chelsea for Tottenham the previous year, broke the ice. Soon the players were mingling together and chatting away. Guest of honour was the FA Cup trophy, gleaming. How must Gillie have felt as he looked at it? It had been his dream to play at Wembley in an FA Cup final and now he was just seven days away.

The night before the final, Tottenham stayed in the Mayfair Hotel in Piccadilly and after dinner they took in a film, before retiring to their hotel for a cup of tea and a chat. Then it was lights out.

The next morning the sorriest player in the hotel was Eddie Clayton, who learned watching television that Cliff Jones was going to be the Spurs sub and he would play no part in the day. "The nation was told before Eddie and he felt pretty sick about it," recalled Frank Saul, the Tottenham striker. "Being dropped from the side when I thought I was playing well was something I knew from years gone by."

Jimmy Greaves recalls that the Chelsea players were rigid with fear before the teams walked out, and that he knew in that moment that Spurs were going to win. Tottenham were relaxed and chatty; there were big names who had done it all before in their ranks, whereas Chelsea's oldest player was Marvin Hinton at 27. In the dressing room, Terry Venables produced a pair of silver football boots and said that whoever scored the winning goal would get them and five pounds out of his own pocket. An unnamed Spurs player bet the Chelsea forward John Boyle that he would not try on one of the guardsmen's hats. He proudly walked into the arena wearing it.

Alan Mullery says the tunnel was a strange place before kick-off. "Although Chelsea had beaten us at Stamford Bridge and we only managed a draw at White Hart Lane, they looked petrified. In fact, Dave Mackay turned round to us and said, 'Look at this lot. We've beaten them already. They don't fancy it.' And he was right. They did look beaten. They were only young kids at the time, and we looked at them and we knew we were winners. We had experience on the big stage and they didn't. Greavsie had been there with England and it was Dave Mackay's third final."

Gilzean, too, had played in a cup final, a European Cup semi-final and had won a league title. In the 1967 final, he was to have an influential effect on the outcome, not least because the Chelsea manager Tommy Docherty, who had bragged repeatedly about his side's chances at Wembley, changed his line-up that day.

Bill Nicholson wrote in his autobiography, *Glory Glory*: "I believe Tommy Docherty made a tactical mistake [...] In previous matches he used Marvin Hinton as a sweeper and took three out of four points in league matches. Alan Gilzean did not like playing against a sweeper, and it showed in these matches. But just before the final, Docherty abandoned the idea and played an orthodox defensive system. When I heard that, I told my players: 'He's done us a favour.' Docherty was a good coach but he was impulsive and changed his mind a lot." It makes sense that Gillie did not like playing against a sweeper. Much of his game was about flicking the ball on for others and one can just imagine a covering defender mopping up everything he played into the space between goalkeeper and back four.

Tottenham Hotspur 2 Chelsea 1
Wembley Stadium, FA Cup final, May 20, 1967
    It was as cool and precise as a surgical operation. Spurs dissected Chelsea

with smooth, polished professionalism to win the FA Cup for the third time in seven seasons. The non-partisan spectators might have complained that it was unspectacular and slow moving. But Spurs brought home the cup by declining to be hustled into a cut and thrust free-for-all. As in the Blanchflower era they successfully dictated the tempo. It was a brilliant tactical battle.

Of course Spurs' first goal could not have been better timed. If there was any luck in this game it was that they should have taken the lead just before the interval. Just after Pat Jennings had magnificently fisted a stinging drive from Cooke over the bar, Spurs moved on to the attack. Mullery blasted in a drive which Harris partially blocked. The ball spun out to Robertson who stabbed home a magnificent low shot.

[…] Alan Gilzean was playing a masterly game, glancing the ball accurately in all directions.

With 22 minutes to go Spurs went two up. Dave Mackay took a long throw-in. Jim Robertson pulled it down to Frank Saul, who in one glorious movement, pivoted round and stabbed the ball home just inside the post.

Spurs seemed to have the game well and truly sewn up. With four minutes to go, however, Tambling headed the ball home in a crowded penalty area. For four long tense minutes Chelsea played as if suddenly they realised they had something to fight for. They moved forward in increasing numbers and the tension was unbearable as they fought for an equaliser. But at 4.40pm, a perspiring, leg-weary Dave Mackay climbed up to the Royal Box to collect the FA Cup from the Duke of Kent. – Tottenham Herald

The significance of Gillie's role in Spurs winning the FA Cup cannot be underestimated, nor should Bill Nicholson's tactical mastery. The Tottenham manager made a change to his formation late on the Friday afternoon as he addressed his players in a team meeting. In midfield, Alan Mullery had sat back throughout the season and Dave Mackay had marauded forward, but Nicholson swapped their roles, catching Chelsea, and even his own players, off guard. "I was very surprised at this," said Mullery. "But not as surprised as Chelsea. They had worked on the theory that Dave would be charging upfield. They never seemed to get over the fact that he didn't."

The subtle change allowed Gillie ample space in which to operate. Bobby Tambling would recall years later that the "superb" Gilzean "destroyed" Chelsea and the Daily Mail History of the FA Cup notes: "[Chelsea's tactics] should have been altered as soon as it became obvious that Gilzean was winning every ball. No goals came from his stream of flicked headers mainly because Greaves was magnificently marked by Ron Harris. But Gilzean's play was like a persistent, prodding finger into Chelsea's midriff, making them twist and twitch uneasily. They were never without the pressure of his presence. Spurs' control and professionalism were so overwhelming it was like watching a high-wire act practising a foot above the ground. They would not slip, and it did not matter if they did."

Everyone had something to say in the aftermath. Bill Nicholson's wife, Darkie, who never watched games lest she jinxed the team, was asked what she was doing when Spurs scored their goals. "The first, I was upstairs in the bedroom, and the second one, I was downstairs in the kitchen washing some lettuce." Saul admitted that he had hit the ball "wrong" for his goal "but I'm damned glad I did, otherwise it would have gone wide". Jimmy Robertson said he had felt like he had won a million pounds on the pools when he scored. Alan Mullery, Jimmy Greaves, Pat Jennings, Mike England and even the Duke of Kent were quoted in the press afterwards.

One man remained absent from the pages of the newspapers. Gilzean quotes were appearing less and less. He preferred not to speak to the press. It makes trying to ascertain what he was feeling, let alone what he was doing outside of football at this time, incredibly difficult. But that was just Gillie. He kept himself to himself.

It would take me almost a year before I found Gillie's thoughts on the final, and even then it was thanks to a chance purchase on eBay: the Tottenham Hotspur Football Book No.7. Even then Gillie's recollections were succinct. "It was the first-ever all-London final and the build-up was tremendous," he said. "There is something about playing at Wembley. It has an aura all of its own. Although I have had many great times at Spurs, I would say that is my outstanding memory."

The 1967 FA Cup final may not have been the spectacle it had promised to be, but it had such a profound effect on the public consciousness that one journalist wrote an entire book on it. The following is an extract from Ralph L Finn's book, London's Cup Final: How Chelsea and Spurs reached Wembley.

Gilzean is an extremely elegant player, and often appears over-casual. He brings out the best in Greaves with his subtle flicks, back headers and shrewd passing. Their understanding is not yet perfect but it is quickly heading that way, and it appears that, within a season perhaps, there will be no more feared twosome in the English league. Many people criticise Gilzean because of his sometimes apparent laxness in passing, but this is often because he tends to think too fast for his colleagues. He is also tending to get stuck in more, having previously given the impression that he was a lazy player.

If he could speed up a little, turn a shade faster, think a split-second faster,

Gilzean would become what every Spurs fan knows he has it in him to be: the greatest all-round centre-forward in the game. Only a slight tardiness in reactions prevents him from being just that. His ground work is supreme, his heading accurate. All it needs is for the two great elements in his play to be fused into one. The whole would make perfection.

If Finn's belief that Gilzean, by now 28, could develop new traits such as speed to become "the greatest all-round centre-forward in the game" comes across as naïve, it nevertheless revealed the kind of realm in which the striker was operating. Yes, there were imperfections in his game; football is an imperfect game. It is chaotic, but there are those who transcend it, even if only for a flash, and they are the ones capable of providing moments of genuine beauty. Gilzean was one.

Eddie Baily was another who noticed a "laxness" about Gilzean at times. Baily was the Tottenham assistant manager for the duration of Gillie's stay at White Hart Lane. He had been part of the push-and-run team constructed by Arthur Rowe at Spurs in the early 1950s. That team won the Second Division and First Division championships back to back, with Baily at the fulcrum of the attack at inside-left. He is one of the stars of the show in The Glory Game, bawling out anyone who moves, or rather doesn't move quickly enough. There are a series of running battles with Martin Chivers. Baily makes a cameo appearance in another magnificent sports book, Gary Imlach's My Father And Other Working Class Heroes. Gary's dad Stewart played with Eddie at Nottingham Forest and he features in one of the chapters.

Imlach's book served as a valuable guide during the early days of my own research. He notes the unreliability of speaking to an older generation and asking them to recall their memories of 40 or 50 years earlier. I had similar experiences. On one occasion, I telephoned Bobby Lennox, the great Celtic striker of the 1960s, to ask him for his opinion on Gillie. "I only played a few games with big Alan," he said. "I only played once for Scotland with him, it was against Wales." I told him that he actually played with Gilzean on four occasions for Scotland, against Wales, Cyprus ... "I was only a sub against Cyprus," he said. He is right, but he also played with Gilzean in two World Cup qualifiers at Hampden, a 2-1 win over Austria in November 1968 and a 1-1 draw with West Germany in April 1969 in front of 115,000. "I can't remember that. You forget these things. What I would say is that he was a lovely man and a wonderful player. A great header of the ball. You can quote me on that."

If I sometimes couldn't remember things that happened 24 hours earlier, how could I expect footballers of pensionable age to remember decades-old events? Lennox put me to rights on another matter, though. I'd been trying to establish the date and occasion of a Scotland team picture containing Gilzean and Lennox. The rolling hills in the background suggested Switzerland, or some other mountainous country.

"Was the Scotland kit dark blue cuffs and collars, no white on it?"

"Yes."

"It was down at Largs, nowhere exotic. It's the hills behind Inverclyde."

Given that Eddie Baily is well into his eighties, and has a reputation for being irascible, it is with some concern and trepidation, that I phone him. Eddie remains as sharp as a tack and every bit as pointed.

"Why would anyone want to read about Alan Gilzean?" he asks with a candour that disarms me. "He passed through a period of being a layabout, didn't he?"

I find myself scrambling for an answer. "Erm, well, he's No.12 on the list of greatest Spurs players and I think he deserves to have his story told."

"Do you know where I was? No.32, bloody disgrace. I don't know who picks these things when they haven't seen people play. My favourite Spurs player was a chap called WG Hall, but I don't suppose you'd remember him. Ron Burgess was another great player. Who gave you my number?"

"I got it from Spurs."

"Bloody cheek," he snaps and I presume he means Tottenham before the subject returns to Gillie. "Where's he living?"

"Weston-super-Mare," I reply. I'm starting to doubt it under this scrutiny.

"What's he doing there, then? Has he remarried?"

I tell Eddie I'm not sure and suddenly he mellows.

"We do talk about Alan Gilzean and whether he's remarried. He was always one of the first to arrive for training. When he came down from Dundee we thought we had a tricky player. He had good feet and being a Scotsman we were quite happy with Scotsmen. We were always up in Scotland looking for players. He added a lot with Jimmy Greaves. He was a good foil for Jimmy and they used to work in tandem. He had good control and an eye for goal and he was a good header of the ball, no doubt about it. He liked a drink, like most players of the time, and I think he thoroughly enjoyed playing with all of the players of the time."

I ask Eddie to expand on what he had meant by Alan being a layabout.

"I go to golf clubs and have a meal and bump into people. It would come back to me on the grapevine that he was living a bit rough in Weston-super-Mare. You've just confirmed it. He left his wife in Enfield. He was friendly with a lot of the people we knew and he lived near me."

I ask whether Gillie was elusive.

"He was like that. He was elusive off the pitch and, I suppose, he was elusive on it. He was like a ghost on the pitch. You wouldn't know he was there."

From the short time I have spoken to Eddie I'm not sure whether this last comment is slightly mischievous. It feels like there is something he is not saying, but I don't get the impression that he's going to, either. I steer the conversation towards football and try to put Gillie's achievements into some kind of context. I suggest that the long-throw routine that Tottenham would later develop when Martin Chivers arrived at White Hart Lane was a footballing innovation and he dismisses the notion.

"All these modern patterns that they talk about now," says Eddie. "They did it all 50 years ago. The game of football has always been 11 men, it's where you put them that matters. They always passed the ball, chipped the ball, volleyed the ball. There were short corners and people who could throw the ball long distances. We didn't invent it. It was a tactic that we used and we would try to get something out of it. When there was a free-kick Ted Ditchburn didn't want a wall. He used to say, 'Get out of the way, I want to see the ball.'

"I always thought Alan Gilzean was colour blind – you ask him."

"Was he? I ask, shocked. "I didn't know that."

"Yeah, we used to have a laugh about it. He'd hit these passes straight to the other team. I used to keep him going about that. If you see him will you pass on a message? I'm 85 and I'm struggling."

Eddie can't resist another barb before he hangs up, though.

"If you phoned up David Beckham he'd expect £10,000 before he would talk to you. These old footballers played the game because they loved it, they would play on Christmas Day because they wanted the fans to enjoy themselves and then they would go home for their dinner. It's not like that anymore."

It's a pertinent point and what he says next is a further reminder of the unequal status of former players. "Is this your first book?" asks Eddie. "You're coming at the back of a queue, you know. Everyone's writing a book: Alan Mullery, Martin Chivers. They're doing one about John White."

I presumed by Alan Mullery's book, Eddie meant Double Bill, the biography of Bill Nicholson, which his former captain co-wrote with Paul Trevillion, the famous football illustrator, in 2005, a year after Nicholson's death. Baily permitted Mullery an interview for the book, in which he revealed the level of antipathy he had felt at the manner of his departure from Tottenham in 1974.

As the Bill Nicholson era came to an end at White Hart Lane, Baily, his deputy for over a decade, felt he should have at least been interviewed for the manager's job.

However, he realised soon enough that Nicholson was keeping things from him and that Gordon Jago, the QPR manager, Johnny Giles, the Leeds United midfielder, and Danny Blanchflower had been into his office for a chat about succeeding him.

Baily told Mullery: "So I grabbed the bull by the horns one day and said to Bill, 'Hey, what about me? Why don't they stick me in the job? I know all the players. I can handle them.' Bill's reply was short and sweet: 'Eddie, I don't think the directors would have you. You've been on overseas tours with the likes of [chairman] Sidney Wale and you've had rows and fallen out with them.' "

Eddie added that he felt that Nicholson's grip on team affairs had slackened with the appearance of Hunter Davies and the publication of The Glory Game.

Back in 1967, relations were still cordial, however. The emotion of the FA Cup final win was saved for the celebrations, but even then Nicholson was not entirely happy. Despite his assertion at the start of the season that he did not care how the team won, he did really. In the dressing room afterwards, Nicholson berated his players for the manner of their performance. Terry Venables says: "It was typical of Bill that he was unable to relax and unwind, even on the night of the cup final, but he was already thinking and worrying about the season ahead."

"Enjoy yourselves," Nicholson told his players at the club reception in the Savoy Hotel that night. "In winning the cup you did more than I thought likely when the season started. But don't get big-headed. You still have to win in Europe to be as good a team as the last." But Spurs would exit Europe at the hands of Olympique Lyonnais the following season after a first round win over Hajduk Split. A brutal away fixture in France demonstrated how loyal Nicholson was to his players. He could hammer them if he wanted, but he would take no nonsense from opponents.

Pat Jennings remembers that there was a mini-riot in the first leg in Lyon, sparked when striker André Guy tangled with Alan Mullery. There followed a free-for-all, with punches being traded. When Jennings raced towards the scuffle in an attempt to break it up he was confronted by hundreds of fans who had invaded the pitch. When the dust had settled Mullery was sent off, but the referee was unsure of who to sanction on the French team. Gillie pointed towards Guy, who was dismissed.

"As we left the field at the interval, Alan Gilzean sensed that the French player might be waiting for him in the tunnel – a huge cavern of a place used for cycle racing with dozens of doors leading to small dressing rooms," said Jennings. "He decided to wait for me to walk with him in the mistaken belief that I would afford him some protection. 'Hi, big man,' he said. 'Keep an eye on me in case that fellow is hanging about.' So I duly walked down the tunnel behind him, looking from side to side to see if anybody was lurking by one of the doors. While I was glancing in one direction,

I suddenly heard a scuffle and looked round just in time to see the French player landing one on the point of Gillie's chin. Then Bill Nicholson suddenly appeared on the scene to separate them. Gillie wasn't amused. It was the last time I was ever called upon to act as a minder."

Mullery notes in Double Bill that Nicholson did more than merely separate them. "At half-time, Guy went to attack Gilzean, and Nicholson had stepped in and Guy leaped on Bill's back. I had been on the pitch playing against this fellow, Guy. He was the ultimate hard man – a real tough nut – and yet Bill simply shrugged his shoulders and flicked him off. I was amazed, and Bill, unmoved, just carried on as normal."

Nicholson could be just as tough when it came to dealing with his own players, particularly when he felt he no longer wanted them at the club. When Dave Mackay was allowed to join Derby County on the day Spurs returned to pre-season training, the players sat down for lunch at one end of a table with Nicholson and Eddie Baily, while Mackay, Brian Clough and Peter Taylor sat at the other end discussing the terms of his contract. The Spurs players could not believe he had been allowed to leave. It came as a particular blow to Gilzean. The two Scots had developed a great friendship, and of all his Tottenham colleagues Mackay had been the one he was most likely to socialise with, sometimes, as Cliff Jones had noted, spending Christmas or New Year with each other.

Steve Perryman, the former Tottenham captain, was a trainee when Mackay's White Hart Lane career was coming to an end, and concurs that the pair were bosom buddies. "Gillie was a true, true fan of Dave Mackay. The stories they tell about Dave Mackay. Dave was a man. If I was playing a game in the morning, I had to get back and work in the tunnel area, and one day this door flies open and he comes out and he turns back and the team haven't come out yet and he's got a ball under his arm. 'If anyone feels like panicking today, give the ball to me.' And this is the last word before they go out. Gillie would say, 'What a man, what a man.' On the pitch, off the pitch, before games and after games, you know?"

One rumour I had heard was that after Gilzean's first training session at Spurs, the players all retreated to their local watering hole and Gillie proceeded to drink them all under the table – even Mackay, who had previously been the heaviest boozer at the club. Alcohol had played an increasingly big part in the post-match ritual at White Hart Lane since the end of the double-winning days. As Matt Allen notes in his book, Jimmy Greaves: "For the opposition, [playing Spurs] was the equivalent of a cup final. As a result the players would find their games emotionally and physically draining and Greaves and his team-mates would work up a thirst every Saturday afternoon. Every pub session was instigated by Dave Mackay. The Scotsman was as hard a drinker as he was player and would often be found propping up the bar, buying the drinks and holding court about the team's performance that afternoon."

But even the double-winning team adhered to the motto, the team that drinks together wins together. Ken Jones told me two stories that further illustrate the point, and demonstrate the close relationship footballers had with the press back then.

"They enjoyed a drink, that Spurs team. They wouldn't get away with it nowadays. John White, Cliff, Dave Mackay and Greavsie, they all liked a drink. I remember one time we were in Czechoslovakia for a game against Slovan Bratislava, and I had been really ill. I'd gone back to my hotel room and there was a knock on my door, it was John White and Cliff. I thought, 'That's nice, they're coming to see me because I'm not well,' but John said to me, 'Any money Ken?' I said, 'Yeah, I've a few quid,' and they took it and off they went for drink in the town.

"When Dave Mackay broke his leg, a couple of us – me, Jimmy Burton, who was Dave Mackay's old business partner, and a few others – went to visit him. Dave still had his leg up in plaster, and when we got there John White was in the bed next to him. He was absolutely legless. He'd parked his car at the training ground at Cheshunt, had a drink and then decided he was going to visit Dave. There were these big, black wrought-iron gates at the Spurs training ground and John had just bought a Humber Hawk. As he took off, he knocked down the big black gates and then drove on to the hospital. When we saw his car outside later on it was a mess. The front grill was completely caved in."

In the absence of any extensive details on Gilzean's capacity for drink, it is interesting to note Greaves' experiences. I had already learned that the two were on a similar wavelength on the pitch and off it. It was not too great a stretch of the imagination to deduce that their drinking habits, and Mackay's, might be similar.

Even Bill Nicholson knew that the Spurs players enjoyed a drink, although to what extent is far from certain. "After a match Jimmy enjoyed a lager," he recalled. "Late on in his career I know Jimmy opened a pub for a friend of his and that might have been the start of his drinking heavily. I had no idea what he was drinking. I know Alan Gilzean was a drinker. He liked Bacardi and Coke. There were a few players who didn't drink at all. Most of them took a lager. There is a lot of free time in football and a lot of energy expended. It is normal to drink and I let them get on with it as it was done in moderation and didn't affect their performances. I was amazed some years later to hear of [Greaves'] revelations about drink and how he became an alcoholic. I must say, he never gave me reason to suspect that he had a problem."

Often, if the team were at an airport or a railway station, Nicholson would give Mackay £10 of his own money for them to have a drink after an away game.

In the 2009-2010 season, Harry Redknapp, the Tottenham manager, disciplined 16 of his squad after they ignored his request not to organise a Christmas party. The players, led by Robbie Keane, had flown to Dublin and spent the night drinking. They told Redknapp they were going golfing. It says everything about how attitudes towards alcohol in football have changed that the players were fined. Keane was subsequently loaned to Celtic for the remainder of the season. It says a lot, too, about modern players that they ignored Redknapp's wishes. It is extremely unlikely that Nicholson's players would have ignored a similar curfew. But then what is known about the dangers of alcohol now was not as widely known then. The players believed they could sweat all the booze out of their systems with a run the following day.

As Allen adds: "Even when the Spurs double-winning team began to break up in the mid-1960s, the drinking culture at the club remained. Joe Kinnear, Alan Gilzean and Phil Beal replaced Mackay, John White and Bill Brown as Greaves' drinking partners, and others around Greaves began to notice he was drinking to excess."

Nicholson started to become concerned only after a trip to a nightclub following the first leg win over Hajduk Split in the European Cup Winners' Cup in September 1967. The Spurs manager sanctioned the night out as a reward after a 2-0 win and the players went to see a raunchy act that involved a well-endowed woman performing tricks with a rope and a tiger skin. Greaves led the way, with 10 pints and 10 shots of slivovitz, a strong local spirit. The following day Nicholson took him to one side and had a quiet word. It was to be the beginning of the end for Greaves. While Nicholson claimed that he had never seen booze affecting his player's performance, within two and a half years he was on his way out of Spurs. In March 1970, he joined West Ham where, ironically, one of his drinking partners was Harry Redknapp.

Greaves would admit that leaving Spurs was the biggest regret of his career, but he would also reveal that he remembered little about his playing days because of booze. "It's amazing how many times I get asked to name my greatest goal," he would say in the 1970s. "People can't understand when I struggle to give them an answer."

He struggles to give me answers, too. Like defenders trying to keep pace with him in his pomp, it takes me a while to catch up with Jimmy Greaves. When I first call to arrange a sit-down interview with him he is on a golfing trip, and a kindly lady at his home telephone number tells me he won't be back for a few days. When I try again two days later I'm told "he's just popped out for an hour, can you try again at six?"

When, finally, Jimmy Greaves answers the phone I am transported back instantly to childhood and Saturday afternoons watching Saint and Greavsie, the football show he hosted with Ian St John in the 1980s. " 'Ello," says Greavsie. It is a voice enriched by many years of pipe smoking. It is instantly warm and friendly and yet I am aware that Greaves, like Eddie Baily, has a reputation for being spiky. Like Baily, too, he has fallen out of love a little with Tottenham and regularly eviscerates the club in his weekly column in The Sun.

However, when I repeat my Gilzean sales pitch for the thousandth time and ask if Jimmy is willing to speak, I am pleasantly surprised. "When do you want to do it?" he asks. I tell him I am due to fly down to London and could come and meet him on the Sunday, but he interjects.

"No, no. We'll do it on the phone. I don't have much to say."

Gilzean's recollections of his old striking partner were always favourable. Pat Jennings, though, remembers that the Scot took some convincing in his earliest days at Tottenham. "Alan Gilzean, another class striker who formed a lethal partnership with Greaves, once admitted to me that during the first half-dozen games he played for Spurs, he thought Jimmy was a lucky player. Alan, like the rest of us, just couldn't believe that Jimmy could so often be in the right place at exactly the right moment to score. But the longer they were together, the more Alan's admiration for Jimmy grew. Alan didn't care for the physical stuff, yet he would willingly have run through a brick wall for Jimmy. That was the kind of effect he had on all his mates."

For someone who remembers little from his playing days, there is a compelling clarity to what Greaves tells me about Gilzean.

"He was the greatest player I played with. I mean, I played with some great players when I played for England. There was Johnny Haynes, Bobby Charlton and Bobby Moore, and at club level there was Dave Mackay, John White and Danny Blanchflower and many others, but I formed a partnership with Gillie and it was a great success. We became the G-Men, we read each others' minds and we knew exactly what the other was going to do. It was a great partnership and it was an unself-ish partnership, we were both good for each other."

I tell Jimmy how surprised I am by his assessment and he qualifies it, but what follows is no less sincere: "He wasn't the best I ever played with, but in terms of what he did for me, he was the best. We both felt a great deal for each other as players and as men. I don't know what came first, the chicken or the egg, whether we enjoyed playing together and hit it off as friends, or whether it was the other way around, but what does it matter? We got on very well and we scored a lot of goals. I thought the world of him. It was a privilege to play with him and to know him."

Greaves once did a television interview in which he joked that Gillie was about 90 years old and lived in a cave in Coupar Angus, but when I mention that his name has been forgotten somewhat in the town he admits surprise. "It is a shame but maybe he prefers it that way. Even I know where Coupar Angus is and I don't think many Jocks do. I drove through it once. I was on my way to Montrose for an after-dinner talk. I flew into Edinburgh and a car picked me up and when we got to Coupar Angus I thought, 'Christ, this is where Gillie is from.'

Apropos of nothing, Greaves adds: "Does he work? I shouldn't imagine he does. My agent deals with memorabilia and he would like to get Alan to sign a few thousand pictures. There would be a lot of money in it for him. Could you pass on that message if you speak to him?"

I tell him I will and ask when the last time he saw Alan was, and whether he has any inkling of why he appeared to go to ground.

"Oh, it's a long time ago. I really don't know. I'm going back to the 70s, I'm going back a long way. If I passed him in the street I'm pretty sure I'd recognise him, but I'm not sure he would recognise me. If you are speaking to him give him my love.

"Everyone has been chasing him and you have confirmed he is in Weston-super-Mare. I think a few of the boys have gone down to see him, but I'm not sure. Alan could come out and present himself now and be a very popular figure, of that there is no doubt. I have no idea whatsoever [as to why he disappeared]. I have heard so many different things. A couple of autograph hunters came up to me after a show in the theatre one night and said they had seen him in Weston-super-Mare and I didn't know what to think, but then they showed me autographs they had got from him and they seemed genuine."

I sense the interview has run its course, but I sneak in one last question and ask him how close Spurs came to pulling off the double in 1967.

"Gillie might know. I can't remember. I know we won the cup. Whilst I was with him for the first part of his career at White Hart Lane, he then had a second part when I wasn't there. There are one or two other players, like Pat Jennings or Martin Chivers, who might be able to tell you more."

I can't resist the urge to say how much of a privilege it has been to speak to him. I wish, almost instantly, I hadn't. Jimmy Greaves is a legend and he's heard this before. Like Dave Mackay, Greaves left Spurs when Bill Nicholson felt his powers had diminished beyond salvation. Unlike Mackay, who would reinvent himself as a sweeper and win the title under Clough at Derby, Greaves' career was nearing its end. Gilzean's, though, was just beginning at Tottenham. He would play until he was 35. Why did Nicholson spare him? Was it affection? Or necessity caused by the decline of his squad? Or, and please pardon the cliché but the simile is apposite, was it because Gilzean, like the finest wine, sherry, whisky or rum, had improved with age?

10

THE SEARCH CONTINUES

"You better win this one lads. I need the bonus. I've got a wife, two kids and a budgie to keep."
– Alan Gilzean, date unknown

I am dashing across London, heading for Maidenhead. I have a 5.30pm appointment to keep with Steve Perryman, the former Tottenham captain and ex-roommate of Gillie during the 1970s. But I have spent rather longer than expected in Bruce Castle museum, sifting through reams of newsprint on an old microfiche machine which took me an hour to get the hang of. When I finally attached the correct spool to the correct coil, it was like discovering an old box of heirlooms in the attic. I found myself shuffling my chair closer to the screen just to get a closer look before the assistant pointed out that the handle on the side controlled the zoom.

There were reports of Gilzean scoring, being sent off, playing exquisitely and execrably. I was amazed that he might have been sold after his first season. The minutiae of his early career unfolded with every turn of the spool, but there was something missing: Alan's voice. Now, as I battle with my luggage, the clock and London public transport, a plastic bag dangles from the end of my suitcase, containing a sample of life at Tottenham in the 1960s and early 1970s but nothing specifically about Gillie's time in London. The detail, for example, that he played cricket for Barnet, would only be of any use if I could speak to someone from Barnet Cricket Club.

Bruce Castle museum is in north-east London, not far from White Hart Lane. Maidenhead is over 50 miles away. It is with some relief that I get across London to

Paddington Station – an hour from Maidenhead – just after 3pm. As I step out of the tube and head towards trains the Tannoy announces: "The next train leaving from Platform 9 will be the 15.30 to Weston-super-Mare." If I jump on it now I could just go looking for Gillie and be done with it, I think to myself. I watch as the train slips away from Platform 9, pulling its passengers and my thought with it.

It doesn't seem like such a bad idea when I learn that my train has been delayed; I panic at the thought of coming all the way from Scotland to miss out on an interview with Steve Perryman, one of my all-time heroes, but the delay is mercifully brief. When I arrive in Maidenhead I dump my bags at my hotel and speed into town: my mission is to pick up a Spurs book for Steve to sign. I am gatecrashing an event that Steve, now director of football at Exeter City, has organised for the club's youth development fund and I want to contribute an auction lot.

The George On The Green is a picturesque family-run pub in Holyport, just outside Maidenhead. The owner, Russell Stone, a fanatical Tottenham supporter, said he would be delighted to allow me to interview Steve before the auction, especially when he heard that I was writing a book about Gilzean. This was a familiar story: Gillie's popularity at Tottenham, and the myths surrounding his retreat from the spotlight, opened doors for me. Sitting outside the 16th century inn, waiting for Perryman to appear, I reflected on how far I had come in the search for Alan Gilzean. I had spoken to most of his team-mates from the Dundee title-winning team, his old scout master, an old school friend and three of his former Spurs team-mates. I was still a long way from getting answers, but a clearer picture had started to emerge. I was confident that Steve would help fill in yet more of the blanks.

Whoever said you shouldn't meet your heroes never met Steve Perryman. This should be exactly how you meet your heroes: suddenly appearing like an apparition from the shadows with a smile and an outstretched hand. He is on his mobile phone. He has mislaid a bag at his hotel. He will spend the course of our interview fielding calls as he tries to recover it. Never is he less than utterly courteous and charming.

Inside, Russell is busying himself with preparations for the evening. A TV shows great moments from Spurs' history.

Steve is smaller than I had expected, but he carries himself with all the assurance of a man who captained Tottenham for 14 years and made over 850 appearances for the club. He is the kind of man one imagines had the maxim 'manners cost nothing' drilled into him as a child.

When his time at Tottenham came to an end in 1986, Perryman joined Oxford United and then took over as player-manager at Brentford, before eventually retiring from football in 1990, at the age of 39, the same year he was appointed Watford manager. He would return to Tottenham as assistant to Ossie Ardiles. Later, he will tell the assembled crowd that his working relationship with Alan Sugar, the then Tottenham chairman, was not good. He forgets his good manners momentarily for that. His time on the coaching staff at White Hart Lane ended in 1994, leaving a bad taste in his mouth for a few years before adventures overseas, coaching in Norway and Japan, recovered his love for the game.

Perryman was a callow youth the day Spurs beat Chelsea 2-1 at Wembley to win the FA Cup in 1967. He would spend the next two seasons attempting to break into the first-team squad before finally making his debut against Sunderland, aged 17.

§

In the August following the FA Cup win, Spurs played out a thrilling Charity Shield with Manchester United, drawing 3-3 to share the trophy. Pat Jennings gave Spurs a 2-0 lead from a long, wind-assisted kick-out, which made him the first goalkeeper at the club to score a goal. A photograph from the time shows Gillie leaping high into the air to celebrate Jennings' historic goal. He was chasing the ball down for a header when Alex Stepney in the United goal misjudged its flight and then found himself stranded between penalty spot and six-yard box as it sailed over his head. United fought back twice, though, from 2-0 down and then 3-2. Nevertheless, that Spurs had more than matched the champions suggested an encouraging season ahead. They had also drawn 3-3 with the newly crowned European Cup winners, Celtic, at Hampden Park a week earlier, in a match which marked Queen's Park's centenary.

Spurs were second by mid-September, but successive defeats to Arsenal and United, plus an injury to Mike England which required surgery, ensured the season ended with Tottenham in seventh, a long way behind champions Manchester City. Disappointment followed in the FA Cup; Spurs surrendered their crown in a fifth round replay against Liverpool at Anfield. Another extended run in the competition had looked on the cards when Spurs defeated Manchester United in the third round after a replay. The second round exit in the Cup Winners' Cup, at the hands of Olympique Lyonnais – the game in which Gilzean had been protected by Nicholson but still managed to get knocked out by André Guy – compounded the ignominy.

Gilzean failed to hit the heights of the previous campaign in front of goal and, despite a brace for Scotland against Wales at Hampden in a European Championship qualifier, he would score just eight for Spurs. None the less, those statistics only tell part of the story. During the FA Cup trip to Old Trafford, in which Spurs forced a 2-2 draw late on, Gilzean linked well with Martin Chivers. Desmond Hackett, in the Daily Express, wrote that "Alan Gilzean, who was becoming a problem player, is now thriving in the company of Martin Chivers. They could develop into one of the greatest scoring acts in the First Division". Tottenham's 89th-minute equaliser at Old Trafford came from a Mike England free-kick to Gilzean, who knocked down to Chivers to score. There was a sense of déjà vu about the goal, but one man was missing: Jimmy Greaves, who had been dropped in favour of Phil Beal. Hackett's prediction contained a remarkable foresight, but inherent too was a recognition that Tottenham's immediate future might be one without Greaves.

The signing of Chivers can be viewed as an acceptance on Nicholson's part that his attempt to use Gillie as an out-and-out centre-forward had failed. There was speculation that Chivers' arrival might spell the end of Gilzean's time at the club. Chivers was signed from Southampton for £125,000 in January 1968 with Frank Saul, jettisoned when Gilzean arrived and so often underestimated by Nicholson, used as a makeweight. From the moment Chivers came into the team, Gilzean was shuffled around the front line and appeared in a number of positions, including left and right wing, before season's end. It would prove to be a season of frustration for Gillie. He was dropped for two games just before Christmas and sent off against Leeds United for aiming a kick at Terry Cooper, the Leeds left-back.

When Gilzean appeared before an FA disciplinary committee in June he was ordered to pay £50 and banned for a week, which forced him out of the first game of the new season, against Arsenal.

The other moment of real note in the 1967-68 season was covered in the official notices pages, when a young Chelsea supporter appeared in court after he confronted Gilzean following Tottenham's 2-0 win over their London rivals. It was a game in which, despite his troubles that season, Gilzean had been, according to one report, "a gleaming jewel", as he commanded the forward line and scored an elegant header.

Amid a number of court reports in the Weekly Herald, which included details of a 13-year-old Chelsea fan wielding a meat hook, appeared the following headline: "Called Spurs star names". The story read: "A 15-year-old Chelsea supporter alleged to have called Tottenham player Alan Gilzean a 'ponce' and a 'fairy' was sent to an attendance centre for 24 hours. PC Christopher Moore said as Gilzean left the ground in his car after the match the boy broke away from a group of supporters and went over to the car, pointing and saying, 'Look there's that ponce Gilzean. Who's a fairy Gilzean?' The boy, a printing engineer from Morden, Surrey, denied using insulting words and said a man beside him did. He said he approached the car because he thought it may have been a Chelsea player who would have given him a lift home."

Gilzean's write-up in the Tottenham Herald for the following season gave an indication of the difficulties Spurs were having in how best to accommodate him in their line-up now that Chivers had arrived. Terry Venables was playing in the inside-left position, Chivers was centre-forward, Greaves was inside-right. That left Gilzean on the wing, something Fanfare remarked on in his annual Spurs review.

> *Alan Gilzean – Another expensive player who is something of a problem boy. One of the most skilful players in the game but the problem is finding the best method of fitting him into the Tottenham team. He ended last season as a winger – a position in which many of his undoubted talents were wasted. It will be interesting to see where he lines up in the League programme this season.*

Again, I thought of Berbatov. A player with undoubted talents who was constricted by tactical stipulations. Formations were changing in football. Jonathan Wilson in Inverting The Pyramid: A History of Football Tactics, writes that Alf Ramsey's England "was a side with no wingers, orthodox or otherwise. Although it continued to be referred to as 4-3-3, it was really, as Nobby Stiles pointed out in his autobiography, a 4-1-3-2, with him as the anchor". It's easy to imagine how this kind of system might have suited Gilzean, either as one of the three or as a striker, but also how it would have militated against him, set up as it was without a natural wide man to supply him with crosses. Nicholson, though, was persevering with a system that did not necessarily bring the best out in Gilzean. A quick look at the shirt numbers Gilzean wore from 1968 onwards tells its own story. This was when shirt numbers meant something, and Gilzean wore them all – 7 (right-wing), 8 (inside-right), 9 (centre-forward), 10 (inside-left), 11 (left-wing). It seems almost perverse that, as the 60s drew to a close, the greatest header of his generation was being asked to play in a wide position, where part of his remit would have been to get crosses into the box. Nicholson, though, was not stupid. Gillie was still asked to attack the penalty area when the ball was on the opposite flank to his. None the less, by playing him wide, the opportunities for him to score with his head were limited. In many ways, this explains a particularly fallow period in front of goal in 1968-69. Gilzean scored just seven – his worst tally in professional football up to that point and just four better than his lowest total, in his final season, which would be blighted by injury.

There were highlights, though. There always were when Gilzean was around and that's why the White Hart Lane crowd loved him. They knew that Gillie was one of those players capable of producing the ridiculous and the sublime. They loved his fallibility as much as his ability to produce pieces of skill that defied convention.

In games against Southampton, West Ham and Nottingham Forest near the end of a season in which Spurs would finish sixth, the G-Men reprised their famous double act with a series of fine performances, Gilzean scoring one and laying on two others for Greaves as Tottenham won three on the trot. The G-Men were back together after Martin Chivers had snapped the patella tendon in his kneecap against Forest (although the real damage had been done by a cortisone injection the previous summer which had weakened the muscle) and missed the remainder of the season.

Chivers reveals in Big Chiv that Bill Nicholson and the medical staff at Tottenham thought he would never play again. It would take two years for him to return to his very best for Spurs, and at his very best he was regarded as the top striker in Europe. His partner would not be Jimmy Greaves, however. In January 1970, following a humiliating defeat to Crystal Palace in the FA Cup, Greaves, Gilzean, Joe Kinnear and Cyril Knowles were dropped for the home game against Southampton. Steve Perryman was another left out, but Nicholson was at pains to say that he was merely being rested. The story made front page news, such was Greaves and Gilzean's standing. Following a dismal start to the season which had brought just 12 wins in 34 matches and 13 goals between the G-Men, Nicholson acted.

There was a sombre mood as the players trudged silently away from Cheshunt after the manager made the announcement. Nicholson told the Daily Mirror: "This was something that had to be done. We have reached the stage where there was no alternative. Now we must rebuild from the ashes. I accept my share of the responsibility for what has gone wrong; now the players must realise they have not been doing enough. The players left out have had a fair crack of the whip. But they haven't been hungry for success. I don't want anyone to get the impression that young Steve Perryman comes into this general criticism. The boy has run his legs off for Tottenham. He was entitled to expect more help and support from those around him."

Only four players who were part of the team beaten at Palace seemed certain of their places against Southampton: Pat Jennings, Alan Mullery, Martin Chivers and Mike England. Asked for his take on events Mullery, the captain, said: "Make no mistake. The lads left out will be back and better than ever."

But Mullery was wrong. The defeat to Crystal Palace was his last game for Spurs. Before the season was out he was part of the deal that took Martin Peters to White Hart Lane. One of the most exciting chapters in Tottenham Hotspur's history was at an end but a new one was about to begin. Gillie sat out the next six games before scoring five goals in the remaining eight games after his return. Chivers scored three. An exciting new, and equally formidable striking partnership, one to strike fear into the most robust defences in England and beyond was forming.

§

It is clear that Steve Perryman still retains a respect for Gillie that stops just short of filial affection. Steve broke into the Spurs first team in 1969 and the pair formed a special bond. I wonder at the reasons for Nicholson's decision to pair a teenager with a man in his 30s, but when Perryman recalls those days it's clear it was another decision Bill Nick got spot on. Perryman was an emerging talent and ready to be fast-tracked into the first team. Gilzean, one of the most respected players in the squad, would see right by him, so it meant a lot to Steve that Gillie was one of his biggest fans.

The others rarely let him forget he was the youngest player in the squad, but Gilzean would often act as a buffer to the merciless stick. It was a master-servant relationship, at times, though. One scene in The Glory Game has Gillie reclining on a sofa in a Bucharest hotel, instructing Steve to fill in his travel documents.

"I sort of assumed that Gillie was older than he was," begins Steve, stirring his coffee vigorously, "so if he was 31 and someone else was 32 I didn't quite know that, but Gillie looked the oldest. Bill Nicholson was clever enough to dictate who roomed with who rather than just leaving it to whoever fancied it. And I suppose it was the master and the ... not the mistress, the apprentice, if you like, and I sort of thrived off of his manner. I thought Gillie was a very clever individual and, of course, I respected him as a player and his opinion of what was happening in our team.

"When you room with someone you have a closer bond. Even if you spent one night with a new player, you'd talk more deeply about things, like your family, the background to you as a person and, therefore, through that extra knowledge of each other's circumstances, you can understand them a bit more. Not that I was a questioner by any means, but he was very good at giving his opinion on players, opponents, tactics, Bill Nicholson, training, all these things you talk about. In all of that was how to live your life, how to enjoy yourself and work at the right time, and you need to play – all of that. It was like an extra education, rooming with this chap."

At intervals the commentary on the TV showing Spurs highlights pierces the conversation. *"Is Gascoigne going to have a crack? He is, you know. Ohh! Schoolboys' Own stuff!"* Steve is looking at the screen and I turn to watch the last frames of a goal I have seen a thousand times: Paul Gascoigne's free-kick in Tottenham's 3-1 win over Arsenal in the 1991 FA Cup semi-final.

"He definitely rated me as a player, which was a good start. I think he had some money that he probably lost, that I was going to be in the England team by the time I was 21 or something. And for some time that was looking good, because I got into the Under-23 team as a 19-year-old. I eventually played a record number of times under Sir Alf Ramsey, but it just didn't go on after Ramsey, or after the Under-23s, and I think there are some reasons for that, but they are not for this discussion. Although I was a passing player when I was young, when I got into the team I had to fulfil the needs of what the team lacked."

"... *And it's still Ricky Villa, oh what a goal!*"

"So when this obviously gifted player like Gillie – the touch, the flair, the flicks, all of this ..." Steve tails off before pinpointing exactly what he means.

"It helped the transition from being a young player. That helped me straight away. If I had got the impression that he didn't like me or he didn't rate me, it would have been a difficult situation, because of the conversations that we had. That's what you do when you stay in a room: talk. You virtually get to your room, throw your bags in the room, get down and eat as quickly as you can and then you go up to the room. That's what you do. At the end of a footballer's week, you actually feel tired enough to go to bed at 8.30 at night and rest, of course. Particularly me at a young age. At that time I used to go home and I would go into our front room and sleep for two hours. I couldn't do that now, but it was this young body trying to get in touch with this physical job and the mental pressure that went with it. Gillie was more than up for that; he lived his life and Friday night was one of his best nights' sleep. But not that you then crash and just go to bed. You got into bed, you had the television on, you relaxed and talked, and eventually you would come to some common decision, probably dictated by him, of when the light should go out."

Like all of his Tottenham team-mates before him, Steve Perryman tells me he hasn't seen Gillie in many years, although he did hear from him once in the early 1990s when he was managing Watford. The phone rang one day and it was Alan asking if there was any scouting work, but Steve had been unable to help because he knew the chairman would not sanction the appointment for financial reasons. Steve told me he had replayed that moment regularly and wondered if it had an impact on Gillie's retreat from the spotlight, adding that if he had thought he was desperate for money he would have paid him out of his own pocket. Before our meeting Steve had said the story was not for publication but now, a few weeks on, he seems amenable.

"I couldn't repay something that he had given me earlier on. He gave me the time, he gave me the confidence, and now I was in a position of leading a club, but I was thinking, 'You can't have jobs for the boys.' I'm not sure I ever put Gillie down as a watcher of games. It didn't fit, what he was asking me to do, but it definitely didn't fit with the club either, because I couldn't put someone on the payroll without justification. I just got the feeling that I'd heard that he'd dropped out [of society] after that, and wondered if he'd made similar phone calls to four or five people and, whatever their reasons were, they didn't go with it; therefore he said, 'Sod you lot, I'm off.' It wasn't as if we were that close after playing, either, but he was entitled to make the call because of our earlier relationship – without a doubt. I'd like to think I could still call him a friend. I hope that he feels the same, but at that moment the friendship couldn't override the job he was wanting. It wasn't as if he was asking me to be chief scout, it was just a little scouting job every week, but arguably the game was getting to the point of business and looking at everything and it couldn't be done."

"Greaves, changes direction so well. Oh, beautiful football, what a great goal! Fabulous goal!" Jimmy Greaves' wonder goal against Manchester United is on, but Steve is concentrating intently.

"He had a great sense of humour, he used to tell me lots of stories, as old pros do to young pros. So it was my link with the old days – I got into the Spurs team in '69 – and what it was like during the war, and when life was a bit tougher.

"There was this one story. I can't remember if we were on tour, but Bill Nicholson was apologising to the chaps and said, 'Look, I understand there was a bit of rowdiness going on last night and there was noise in the corridors and I'm really, really sorry if you were disturbed.' "

Steve starts to smile as he recalls the scenario. He mimics Gillie's accent: " 'Aye, Bill, yeah, there was a bird knocking on my door at three o'clock in the morning,' and then everyone's ears shot up." He pauses for effect before the killer punchline is delivered: " 'She was trying to get oot.' "

Steve and I are still laughing when he adds: "I could never enter that banter, but I could live off his. I always say that I didn't speak for 18 months, simply because the banter between those players was right to the point. As a young player you haven't got the wherewithal to handle that, and so my instinct told me, 'Shut up until you're ready.' But Gillie, in a way, would be a little protective of me, because we were forging this partnership. Sometimes people would say to me on a bus or a train, 'Hey, you, noisy. Shut the fuck up,' and he'd say, 'Leave him alone,' in that type of fatherly way, almost as if to say, 'He's with me.' Just a very, very nice chap. A good man. Lived his life, enjoyed his life, but he worked very hard."

Steve arrived at Tottenham with a glowing reputation. He had been scouted by the cream of clubs across England and when he signed had the pick of Tottenham or Chelsea, the team they were about to face in the 1967 FA Cup final. Tommy Docherty offered him all sorts of incentives, but there was something about Bill Nicholson's quiet, indifferent manner which persuaded him. Nicholson's treatment of his players bordered on disdain, but it was aimed at keeping them grounded.

"They started giving me complimentary tickets to go to games during '67. Then

Bill Nick asked me if I was going to sign for Spurs just before the 1967 cup final. And then he said: 'Because if you're not, you're not getting a cup final ticket.' He wasn't all over you and that's how it remained ever after, always looking to keep you down.

"I think it gave me longevity, because I never really fancied myself as a player, so that made it nice when people like Gillie were saying, 'Cor Steve, you were the man, you did well today.' I never really thought of myself as doing well. I knew I'd worked hard, but I'd say, 'I gave two throw-ins away.' I'd be thinking more about that than the good things I'd done. You're never happy with yourself, you keep striving on, which I thought was good, but it was very important to have people around you that appreciated you, too, and Gillie was one of those."

Eddie Baily used similar tactics when Perryman was called up for the pre-season tour of North America at the end of the 1968-69 season. Gillie had been named in the Scotland squad for a World Cup qualifier against Cyprus, and a place had opened up in the party. It was a chance the young Perryman, who was playing as many as three games on a Saturday, seized with both hands. "I played this one night game at Cheshunt, on that very good pitch we had that was like Wembley, and the way of the club then was to not let anyone get above themselves. If you were starting to make a name for yourself the coaches would be coming down harder on you. I finished this game at Cheshunt and Eddie Baily said, 'Perryman, you must be a good player.'

" 'Well, what do you mean?' I asked Eddie. 'Well, you must be a good player because I've just seen a list on the noticeboard in that changing room there that is suggesting that you've got a chance to go to America on tour with the first team. Now I can't actually believe that's right, but I've seen it with my own eyes, so I suggest you better have a look at it.'

"He said this because he actually believed that I wouldn't look at it, because I had no need to. So I went on the tour on the understanding that Gillie was away with Scotland and when he'd finished he was going to join us and I would go home. I played the first two games, Atlanta and Baltimore. Then we were going to Toronto for a tournament. Eusébio played for Toronto, on astroturf, Fiorentina were there.

"Gillie turned up and I was supposed to have gone home, but a lad called David Jenkins had got sunburn on the top of his feet – sunburn on his feet, you can imagine Bill Nick. Anyway, Bill Nick sent him home and allowed me to stay. So, in a round-about sort of way, Gillie had a part to play in me becoming part of the first team.

"In Toronto, you realised how many Scottish people there are around the world. I'm not sure I was rooming with Gillie then, but there's always people who turn up at hotels – friends of brothers, relatives – and it just seemed like Toronto was full of Scots. He was a very laid-back character. I can still see the saunter."

This was something I had heard before, his generosity with Scots he met on trips. It tallies with what Bill Nick had said about him following the bagpipes, with Cliff Jones' memories of Amsterdam and the recollections of Graeme Souness, who says that when Dave Mackay left Spurs, Gilzean pulled him aside one day and said, "Right, we're the only Scots left. It's you and me against the rest of them. Okay?"

Steve told me on the phone before we met that he was once accused of not liking Scots. "There were people who I didn't always get on with in the team who happened to be Scots, but that's not the same thing. Ask Gillie whether I don't like Scots."

At that Steve breaks off to take a call about his mislaid bag. The hotel has found it and he is so effusive in his thanks that I wonder if his medal collection is in the bag. It is clear, too, that this is no act for my benefit. Steve is just one of life's nice guys.

"I'd really like to know if he likes me or not," he says, thinking out loud after he finishes his call. "I hope we haven't fallen out. I really, truly hope that we haven't, but if you speak to him say Steve sends his regards and see his reaction."

Gillie's approach to his career at Spurs reflected the Presbyterian values he was brought up with: hard work and plenty of it. His social life demanded it, too.

"I would be aware that Gillie had had a good night out, but not to that extreme. I remember the players being in awe of Gillie with the knowledge that he'd had a night out. On a Thursday, we used to do this 10-lap run and we had to put one person up as a special challenge to beat him, otherwise he'd batter us about his running prowess. Sometimes they would beat him and other times they wouldn't and the rest of us would just be going the normal speed and watching this race unfold. But that would be even after a night out. He enjoyed it, but he worked hard after it, that was his reasoning behind it. You had to pay for a good night out by working hard."

Much is made of old footballers' propensity for booze, but in many ways it was merely an extension of the working man's life. There wasn't a curfew at Tottenham, as such, and Nicholson had a laissez-faire attitude to it. Steve admits it was rooted in the culture of football at that time.

"If you come home every night and your father has a drink by the fireside, there's a fair chance that you might do the same thing. I'm not saying Gillie's did, but that was more evident then than today, even though everyone talks up the alcohol problem more now. You were a pro, you worked hard, you played hard, you enjoyed yourself after. It was almost like that was the thing to do. I have to say that I got into that same routine, and sometimes led by Gillie. Not to any extreme, but I would probably be out to one or two o'clock in the morning after a game when it probably was best for my body not to be doing that, and I got to know a lot of the people he was friendly with. I knew that he had this favourite Greek restaurant up in the West

End. He invited me there and they would be throwing the plates and all this sort of stuff, it was fantastic.

"Is Gillie still playing golf or is that beyond him? They played at Crews Hill in Enfield. They'll have some stories about Gillie there. The one you should speak to is a Doctor Curtin. Doc Curtin, the captain. We had a function two years ago and he was there. Lovely guy, would have almost been in more scrapes than Gillie."

"Was he a drinking partner?" I ask.

"Captain of the golf club. A lot instigated around that."

I will later send an email to Crews Hill Golf Club asking about Doc Curtin's whereabouts, to which I receive no response.

I speculate on the similarities between Gillie and Greaves and wonder if Steve had seen it too. "I just knew that they were called the G-men and they had some sort of understanding. It was telepathic. Gillie flicking on and Jim's in. So why didn't they room together? Quick-witted for sure; stories for sure; they kept themselves to themselves, yeah. They were similar."

Every so often Steve pauses, looks at an undefined spot in the distance and transports himself back to a different era. A half-smile is never far from his lips; he speaks carefully and with consideration, as if he is mulling over a great philosophical question deserving of his full attention. He recalls one time he approached Nicholson for a pay rise, buoyed by the knowledge of what Gillie was earning. Perryman was earning £28 a week, some way short or of what his room-mate got.

"I knock on his door, go in and he says, 'What do you want, Steve?'

" 'New contract, Bill.'

" 'What do you want?'

" 'New contract.'

" 'What. Do. You. Want?'

"So I said, 'Well, I shouldn't really know this, but I've been in your team three years, never come out ...' I'm quite pleased having the front to say this to him. 'I'm earning £28 a week and Gillie tells me, and I know he's a great player and I know he's a goalscorer and I know he's an international, he earns 95 quid a week. So, after three and a half years, I think I should be a bit closer to him, to the big players.

" 'Last chance, what do you want?'

" 'Well, thirty.'

" 'Thirty? Thhhhirrrty? You want £30 a week to play for Tottenham Hotspur?'

"Jimmy Greaves always says that Bill Nick was one of those old-fashioned people who thought you should pay to play for Tottenham Hotspur. So he didn't make it easy for anyone, but you were very happy to be at that club and what it stood for. The way that you were treated, it sort of didn't matter. The money didn't matter. I think you have to fit at a club and Gillie fitted, unbelievably. And those people could be very critical, very hard, particularly that era because they saw '60-'61. They could compare you. Bill Nick compared you as well, and for them to be in such awe of Gillie, having seen the double team, meant a hell of a lot. It was almost as if they thought Gillie was capable of being in that team. They nearly did the double, that team."

Steve is gazing into the distance again. "They had a funny sort of relationship. I lived off every word that Bill Nick said, I took everything to heart, and if he gave me a 'well done', which was very rare, it was all my birthdays in one. But he would sort of get mischievous with Gillie because he thought that was the way to him. And he'd say, 'Gillie, we're in white today.' Alan had this thing where, you know when the front man gets the ball and he looks up, and then he would try and hit the winger? Well, he'd play *their* winger in."

Steve is laughing. We're both laughing, but it means more to him because he can see it in his mind's eye. He knows what it is really like to try to send the winger away. The story demonstrated the warmth Nicholson had for Gilzean, in contrast to, say, Martin Chivers, with whom he had many battles over his perceived lack of effort.

"I liked Gilly," wrote Nicholson in his memoirs. "He was easy to talk to, never moaned and got on with the job in an uncomplicated way. He was an unorthodox player, different in many ways from Bobby Smith. He was more of a footballing centre-forward and started his career as an inside-left. He didn't head the ball full on like Smith. He preferred to glance it as he turned his head. It was not a style you could coach in anyone, because the margin of error was so small. [...] Sometimes I would chide him: 'Where did you learn your football? What were you trying to do?' He would hit a ball into space up the wing and expect someone to be there to meet it. 'If the man is not running, play to feet,' I would tell him. 'You're not in Scotland now.' He would take it in good spirit. I could be open and frank with him and he wouldn't get angry or sulk. He was very trustworthy and likeable. Away from football, he was something of a loner, a quiet, unaggressive man. It was a tribute to his fitness that he was still playing for us at the age of 36."

(Gillie was actually 35 when he left Tottenham but given his appearance it wasn't surprising Nicholson added on a few months; the hair on top had almost entirely disappeared). Nicholson's affection for Gillie seems to have stemmed from his sanguine approach to the game. Gilzean is almost unique in this respect. Praise for his players from Nicholson was rare, particularly during his days as a manager, but his relationship with Gillie was different.

"I always remember that Bill's way through to Gillie was by taking the rise out of him or his way through to him was with a joke," remembers Steve. "I don't know that he had that with many other people. I think he treated Gillie differently. Not better, differently. I think Bill Nick thought, 'I know what you are Gillie, but I like it.' There was an acceptance of his way. He never said to me, 'It might be right for him, but you be careful.' It was never like that. He would let me be. Gillie could invite me out and I could say yes or no. Players always went out. We always stayed away on midweek games. We never got back that night. This was always by train and you had to get the first train out by morning. Gillie would say, 'Stevie, we're going to so-and-so, and more often than not I'd say, 'Gillie, not for me, not for me.' And he'd say, 'Okay.' It's not like he was saying, 'You bastard, we're a team, come on,' which a lot of people do. There was a care there, plus I think he knew that I had my own mind."

Steve had told me that a Spurs player once observed that it looked like Gilzean was playing the game in carpet slippers. It struck a chord, not least because I had read that he soaked his boots in water before games. I imagined Willie Gilzean cleaning a paintbrush while telling his son to look after his tools. Bill Nick seemed to think it was because Gillie had grown up wearing the old-style boots. But who knew?

This felt like as close I was going to get to Gillie, vicarious reflections of the man himself. Throughout my search there had always been a side missing. Alan Gilzean the person, the father, the husband and the son. To the Spurs players and even Steve Perryman, who roomed with him, he had always been something of an enigma, a man who left his private life outside the dressing-room door. In the absence of any hard information it had been left for others to speculate on his life. It was what I was doing, although the insight I was gaining seemed to be the only real insight any of his contemporaries had of him. I ventured the idea that Gilzean had viewed football as merely a job, despite having reached the conclusion that this was nonsense.

"It never came across to me that Gillie thought it was a job," says Steve. "I think Gillie was just a star in his arena on his stage; that's where he came alive, and then off the field he became very ordinary. He strolled around, his head used go from side to side and he had this walk. He had these driving shoes, ultra casuals. Always dressed in a golf style, rather than how a footballer would have dressed then. Just ordinary, very ordinary. He was very private. I never visited his house. Never, no. And yet, I drove past it and I wouldn't think that I had the right to go in. I think he lived a double life. He was a little bit the star in the shirt, but he just went back to normality. His wife was a policewoman, wasn't she?

"He used to have this circle of friends that came to the games. English, from around the Hertfordshire area. They were business people that he met and he would have a drink after the game and they would invite him out. In a way, you could say 'hangers-on', but they weren't. They were giving as much to him as he was giving to them. But he'd always arrange their tickets for them; he'd be on the phone and I'd see him writing envelopes. He was an educated writer. There was a little bit of elegance and an artistic side to it. So when he became a transport manager I could see him keeping ledgers and stuff. I could see that being part of what he did." It reinforces the idea that football was not a job Gillie had pursued, it had chosen him.

"I was vice-president of a club called Yeading when I was younger – '69, '70, '71, '72, the Gillie years," says Steve smiling. "They always wanted me to invite someone. It was a long way to travel, but Gillie was great. I know that if I invited four people one would be Pat. I probably had Gillie twice because there was no-one else I thought I could ask or no-one else would accept. But Gillie was great. For banter, whatever. And he was not the Mr Big. He had this way that was normal and he was elegant. If I had 20 kids here I would be signing quickly, almost not wanting them to wait, but he would deliberate over it and he had a great signature. I can still do the signature."

Steve signs the notebook in which I have been transcribing my shorthand. He is unhappy with his first attempt and tries again. "I haven't done that for ages but … something like that. You have a look at Gillie's autograph and that won't be far away. I might be getting the image wrong in my own mind but he was very thoughtful. It was like he would be thinking before [he wrote], sort of studious in a way. He wasn't what I would call a typical footballer, as such. I think he used the pen and paper more than I saw anyone else. Just taking notes of tickets or what he was due. I don't know, he was just a notetaker. He came across to me as educated. Whether he was or wasn't I don't know, but to have the handwriting that he had and his manner, he was a bit studious. And I seem to remember that he was good with words, his spelling."

I ask Steve if he has any theories as to why Gilzean has not been seen at Spurs. He revisits the idea of him being a down-and-out, but he too thinks it is ludicrous. He ventures that perhaps there need not be any great mystery. "It could be that we all hear the same thing and we're all retelling it and then someone mentions Gillie and we all say, 'Yeah, Gillie's not doing so well.' And I hope that's not true, because I just think he was very private and the longer you get away from your togetherness as a team, of course you are going to see less and less of each other."

The interview is shifting slowly towards its end when there is a knock on a glass-fronted door to my left. When I turn to look at who is entering I let out a gasp – Ossie Ardiles and Ricky Villa are standing not more than a foot from me. "This chap is writing a book about Alan Gilzean," Steve says. "Ah, I see," says Ossie, before Steve ushers them towards a table where guests are starting to mingle.

Just as Steve and I wind up the interview he says, "It was very kind of you to buy the book, but we have plenty of stuff for the auction. I'll sign it for you, get Ricky and Ossie to sign it, and you keep it."

The interview over, I sit down at a table with an elderly gentleman with a hook nose and white hair and a younger man whom I presume to be his grandson. "I'm writing a book about Alan Gilzean," I tell them, too eager to please or to buy credibility, I'm not sure which. "That's why I'm here, I've just interviewed Steve Perryman."

"Where is Gillie these days?" asks the elderly gent, introducing himself as John.

"I believe he's in Weston-super-Mare. The book was mentioned on Talksport last week, on the Alan Brazil show."

"Was it? I'm very friendly with Alan Brazil. I'll phone him and ask him. Can I borrow your phone, the battery on mine is about to go flat."

After John hangs up the mood at the table changes. There is a brusqueness in his voice as he announces: "Alan says he has been in touch with Gillie and that he's a very sick man and that he doesn't want a book written about him." There is little doubt as to what he thinks of the enterprise. I wonder how I am going to see out the rest of the night sitting beside someone who a minute earlier had been all smiles. The conversation is stilted as we tuck into bangers and mash. I ask John what he does.

"I work in the entertainments industry. I sell tickets to sporting events. I was at the American Football at Wembley yesterday. Alan Brazil mentions me in his book and says that if ever he needs tickets I'm the man he comes to."

The New England Patriots have just played the Tampa Bay Buccaneers in the NFL's annual game in England. I watched the match in my hotel room. I tell him I love American Football. "You came all this way and didn't go to the game?" he asks. He refers to Perryman as 'the skipper' and it's clear he's well-connected with Tottenham. "You should try talking to Dave Mackay," he says.

We manage to pass ourselves for the remainder of the meal and then Steve announces that he will be hosting a Q&A session with Ricky and Ossie, at which point John excuses himself and transfers to the opposite end of the bar. The younger man, who I assumed to be his grandson, remains seated.

"Are you not with John?"

"No, I've never met him before."

"He doesn't seem to like my book idea."

"I wouldn't listen to him. I think the book is a fantastic idea."

Before the night ends, I speak to an assortment of people who tell me the same thing. At one table I tell a gentleman in his late 50s or early 60s and his three sons about the book. "Ask him does he know what Gillie's nickname was," the man says to his boys.

"Of course he knows, he's writing a book about him," says one to his old man.

"It was the King," I reply, anxious to demonstrate my credentials, before relaying the story about Gillie, the boxing glove and the scout hut in Coupar Angus, and then launching into a diatribe about why Gilzean should be inducted in the SFA Hall of Fame and how I believe his name has been lost to the wider public.

"He was my favourite ever Spurs player. He was magnificent," says the father when I finish. "Thank you for doing this. It's about time someone did."

§

The following day I make the reverse trip from Maidenhead back to north London. My destination is the British Newspaper Library at Colindale, at the fringes of the Northern Line. The library is a vast, red brick building which houses hundreds of millions of printed words dating back to the 19th century. I have a hunch that I just might find something on Gillie here. After negotiating the Fort Knox-style security procedures (I need two forms of ID to get through the door and I'm required to sur- render all my belongings in return for a pencil and a plastic bag) I find myself staring at a logistical nightmare: how to pare down Gillie's 10 years at Spurs into manageable chunks. A general search of the library's database reveals hundreds of references. But one newspaper cutting, from the Daily Express, proves of particular interest. 'Gilzean signs for Spurs ... and here's how he did it'.

Beside the headline is Gilzean's signature. I'm amazed because I've seen it before. It could just as easily have been written by Steve Perryman.

11

THE KING OF WHITE HART LANE

"The difference between Alan Gilzean and the majority of his peers was the gulf between a Van Gogh and a competent, even excellent painting by a lesser artist. A cursory glance at the canvases by anyone but a true connoisseur might offer the impression that there was little to choose between them; closer examination, of course, would reveal the subtlety of colour, composition and texture that lifted the Dutch master into a class of his own. So it was with the King of White Hart Lane, who provided the Tottenham fans with everything they demand of their idols – sheer quality invested with character and style."
– Ivan Ponting, Tottenham Hotspur Player by Player

The 1970s were a shit time to play football. Flair players got kicked to bits on pitches that a farmer wouldn't graze cattle on. Psychopaths in shorts spent their afternoons trying to maim anyone who dared to go past them on the pitch, while a section of sociopaths who looked on sometimes did their best to maim anyone who dared to get in their way off it. Football was changing, gone was the sedate tactical game, romanticised by Danny Blanchflower.

The idealism of the early 1960s, of push and run and of playing football the right way, was becoming a fading memory. Nicholson held firm to his principles, but he was pushing against the tide. Now, it was win at all costs – he had admitted as much back at the start of the 1966-67 season when he gathered the players together.

Steve Perryman, for example, had made a name for himself in the reserves and youth teams as a passing player, but he could tackle and had an insatiable appetite for hard work. Immediately, he was thrust into the role of midfield enforcer. Perryman had his career shaped by Tottenham's need for pragmatism in an age when thuggery prevailed over flair. "I came into a team that had too many chiefs and not enough Indians and I was an Indian, although that wasn't actually my role as a youth, I was a passer. Of course, I always had industry and effort, but that was called upon even more as a young player in the team."

It was a chronic waste of Perryman's abilities and it speaks volumes for him as a footballer that he managed to alter his game. He received the Football Writers' Player of the Year award in 1982, after 13 years of consistency for the club.

The redeployment of Perryman was not the only concession Nicholson would make to tactical pragmatism: he helped invent the long throw. As the 1970s began, Spurs were once again drifting, much as they did during the years after winning the double. However, there was cause for optimism in the opening months of the 1970-71 season. Gilzean and Chivers were showing signs that a burgeoning partnership was forming, and not just in their link-up play. Bill Nicholson and Eddie Baily had noticed that Chivers was able to throw the ball tremendous distances.

In Big Chiv, Chivers says he used to practise daily until his shoulders ached, and that the Spurs management team devised two tactics. "The first was for me to pin it on the glossy head of Alan Gilzean at the near post and for him to flick it on to Martin Peters coming in from behind. The second involved waiting for Mike England to run forward to meet the ball at the penalty spot."

Once, for a televised competition at Stamford Bridge, he had thrown the ball 130 feet but had been disqualified because his toe had touched the line. He put his ability to throw so far down to his broad shoulders. It made sense to utilise Chivers' throw when Spurs had the greatest header of the ball in world football. One picture from this era shows a game between Tottenham and Wolves. Inside the box, Gilzean is presumably awaiting a throw from Chivers; there is a Wolves defender in front of him, one to his left, one to his right and one behind him. The four stand expectantly, and incongruously close. They look apprehensive, if not frightened, and they had good reason. Chivers to Gilzean was a deadly weapon in the 1970s.

Perryman told me that it was his job to utilise his accuracy from dead balls to give Spurs another edge. "One of my first jobs in the team was to take a near-post corner," he said. "I could have hit the spot between five and nine out of 10. Obviously they chose me for a reason, but it didn't matter whether it was five or nine out of 10 because Gillie would have got it every time. We scored a lot of goals that way and I think that's why we were successful in Europe particularly because, although we were a good team as well, if the football didn't work we'd score at a near-post corner or a long throw. We had overlapping full-backs, Cyril Knowles and Joe Kinnear, and they couldn't cope with that either, and then it would be something else. That's why you have to have the Bailys and the Nicholsons of the world thinking of these ideas."

When I mentioned to Steve that Eddie Baily had told me that the long throw wasn't an innovation, he looked surprised. "I think it was," he said with certainty. Not for the first time, I wondered whether Eddie had been deliberately provocative.

Pat Jennings also said Gillie's prowess in the air was something he had looked to capitalise on – and that it was Gillie's bald head he had been seeking when he scored against Manchester United in the 1967 Charity Shield. "At goal kicks from the deck or out of my hands, it was always Gillie I was aiming to hit," says Jennings. "It was something we worked on. Gillie would take up a certain area and I would try to hit him, and he was so good in the air. He would just come across the first defender and he would get a flick-on. The day I scored the goal in the Charity Shield I was basically aiming for him. Alex Stepney came out thinking he would pick up a miscontrolled ball from Gillie and, of course, it missed Gillie and Stepney was in no-man's land. With the next bounce it was in the net. But he was always my target, Gillie."

One of the main beneficiaries from such prolific service was Martin Peters. He had struggled in the opening weeks of the 1970-71 season, but had gradually started to find his feet. By early December, he had scored 13 times, mostly after making late runs to convert Gilzean knock-downs following Chivers throw-ins. Spurs sat third in the league and had reached the League Cup semi-finals, but it was a game in an earlier round that emphasised the importance of the Chivers-Gilzean-Peters triangle.

Tottenham 5 West Bromwich Albion 0
White Hart Lane, League Cup fourth round, October 28, 1970
    Four goals in a power-packed second half must make Spurs hot favourites for Wembley. [...] They brought their unbeaten run to a lucky 13 with a super-efficient display of fast and frenzied soccer. Martin Peters crowned a magnificent performance with his first hat-trick for Spurs and Alan Gilzean scored twice to complete a rousing evening for the 31,598 crowd.
    [...] It took until two minutes before the interval before Spurs went ahead, and then it was under rather suspicious circumstances. Phil Beal pushed the ball to Alan Gilzean who seemed offside. But no linesman's flag was raised and Gilzean moved forward to score with a low drive. [...] From the 68th minute onwards, Spurs moved into top gear. Pearce and Gilzean combined and the ball went into the middle for Peters to stab it home.
    Eight minutes later a long throw-in by Chivers was headed on by Gilzean

for Peters to crash the ball home. Ten minutes to go, and Gilzean drove the ball
home from a fine cross from Mullery and it was Mullery again who flicked the
ball over in injury time for Peters to complete his hat-trick.
  – Tottenham Weekly Herald

The move involving Chivers, Gilzean and Peters would be repeated often
throughout the season. The long throw yielded goals in wins over Motherwell in
the Texaco Cup, West Brom (again) in the league and Sheffield Wednesday and
Nottingham Forest in the third and fifth rounds of the FA Cup. Nicholson's decision to utilise Chivers in this way contradicted the idea that the main striker should
always take up a position inside the penalty area, no matter what the set-piece. If
not an innovation, it was, despite Eddie Baily's protestations, certainly something
that hadn't been seen for quite some time. The tactic was mimicked by Arsenal and
Chelsea, who, like Spurs, also instructed their main strikers, John Radford and Ian
Hutchinson respectively, to aim long balls into the area from the touchline.

Spurs' goal against Forest was such a fine example that it featured in an article
entitled The Long Throw in the Book of Football magazine:

Spurs forced a throw-in on their right flank some 30 yards from the Forest
corner flag. Chivers, as usual, was deputed to take the throw. As he picked
up the ball, Alan Gilzean [...] was loitering innocently at the far side of a
crowded goal area. He was tightly marked, Chivers threw the ball towards the
goalmouth, but to the near side of the goal area. Suddenly, with perfect and
unpractised timing, Gilzean sprinted 12 yards and was the first to reach the
ball with his left temple, skilfully directing it behind him with sufficient power
to send it gliding towards the far side of the goal. That Gilzean scored from so
delicate an angle was a testimony to his deft touch [...] but even had his header
been less precise, the move was still very dangerous once Gilzean had got his
head to the ball. The deflection could have made a goal for an onrushing col-
league ... Gilzean could direct and deflect the ball at amazing angles. Most of
Spurs' long throws were aimed at him. The opposition knew this but, by timing
his runs and using other players as decoys, Gilzean was still able to make his
penetrating flicks to unbalance defences.

Tactical considerations aside, Tottenham's upturn in fortunes in the 1970-71
season were helped by the blossoming of Gilzean and Chivers into a partnership as
effective as the G-Men had been. Arsenal won the double in 1971, but had Mike

England not sustained another serious injury Tottenham might have run them close. Early in that season, Gillie and Big Chiv combined to devastating effect in a Texaco Cup game against Dunfermline in which Chivers scored a hat-trick, assisted twice by Gillie: an inch-accurate centre for his second goal and a flicked pass for his third. Tottenham's other scorer was England ... from a Chivers throw-in.

By the time Spurs faced league leaders Leeds United at Elland Road on January 9, they still had a remote chance of winning the title, requiring a victory to keep their hopes alive. They were fourth in the table and trailed Leeds by 11 points but with two games in hand. Arsenal were second, a point behind Leeds. It would prove to be one of Tottenham's finest performances of the season, resulting in a 2-1 win which would hand the initiative to Arsenal, but also resurrect their own, distant title aspirations.

The Tottenham Weekly Herald notes of Gillie's performance at Elland Road that: "[He] can hardly have worked so hard for his side. He was here, there and everywhere, and it was his persistent worrying that led to the Tottenham goals." Chivers got both, the second coming from a fine pass by Gilzean.

Leeds had earned a deserved reputation as the dirtiest team in football. Don Revie, their hard-nosed manager, was ahead of his time in many ways: he was tactically astute and utterly vigilant in his preparation. He would compile dossiers on opposing teams and their players. He was particularly enamoured of Gilzean.

"[Gilzean is] one of the greatest touch players in Europe," he once said. "Watch him when goalkeeper Pat Jennings has the ball in his hands ready to clear. Gilzean moves into the inside-right position. A defender will mark him tight, but Alan will take that huge clearance on his chest, have the ball down and played away to the toes of a mate before the tackle goes in."

Revie would overlook Perryman repeatedly for England, while Gilzean had placed a bet on Perryman to play for England by a certain age. There were no winners in this state of affairs: not Revie, a disastrous England manager, not Perryman who would go on to win just one England cap, making his one and only appearance as a substitute against Iceland aged 30, and not Gilzean, who lost his bet by about 10 years.

Billy Bremner, Revie's captain at Leeds was also a Gilzean fan. "You can't tackle him out of a game because you will get skinned as soon as you commit yourself. Spurs play a lot of one-touch and it might look easy, but just try to take a ball out of the air and sidefoot it on the volley at the exact pace and angle you need and you will find it is one of the hardest things in the game."

The win at Elland Road in 1971 was revenge, of sorts, for a game played three years earlier. Revie had sent out his players with instructions to win at all costs. It resulted in Gilzean's dismissal, the third in his career, for retaliating against Terry

Cooper, the Leeds left-back. Shorn of one of their best players against one of the best teams in the country, Spurs played for a draw and were criticised in the local press.

The Yorkshire Evening Post's reporter, Phil Brown, said "it was sad to see a side with the gallant reputation Spurs have maintained so unscrupulous in stopping opponents. Playing for a draw is one thing, and is a big thing in modern football, if to its detriment as a spectacle, but playing it like Spurs did is not forgivable."

This conveniently ignored the part Leeds played in reducing Tottenham to 10 men, and the manner in which they secured their 1-0 win. Jennings and Gilzean were jostled and buffeted throughout. When both snapped, Leeds were given a penalty and a sending-off. In his autobiography, Jennings reveals the level of provocation. "A Leeds player ran into me on the first occasion I went to gather a cross from the wing – and that treatment was repeated five or six times in a tough but goalless first half."

After half-time, Mick Jones banged into Jennings and both fell to the ground. When the goalkeeper tried to get up, the Leeds striker used his legs to pin him to the turf. "Mick must have thought I was going to have a swing at him and decided to get in first by planting a right-hander on my chin. That was too much. I lashed out with my foot and kicked his behind ... I was spotted by a linesman who instantly put up his flag to draw the attention of [the referee who] not only booked me but added what I regarded as insult to injury by awarding Leeds a penalty. "

Peter Lorimer scored and, when Gilzean was sent off 10 minutes later, all hope of a Spurs comeback disappeared down the tunnel with him.

Ian Mackenzie, Gilzean's best man, recalls that he "never personally criticised an individual – although he did consider that Norman Hunter kicked anything that moved above the turf!" There was hardly a team in England that didn't hold some beef with Leeds, or their defender 'Bites Yer Legs' Hunter. It was not just Brian Clough, whose ill-fated reign at Leeds was brought to life in David Peace's novel The Damned United, who thought Revie's tactics beneath contempt.

As Jennings notes: "Like many other people [...] I have often wondered if they sold themselves short by trying to be too clever; whether they might not have been even more successful if they had been a bit more lovable. I know the policy at Elland Road was to win points rather than friends but the side was oozing with talent."

Just as he would become an easy target off the pitch because of his silence, Gilzean was an easy target on it. He rarely reacted to the blows he would receive on a Saturday, and the provocation was extreme. "The dirty players are once again making their presence felt, and that is a bad sign," he said at the start of the 70s. "Full-time refs with the chance of a career in the game would probably help." It was inevitable that there would be a consequence to the late tackles and snide kicks. In Gillie's case it was the knees that felt it, specifically the right one. As his career wound down at Tottenham, the punishment meted out would start to catch up with him.

But, for now, he was still a force in English football. In many ways, though, that victory at Leeds in 1971 was something of a blip. Inconsistency dogged Tottenham's season and again injury to England – a fractured shin bone – proved crucial. By beating Leeds, Tottenham brought to an end a five-game sequence without a victory stretching back to November. True to form, they lost their next game at Southampton, before a 2-1 home win over Everton was followed by a four-game winless streak. They recorded just two league victories between November 14 and March 13.

In between, they beat Bristol City over two legs in the League Cup semi-final, Gilzean scoring the goal in a 1-1 draw at Ashton Gate before Chivers and Jimmy Pearce struck at White Hart Lane to take Tottenham into the final against Third Division Aston Villa. The game brought Gillie his second medal as a Tottenham player, but it might have ended differently had Villa taken one of their many chances.

Tottenham Hotspur 2 Aston Villa 0 –League Cup final, Wembley, Feb 27 1971

Aston Villa trudged off the Wembley pitch with the stunned, disbelieving expressions of men who couldn't accept they had lost the League Cup final. It was snatched from them by two late goals from Martin Chivers.

Tottenham's players walked off wearing the sheepish smiles of men who knew they didn't deserve the trophy they were about to collect.

Eleven minutes from time [...] the First Division side were tottering on the brink of extinction when they emerged from a spell of memorable pressure with a breakaway upfield thrust that was its own tribute to their ability to survive. This was not the calm superiority of class finally showing through. It was the spur of sheer desperation having its effect at last.

Alan Gilzean put outside-left Jimmy Neighbour in the clear, one stride inside the corner of the penalty area with a superb through ball. Neighbour struck fiercely and although John Dunn, diving to his left palmed it away with one hand, it fell in front of Chivers who slotted it home.

The assets that have made the big man the striker of the season were seen again two minutes later. In the tiniest space he managed to retain control against a challenge [... he] turned on the ball, despite the lurking attentions of left-half Brian Tyler further restricting his time and room, and managed to find enough of both to hit the net.

Until the explosive flash of class from Chivers it had been difficult to single out one Spurs man who had played up to what is reasonably expected from footballers of their class and reputation. Spurs had only one real spell of initial authority – the opening minutes when it seemed that the class and calm rippling outwards from Alan Gilzean would be too stern a test for Villa.

[...] The impression that will remain in the memory will always be one of slight disappointment and sympathy for the underdogs who deserved better.

– Daily Mirror

Tottenham's patchy form meant their remote chance of winning the title had evaporated by the time Arsenal arrived for the penultimate game of the season needing just a point to take the title. I had heard a rumour that Gilzean had placed a bet on Arsenal to win the double in the 1970-71 season and had missed "easy chances" on the night Bertie Mee's side won the league at White Hart Lane with a 1-0 win. The tale was apparently well known in the Stag and Hounds, where Gillie drank. Its veracity hardly stands up to scrutiny. Why would any professional footballer confess to such a crime, for that's what it was, and in a bar of all places? It ignores, too, the fact that, at one stage of the season, Tottenham had been live outsiders for the league and Gilzean was in the midst of one of his best spells at the club.

Local pride was at stake and the accusation that Gilzean deliberately missed chances to hand Arsenal the league, just five days before they were due to face Liverpool in the FA Cup final, is laughable, not least because of the contempt Gilzean had for Bob Wilson. His views on Wilson's call-up for Scotland in 1971 were well-known to his Tottenham team-mates.

Wilson would not play for Scotland for another five months, but there was speculation that he was attempting to do so. As Chivers points out: "Gilly was a quiet, mild-mannered man and I only saw him grow horns on one occasion. I have never known Gilly go for a player like he went for Bob Wilson that night. Basically, Gilly felt that Wilson had bought a Scottish cap. He wasn't going to get in the England side, so he had found a Scottish relative and qualified for the Scottish team. Gilly – as passionate a Scot as you will ever meet – was absolutely mad about this."

Chivers recalls that Gilzean spent the evening banging into the Arsenal goalkeeper, who had a habit of rolling the ball into space to gain ground, before picking it up. On each occasion, Gilzean clattered him. Indeed, according to Phil Beal, he had asked team-mates to orchestrate the event. On the third occasion he injured Wilson's ankle. Again, it makes the idea that Gilzean was betting on the outcome seem outrageous, especially as these were the days before substitute goalkeepers. Why, if he wanted an Arsenal win not just that night but in the cup final a few days later, would he risk injuring their goalkeeper? Chivers recalls that after the game Wilson left the dressing room on crutches, passing Gillie and his strike partner on the way. "You big soft bastard, and you were lucky sods tonight," Chivers recalls Gillie saying after Arsenal's 1-0 win.

"I know that would be untrue," says Beal of the rumour, echoing what Pat Jennings told me at Morris Keston's book signing. "You don't do that type of thing. Bill Nicholson used to come into the dressing room and say there are two cup finals every year. Arsenal at home and Arsenal away. We hated each other. Off the pitch we had a drink together and a chat, but it was a different story on it. If there were remarks going around like that, I would condemn them. I think it's a ridiculous thing to say. He really did have a hatred for Bob Wilson. He would say, 'Give me the ball near Bob Wilson.' He would clatter him."

The physical battles would get worse as the 70s progressed; Gilzean shrugged and carried on. It was the same in Europe. The Glory Game focuses extensively on Tottenham's match with Rapid Bucharest in the third round of the UEFA Cup, giving over a whole chapter (The Battle of Bucharest) to the game. Gilzean is kicked, prodded and goaded repeatedly, but gets up, dusts himself down and continues playing.

Spurs went into the game on December 15, 1971 with a three-goal lead from the first leg. Gilzean had set up the first goal for Martin Peters with a trademark flicked header, but the return game was anything but easy. Spurs won 2-0, but the Romanians spent 90 minutes kicking lumps out of their opponents and seemed specifically to have targeted Gillie. As Hunter Davies notes in The Glory Game, Gilzean was punched brutally in the kidneys by a Romanian defender. The same player then took a running jump at him and ran both sets of studs down Gillie's legs.

"I can honestly say that in all my experience of football I have never played in a dirtier game," he would later remark. "I was forgetting about the 70-30 balls, let alone the 50-50 ones. I understand they destroyed the film of the match and I am not surprised. It would have made The Godfather look like a Walt Disney cartoon."

That same season saw Gilzean score his 100th goal for Spurs in all competitions, against Leeds. It was one of the finest of his career, receiving a ball from Chivers before beating two men and hammering a shot past Gary Sprake from 25 yards.

There is little point in this author trying to outdo The Glory Game and paint the 1971-72 season as something else. Whatever shortcomings I feel there are in the book pertaining to Gilzean, it is still an excellent account of life behind the scenes at a football club. It was so illuminating that the players, who had copy approval and received part of the profits from it, asked for certain bits to be removed.

As Mike Langley in The People wrote in his review on October 29, 1972: "It's been suggested that Chivers, Mullery, and even Mrs Nick might make [...] a point of smashing Mr Davies' front teeth down his throat. But no-one mentioned that he'd an arrangement with the club. That each player, and fan, Morris Keston, read and approved his individual chapter [...] Far from doing Spurs down I'd say he's glossed over a few sensitive details."

It says much about The Glory Game that it is remembered almost as much as the fact that Tottenham ended the 1971-72 season winning the UEFA Cup. It was another productive year for Gillie. He ended it with 22 goals including four in five FA Cup matches. He saved one of his best performances for a game in which he did not score, though. The 3-0 home win over Crystal Palace on September 18 brought up a personal milestone for Gilzean, who was now just a month short of his 33rd birthday. The Weekly Herald report contained the obligatory cliché: "Alan Gilzean was out of this world. Gilly was playing his 300th game for the club, but it was surely his best. He improves with age – just like a good wine."

There was speculation at the start of the season suggesting Gilzean would struggle to play, as Bill Nicholson had bought Ralph Coates from Burnley for £190,000. A few weeks after Coates' arrival, Hunter Davies sat in Gilzean's garden drinking beer. He asked Gillie if he was worried about losing his place to a player hailed as the new Bobby Charlton. "No, he won't get my place," Gilzean said. And he was right. He was a virtual ever-present during a year in which Coates struggled to settle.

Gillie's contract had expired the previous summer and many felt Spurs would follow the same policy as they had adopted with other long-serving players: allow them to pick their clubs and leave for a nominal fee. When Dave Mackay and Bobby Smith had been allowed to depart for Derby County and Brighton respectively, it had been for a mere £5,000, thus enabling them to negotiate contracts worth £10,000.

It had been expected that Gillie would join Mackay, now winding down his playing days at Swindon, but he went on the club's close-season tour of Japan without signing a new contract. The usual misinformation followed. "I've heard all the rumours. I'm told I'm going into the hotel business in Perth, that I'll move on. I still think I'll be a Spurs player next season." And he was.

"You are as old as you feel," he added. "I see no reason why I should not carry on playing in the First Division, especially with the present Spurs set-up. They are as good a side as I have played with since I moved to White Hart Lane."

Those words were backed by deeds, too. In a 3-1 win over Carlisle United in an FA Cup third round replay at Brunton Park, he played through illness, yet produced another masterful performance. "He was feeling queasy and we were not quite sure whether or not he should play. Gilzean is such a great professional I left it to him to make his own decision," Bill Nicholson told the following day's Daily Express, which described the first goal thus: "Gilzean, who seems to collect seconds all to himself to decide what to do next, coolly delivered the ball to Martin Chivers. When Chivers shoots there is no resistance, nor was there last night."

The description for the second goal was no less effusive: "Martin Peters, a great player this night, calmly took over, crossed, and Gilzean, the greatest header in modern day football, almost calmly nodded the ball into goal." Chivers completed the scoring with another powerful blast, after "an elegant pass by Gilzean".

Gilzean had metamorphosed again, as he had done when first joining Spurs. Then it had been the darting runs of Jimmy Greaves he had gilded. Now it was the languid, striding Chivers whom he was feeding. Chivers has nothing but admiration for his striking colleague and, while he refused to speak to me about him, he is sufficiently quoted elsewhere. "He was good at scoring goals and we worked very well together. He took a lot of stick up front, same as I did in those days because it was a physical game. I had to read what angle that ball was coming off that shiny bonce of his and I must have worked it out during my time with him. He was the fittest player in the team if he wanted to prove a point, but he rarely did."

The same allegation would be levelled at Chivers. For a spell in the early 1970s, he was simply the best striker in the world, but only, as Ivan Ponting notes in Tottenham Hotspur Player By Player, "when he was in the mood".

Chivers had power, pace, intelligence, technique, flair and prolific finishing ability, but the one criticism was something he could do nothing about. It was said that he lacked a killer instinct. Bill Nicholson would instruct defenders to clatter into him in training to goad him into action, but it never worked, the placid, sensitive Chivers becoming more and more disaffected with his manager until the relationship strained so far that Nicholson placed him on the transfer list. It was only in later life that he sorted out his differences with his former manager, the two becoming close friends.

Gillie's partnership with Chivers had fringe benefits. The tentacles of commercialisation were reaching into football and, as one of the English game's most potent strikeforces, there was an increasing demand for their services – though the rewards were far removed from those on offer to players today. One newspaper report from the time shows the two opening a stereo equipment shop on Tottenham High Road in December 1972. Chivers recalls that he and Gilzean were asked to open a garage, for which they received a crate of beer. A year later, Gillie was promoting a chain of carpet stores. An advert shows Gillie being given a tour of the Edmonton store. He is quoted as saying: "The range of grades and patterns I saw at the store was terrific. The only problem I had was making up my mind which one to choose."

By 1974, Gilzean was developing a portfolio of businesses which he helped to promote. The illustrator Paul Trevillion notes that, with the World Cup in West Germany approaching, he asked Gilzean if he would be prepared to put his name to a heading wallchart for the biscuit company Wm Macdonald & Sons, and he agreed. The idea came from an illustrated interview Trevillion had provided for The People in 1972 on Gilzean's heading ability. The interviewee? A certain Bob Wilson.

"Gilzean's not a power header of a ball – not like Ron and Wyn Davies. When they head the ball it really goes. Even so, I'd rather face those two than Gilly. With them, you know what to expect, so you're moving fractionally before they hammer it. You're in with a chance. But Gilly is impossible to read – and if you're foolish enough to try, it's odds on he'll wrong-foot you. And when a goalkeeper's off balance he can be made to look a mug." Not least when there's a maniacal, bald Scot charging at you, Bob must have thought.

The readiness with which Gilzean was prepared to offer his services runs contrary to the idea that he was diffident. So, too, does the knowledge that he was regularly photographed at charity events or awards ceremonies for local boys football clubs at this time. More likely, it seems that there was a metamorphosis going on off the pitch, too. London life was far removed from the country upbringing Gillie had experienced. He had become more streetwise. He had a public persona and a private one. And it seems he was more of a public figure than I had been led to believe.

Sifting through the offprints from Bruce Castle museum I found pictures of him at a celebrity night to raise money for the elderly and children's homes, and at a charity evening at the Lord Palmerston pub in King's Road, Fulham for the family of Sonny Walters, the former Tottenham winger who died in 1970. There were other shots of him at a golf day in Welwyn Garden City, him receiving the Norwegian Spurs supporters' club player of the year award and an appearance at the Lordship Junior Football League's presentation dance.

David Leggat, then of the Tottenham Weekly Herald, recalls a man who loved to socialise. "He went to a lot of supporters' events," says David, who spent the 1972-73 season as the Spurs beat reporter before moving to the Daily Mail then The People. "I think that's why they identified with him so much. Gillie was a fearsome drinker and a heavy smoker. He would have a triple Bacardi and 20 Rothmans. He liked a good bucket on a night out, but it wasn't hedonistic by today's standards.

"The players would go to the Bell and Hare after games, which was just across the road from White Hart Lane. It didn't open until six in the evening and after a home game the players would get in by the back door. Gillie would sneak me in and we would have a drink. He was quite happy to mix with the fans. Afterwards they would come into the bar and you would see him standing there in conversation, with a drink in one hand and a cigarette in the other. I would go along to fans' functions and he would be there – a good night out was great for him and the fans took special delight in knowing him. I think that's why he was so popular with the supporters."

David, a Rangers fan, tells me that he first encountered Gillie in 1962, when Dundee had thumped the Scottish champions in the Glasgow fog. "The first time I saw him was as a kid, when he scored four at Ibrox. When I first met him I told him this and it became a big gag between us. We developed a friendship after that. He was a very nice guy, he was Joe Ordinary with his bevvy in one hand and his fag in the other. He wasn't flash or fashionable. It was the time of bell-bottom flares. If you ever watch the Big Match Revisited with Brian Moore, you'll see the suits they were wearing, but Alan wore a plain grey suit with just ordinary old-fashioned lapels.

"On a Saturday night he would go around the Hertfordshire area. He was friendly with Ricky Prosser, who owned a haulage company, and a guy called Mad Mike Madison, who was Ricky's transport manager. Jimmy Burton, who was Dave Mackay's partner in his tie company, was also part of the scene. He was a bit of a ducker and diver and did a stretch for handling counterfeit money.

"Gillie took me out with these guys to country clubs. I was earning a wee wage as a newspaper reporter but it didn't matter to them. I was a friend of Gillie's and that's all that mattered. A few weeks before England played West Germany in a European Championship game – it was the one where Gunter Netzer ripped the pish out of England – Gillie took me to this restaurant in Soho. Sitting at the table opposite me were Franz Beckenbauer and Bobby Moore. A couple of minutes later, they were over and sitting at the table with Gillie and I'm thinking, 'Fuck me, it's Franz Beckenbauer and Bobby Moore.' But that was Gillie. Wherever you went, everybody knew him and everybody loved him. He had a shyness and he didn't hog the limelight. He was just a nice guy, because there was no side to him. Everybody loved him.

"He had a couple of party pieces when he had a few drinks. He had a favourite Greek restaurant, I can't remember the name of it but it was in Goodge Street, on the fringes of Soho. The waiters would throw the plates to Gillie like a frisbee and he would glance them off his head and into the wall to smash them.

"He would do this other trick where he would catch a two-bob coin on his forehead and then roll it down his face, let it fall and catch it on his foot. Then he would flick it up into his top pocket."

But he was anything but a two-bob player, recalls Leggat. "I remember seeing him at White Hart Lane against AC Milan in the semi-final the year they won the UEFA Cup. Gillie got absolutely battered and he played a lot of the game with balls being knocked up to him with his back to goal. The Italians were hammering into his back the whole game and he never shirked it or shied away. He had this wonderful ability on the ground and with the ball at his feet. He would flick it with his right foot and swing away to his left for the return pass."

Steve Perryman said this was a typical Gillie game. He had a score to settle against Milan, exactly 10 years after Dundee had lost to the Italians in the European Cup semi-final. Here he met another old friend, Karl-Heinz Schnellinger, the defender detailed to mark him when Dundee faced Cologne. Watching the game, it is clear that Gilzean is motivated by a sense of injustice. He gesticulates wildly as the referee ignores the Italians' cynicism. He throws himself into challenges with a ferocity that his critics habitually complained was lacking from his game. I asked Perryman if he felt football was Gillie's release. "There is no doubt this game was a chance to express himself. I've got a tape of it because I scored two goals, and it's a great tape of Gillie. You just felt in this game he was saying, 'Oh you're tough? You're Italian and you're tough? We'll take second best, will we?' Bang, bang, bang. He was saying 'ach' to the referee and waving his arms. These days it would be all mouth."

Schnellinger and Gilzean were booked as tempers began to fray, Gillie's ire increasing every time he was penalised for a succession of decisions which, over the course of the game, rendered him unable to challenge for a header.

In the build-up to the Milan game Gilzean had again been asked about his future plans, but he remained as non-committal as he had the previous December. "In my eight years with Spurs I've played no more than three or four reserve games. Until you feel you are going to be a permanent reserve you don't worry. I like to concentrate on getting on with the game instead of fretting over off-the-field matters. Only when Bill Nicholson tells me I'm no longer a first team man will I think of leaving Spurs."

Spurs' 3-2 aggregate win over Milan had far-reaching benefits. Tottenham had beaten one of Europe's finest teams, their opponents in the final were Wolves, and Martin Chivers always scored against Wolves: he had already done so three times that season. Gilzean had scored twice against the Midlanders but, as would so often prove the case for him in showpiece finals, he could not repeat the trick. When Spurs came away from Molineux with a 2-1 win, courtesy of two excellent Chivers goals, the scene was set for another memorable European night at White Hart Lane. Gillie, though, was subdued as Tottenham secured the UEFA Cup at White Hart Lane with a 1-1 draw a week later. Again, it seems somehow symbolic and appears to define his career: one of baffling brilliance, of redefining the word enigma.

The Glory Game season had other seminal moments. A week after the Battle of Bucharest, Tottenham played Chelsea in the first leg of a League Cup semi-final.

Gilzean, battered by the Romanians, missed the game, as did Perryman and Peter Collins, but watched as Spurs lost 3-2 at Stamford Bridge. The result left Tottenham needing a goal at White Hart Lane to win on aggregate. It arrived on the stroke of half-time when Gillie, now recovered, nodded down for Chivers and he lashed a volley beyond Peter Bonetti. But, after sustained pressure, Chelsea found an equaliser in the second half, to move back ahead on aggregate. Then, with eight minutes remaining, Martin Peters sent the Chelsea goalkeeper the wrong way from the penalty spot to leave Tottenham 2-1 up on the night. Just one minute remained when Alan Hudson took a free-kick near the corner flag. The Chelsea winger mis-hit his cross but, as the ball trundled innocuously towards Cyril Knowles, the defender opted to boot the ball clear and it slithered under his foot and into the net.

Hunter Davies describes the desolation in the Spurs dressing room: "They sat like shipwrecked hulks, naked with their heads bowed, their faces in their hands, unable to move. Knowles seemed to be crying. His eyes were red and swollen. His arms were shaking. No one could look at anything else ... at that moment their little microcosm seemed to be a microcosm of all human disasters."

And then, slowly the inquest begins.

"Fucking tragic" and "What a fucking goal. I've never seen such a fucking goal. I'm definitely not going upstairs. They can stick their reception," Gilzean is quoted as saying. "There'll be some spewing up in Tottenham tonight. I couldn't stand seeing anyone. I'm going straight home."

A few months later, when The Tottenham Hotspur Football Book was published, Gilzean told the author, Peter Smith, that the defeat to Chelsea and missing out on Wembley ranked "as one of the biggest disappointments" of his career. The League Cup had been much-maligned since its inception and had been compared unfavourably to the FA Cup. But the guarantee of a European place had changed matters.

"Every game means as much as the biggest FA Cup tie when it comes to effort from the players. Defeat at the last hurdle before a second Wembley final in two years was a hard pill to swallow. But the manner of our exit was what sent everyone into a state of depression which took weeks to wear off. Ninety-nine times out of a hundred Cyril would have planted the ball firmly towards the other end of the pitch.

"I can remember being frozen to the spot when the ball went in, with my mouth wide open. I just could not believe it. My mind strayed back to the previous time we had lost a League Cup semi-final. Then Arsenal beat us – and again it was a last-minute goal that proved our downfall. But the goal John Radford put past us in 1968 was a great one – this time there was no such compensation. After the match our dressing room was like a morgue. None of the team said a word. Everyone felt too choked in themselves to talk. Even Bill Nicholson said little. That is what Wembley means to players. When you have been there and experienced the emotion and glamour of the occasion it becomes the peak of your ambition. Which is why Spurs are determined to be back there this season."

Tottenham would endure another mixed season in 1972-73, the penultimate of Gilzean's senior career. But they would indeed reach another League Cup final.

Tottenham Hotspur 1 Norwich City 0 –Lge Cup final, Wembley, Mar 3 1973

There are very few things that anger footballers more than to be compared unfavourably with great teams of the past. The present Spurs side have suffered more than most from that sort of thing [... But] the present side deserves a place of its own in soccer history. Three cups in successive seasons is a tremendous achievement [...] It's going to be a long time before any other team emulates the success of the present Spurs side and the feat may never be seen again.

It wasn't a classical final – but don't blame Spurs for that. Norwich didn't exactly adopt tactics based on open, attacking football.

The main thing is that the League Cup is now back at White Hart Lane and the men who brought it back have written another glorious chapter in the Tottenham Hotspur legend. Undoubtedly the hero of the day was Ralph Coates with his cracking 20-yard winner. It came after a shrewd bit of thinking by Alan Gilzean, who had been marked tightly by David Stringer. When Spurs won a throw-in in the 72nd minute, Gillie drew Stringer away from the near post. That created space for Martin Peters to move in. He got his head to the ball and turned it across the goal. Gilzean helped it on towards Mike England but David Cross pushed it clear. The ball went as far as Coates who smashed a low, right-foot drive past Kevin Keelan. A goal which was fit to win the cup.

– Daily Mirror

David Leggat remembers the League Cup final for personal reasons. "Gillie was very kind to me. The editor of the paper came to me and said he wanted a first-person piece but, of course, this was a small newspaper and there was no money to spend. So I asked Gillie if he would do it and he said, 'What will I get?' I told him I could buy him a drink. He did that for me."

The campaign ended with Gilzean third in the voting for the Football Writers' Player of the Year award. It seemed that recognition was coming for his body of work, rather than a specifically good season. Pat Jennings won, but rather than express disappointment, the ever-humble Gilzean was merely chuffed for his team-mate. "Yes, it would have been great to win, but it couldn't have gone to a better choice."

His apogee that season had come in a game which Spurs drew at Southampton. The press raved about him. He did not score, but he gave the kind of performance which had become the hallmark of his time at Tottenham. The Observer described "the Grand Master" giving a "display of skill and energy [which] was pure delight". The report continues: "Tottenham scored first after 15 minutes. Gilzean (who should and probably has written a treatise on heading the ball) nodded back to Pearce who spotted Chivers moving fast down the middle. The centre-forward collected the ball as if he owned it and placed a well-angled shot past Martin." Spurs couldn't find a winner after Mick Channon equalised, but came closest when Gilzean "scarcely without looking, flicked in a rising ball which Martin scrambled over the bar. A fitting note to end on."

As David Leggat says, the fans loved him. Few players in Tottenham's history have had as many songs penned in their honour. It was not just Spurs supporters, either. He is a prominent figure in Hector Nicol's The Dundee Song, written in 1962. He is the only player to have both names included in the song, although this might merely be down to lyrical considerations.

There was The G-Men, which contained the line: "We've got the G-Men. In Greaves and Gilzean, they are the world's best goalscoring machine." To the tune of The First Noël, they sang: "Gilzean, Gilzean, Born is the King of White Hart Lane." And to the strains of Land of Hope and Glory they belted out: "I know Alan Gilzean. And Alan Gilzean knows me."

One fan, Martin Lee, believes he was the first to sing Born Is The King: "My friend John Moody and I claim legitimately that we were the Spurs fans who made up the song. It was on Boxing Day during the 1964-65 season. We were on our way home on the train from Nottingham Forest – our only away win that season – when being Christmas, the Christmas Carol Noël Noël was being played and we changed the words to 'Gilzean, Gilzean'. Soon the whole train full of Spurs fans were singing the song. We still talk about it in the pub before games to this day."

The Dundee Song is still played at Dens Park today and ends with the rousing, "For there's Robertson, Penman and Alan Gilzean, With Cousin and Smith they're the finest you've seen. A defence that is steady heroic and sure, Liney, Hamilton, Cox, Seith and Wishart and Ure."

But it was not just Dundee and Tottenham supporters who sang of Gilzean, Celtic supporters did too: "We don't need your Colin Stein, Eusébio or Alan Gilzean, We've got someone twice as good, We've got Harry, Harry Hood

His presence in so many terrace chants is probably an indication of the esteem in which he was held. Hunter Davies noted it in The Glory Game. Every Dundee and Tottenham team-mate I spoke to talked of his special relationship with supporters and Revie, the hugely successful Leeds United manager, had seen it. He loved nothing better than displaying his mastery of the ball in games. He would trap it with his backside in the warm-up to delighted cheers from the home support. His flicks drew spontaneous applause and his goals raucous cheers. He was the King of White Hart Lane. The stadium rang out to his song every week, and his relationship with those fans bordered on cult status. Yes, Nicholson had sacrificed something of his principles by adopting a more uncouth approach to scoring goals, but Gilzean provided beauty and grace and, by turning it into an art form, his name became synonymous with heading the ball. He transformed it from the bludgeoning style of the likes of Lawton, Mortensen and Lofthouse, who bundled goalkeeper, ball and anyone else into the net, into a near-surgical practice which required guile, timing, accuracy and above all, intelligence.

When Miljan Miljanic, the Red Star Belgrade coach, came to watch Tottenham on a scouting mission ahead of his side's UEFA Cup match with the London club in 1972, he was so impressed that he said: "If ever a Football University is founded Alan Gilzean should be appointed as the first professor to lecture on how to use one's head and to play with one's head." Miljanic, who would later manage Real Madrid, was named by World Soccer as one of the game's 50 most influential coaches in 2010.

Gilzean scored what he later claimed was one of his favourite goals for the club when Spurs beat the Yugoslavs 2-0 at White Hart Lane, a few weeks later, to confirm what Miljanic had feared. "Big Chiv had put us one up, and in the second half, just as Red Star were beginning to come back at us, Martin Peters gave me a great pass to round off a fine move which started in our own half. I felt really good after scoring that. I knew it was a good goal," Gillie said in a rare moment of public pride.

But it was not just great coaches who recognised his impact on football in the 1970s. Gordon Banks, then the world's No1. goalkeeper, claimed Gilzean was the forward he feared most. "Gilzean is superb in the air, and extremely strong for someone of his build. He's one of those cunning lads who can find good positions. Even when not scoring himself, he lays on chances for others with those deft flicks of his."

But perhaps the greatest compliment came from one of the finest players of his generation, Johan Cruyff, himself no slouch in the air. Tottenham travelled to Amsterdam for a benefit match against Ajax at the Olympic Stadium for Sjaak Swart, then, aged 35, the oldest player in the Dutch league. Spurs were paid £4,000 to provide the opposition for the game and there had been talk of Pelé and Eusébio guesting for Ajax, only for the plan to fall apart. Spurs lost 4-1, but Gilzean, just a few months younger than Swaart, displayed his usual elegant prowess and prompted Cruyff to remark: "Gilzean impressed me with his heading ability. He won nearly every ball in the air; he is just great with his head."

At the end of the game, the Ajax players carried Swaart shoulder-high around the Olympic Stadium. It was an act the Spurs players would replicate 11 months later as Gillie played his last game on an end-of-season tour to Mauritius.

His Tottenham career had been in decline from the start of that season. In August 1973, the Sportsman 68 Club held a dinner in his honour and, during his welcoming speech, Gilzean hinted at what was to come. "Everybody says, 'When are you going to pack up?' and some send me congratulation cards for my retirement, but I enjoy football and when I finally have to give it up it will be something out of my life. I will keep on going as long as Bill Nick needs me."

But it was becoming increasingly apparent that Nicholson did not need him. There had been press speculation about a move for Southampton's Mick Channon that did not materialise, and there was optimism that Chris McGrath, who had scored a clutch of important goals during Gillie's absence through injury, would make the step up from the reserves. McGrath's form would ultimately deny Gillie the chance to play in another UEFA Cup final, this time against Feyenoord.

It was the third season running that Spurs had reached the latter stages of the tournament. The previous year they had lost to Liverpool on away goals and this was a chance to right that wrong.

But it was a game that would be remembered for violence off the pitch, as Spurs and Feyenoord fans clashed on the streets of Rotterdam and then in the De Kuip Stadium. Eyewitness accounts say there were tears in Bill Nicholson's eyes as he appealed to the Tottenham supporters to calm down and was largely ignored. The trouble, and Tottenham's 4-2 aggregate defeat coupled with a poor start to the following season, would persuade the most successful manager in the club's history to call it a day. Eddie Baily left at the same time to take up a position with Essex Schools, when he had thought he would take over from Nicholson. It triggered a decline that would end in relegation in 1977. Spurs would return to the top flight the following season, but it would take another three years before the glory returned when Steve Perryman, the one player still connected to Nicholson's second successful Spurs side, lifted the FA Cup after a Ricky Villa-inspired win over Manchester City in 1981.

During Gillie's final season, he was limited to just 23 appearances. It was feared that there was a cyst behind the right knee, but an exploratory operation in January 1974 revealed that there was no significant problem and he was able to resume for the rest of the campaign. Nevertheless, it was clear that time was starting to catch him. He was now playing regularly in the reserves – one of the benchmarks he had set himself – and not just because he was returning from injury. McGrath was having a decent season, but after the 1973-74 campaign he would play just nine more games for Tottenham, not least because Spurs had trodden a well-worn route to find a replacement for Gilzean.

John Duncan, who had scored 109 goals in 188 games for Dundee, arrived at White Hart Lane for £150,000 just as Gillie was departing. He had already been given a nickname for his prolific goalscoring and his proficiency in the air. "One day we were in the [Dundee] dressing room and we were trying to come up with nicknames and George [Stewart] suggested 'Gillie'. It just stuck. I had watched him in the reserves as a young boy and later in the first team, so it was a real boost to my confidence to get the nickname, but it didn't go any further than that," says Duncan, who would go on to register 62 goals in 120 games at White Hart Lane.

The tragedy was that at the start of season 1973-74, Gillie had been on course to break the 100-goal barrier. He would have become the first Scottish player to reach a century in the league in both England and Scotland. A season later, Neil Martin, who played for Queen of the South, Hibernian, Sunderland, Manchester City and Coventry City, would achieve that feat in the colours of Nottingham Forest.

Gilzean managed just three goals in that final season but had the satisfaction of scoring one in his last game, against Newcastle at St James' Park. It was only his fourth start since the previous December, but there were, according to the Tottenham Herald, "touches of vintage Gillie magic". Nine minutes remained when John Pratt and Mike Dillon combined to allow the King "a fitting end to a great reign".

In February 1974, Gilzean announced that he had yet to make up his mind on what his future held. He described as "nonsense" a Sunday newspaper article which claimed he had already agreed to finish his career abroad, but it appeared certain he was preparing to abdicate his throne. "I don't want to make any decision until the end of the season when my contract runs out – that will be the proper time," he told Harry Harris, then of the Weekly Herald but later of Fleet Street fame. "Then I will look at any offers and make up my mind."

There was a suggestion in that article that Spurs would offer Gilzean a contract extension, but it never materialised. Nevertheless, he was still a Tottenham player by the time the team travelled to Mauritius in June. Steve Perryman told me about Gillie's last trip away with Spurs. He enjoyed it, by the sound of things. "Bill Nick wasn't there. Eddie Baily was in charge and there was a nine-hole golf course on the beautiful white sands at the hotel. We played three games and won the first by six goals, then we won the second by five goals. But stories were going around about how he was enjoying the trip and this was Gillie's last trip, so we were definitely having a good time. We put everything on the room bill, whatever it was – six vodkas, two rums and Coke, whatever. Gillie was just like, 'Put it on the room.' So one night Eddie Baily calls this meeting and says, 'Chaps, I've just seen the room bills and the guvnor's going to go berserk. This just can't happen.' "

Pat Jennings takes up the tale in his autobiography: "There was a bill of £400 outstanding for the drinks we had ordered with our meals. Spurs were refusing to pay it. We hadn't been hitting the bottle. The players had been relaxing on an end-of-season trip and divided between about 18 of us, spread over a couple of weeks, it wasn't an outrageous sum. But the Spurs directors said it wasn't the responsibility of the club, and we would have to cough up.

"Alan Gilzean, who liked a drink, was so incensed at what he regarded as the mean attitude of the directors that he was ready to sign a personal cheque on the spot – but the rest of the lads insisted that the bill must be split equally between us. We knew the tour sponsors couldn't afford it, and the last thing we wanted was to give our hosts the impression that the Spurs players were free-loaders. Our personal reputations, quite apart from the good name of the club, were at stake.

"That was when our African friend came up with a bright idea. He pointed out that local bookmakers were offering odds against the correct score of our final match, and if we could win by a certain margin we could raise the cash to pay our debt.

"We held an impromptu team meeting and decided that 6-0 was about right. The odds were 10-1, so we had a whip-round and duly invested £40 to win us £400.

"It wasn't easy, for the home goalkeeper had an inspired match and pulled off a series of spectacular saves. Even when Spurs went 5-0 up he was diving all over the place, turning shots round the posts and over the bar. There was no more than 90 seconds left when we scored our sixth goal among scenes of jubilation that must have convinced the crowd that the sun had got at us."

The match was an emotional one on another level. Gilzean was led out before kick-off by Eddie Baily and was presented with two large ornamental cockerels by Steve Perryman and Martin Peters. He was clearly emotional, according to press reports, but it did not stop him from doing his bit for the team, scoring a hat-trick to help his side to the 6-0 win needed to secure their £400. At the end of the game, a brass band played 'For he's a jolly good fellow'.

Harry Harris reports: "The team did a lap of honour and as a final tribute to a great player and friend they carried Gilly shoulder high as they ran around the uncovered brick stadium. The sun seemed to agree with Gilzean as goals shone bright on tour. He scored seven of Spurs' 17 goals in the three games. That could well have made him decide finally to end his playing days in the sun with a South African club."

It was Ricky Prosser who drove him to the airport on the night he left London for his new life on the other side of the world and he remembers that Gillie's bags were packed to bursting when he went to check them in.

"He put his bags on the scale and they were over the baggage allowance," says Ricky when I speak to him by telephone in May 2010. "But he had no money to pay for them, so I gave him the £80 to get his bags on. We were great, great friends. He never acted like a star, he was just an ordinary bloke. But I've not seen him for over 10 years – he just disappeared. I hope he's well, somebody said he's very ill. I tried looking for him on the internet but I couldn't find him."

Ricky first got to know Gillie through Dave Mackay. "My wife and kids used to play football with Dave's wife and kids in their living room, and Dave was big friends with Gillie," he says. Ricky followed Spurs around the country every week, often staying in the same hotel as the players. He would see Alan most Saturdays at the hotel or when they went out to one of the country clubs David Leggat told me about. "There was one called the Starlight Rooms in Enfield and another called the Bush Hill Country Club in Hatfield." The Starlight Rooms was affiliated to Enfield Town Football Club and used to put on variety acts each week with singers and stand-up comedians; Bush Hill Country Club had a similar set-up.

"We had some good social times together," says Ricky. "He was just good fun to be out with. He liked a drink; we used to go to Newmarket races. I'm not a betting man, but I liked to go along and watch. He played golf with another friend of mine called Captain Jim, but he's dead now. They played at Crews Hill and we used to have a day out golfing every year at Beckenham in Kent or the Isle of Sheppey. He was very friendly with Mike Madison, my transport manager. Gillie and him were out all the time. But he's dead now, too."

The South African club Gillie agreed to join was Johannesburg's Highlands Park. Known as the Manchester United of South Africa, they had won trophies in all but one year since their inception in 1959. In July 1974, he signed a two-year contract despite interest from Luton Town, newly promoted to the top flight, Portsmouth and Fulham. Yet, within three months, Gilzean would be back in England.

12

"It's Alan Gilzean"

If Alan Gilzean really did live as a down-and-out, why should I be the one to expose it? What right had I to interfere in an old man's private affairs? The only answer I can give myself is that I was writing about him for the right reasons: to give him some kind of recognition for his achievements, to give him his rightful place in Scottish and English football history. Jimmy Greaves, Gordon Banks, Cliff Jones, Johan Cruyff, Miljan Miljanic, Don Revie, Phil Beal, Alan Mullery, Hugh Robertson, Ian Ure and Pat Liney couldn't all have been wrong, could they?

That supposes, though, that Gillie wants any kind of recognition. Perhaps, as Greaves had said, he was happy to live the quiet life.

My car is clinging to the steepest hill I've ever been on as I drive from Dundee to Coupar Angus. The sun casts verdant shadows in the valley beneath me. There is a seduction in the air and that hill is pulling me ever nearer to my destination. I understand cricket, country walks and summer fetes in that drive down through Tullybaccart. The car feels like it could topple over or slide down if I so much as take in the scenery. 'Tullybastard', Jim Crumley's father called it in The Road and Miles as he remembered his grandfather's tales of woe as he delivered barrels of beer by horse and cart to Coupar Angus. He had remarked on the miracle of Gillie – the biggest surprise was that he'd come from the 'Couparry'. "All berries and coo shite".

But to me, resplendent in sunlight, the drive through the hills is energising. Can there be a more apposite metaphor for the journey I have undertaken in search of Alan Gilzean? Here I am driving towards a meeting with, in no particular order, his best man, an old schoolfriend, a former team-mate and a local football coach who used to pick berries with Alan's mother, on the very road that Gillie used to travel daily as his football career was starting out.

The sun is shining and my pulse is quickening: this is, after all, the birthplace of a Tottenham legend. When I finally pull into the car park at the Red House Hotel I am a good half an hour early.

A few weeks earlier, Ron Ross, the old schoolfriend, and I had a number of telephone conversations about Gilzean. I could tell Ron was excited. He was sports editor of the Dundee Courier for many years and he is now retired, but the journalistic antennae are as sensitive as ever. He told me one lovely story about a colleague, Adrian Arthur, who upon finishing his shift early one morning received a phone call from the door-man at the Dundee Courier offices to say that there was a Mr Revie downstairs looking for directions to the Lorimer household in the Douglas area of the city.

"It being nearly 3am, Adrian seemingly told him to hang about and he would escort Mr Revie to the address. This he did on his scooter, since these were the days before sub-editors could afford cars and, I think, was asked into the Lorimer house along with Don Revie, where he witnessed the historic signing of the teenage Peter."

On the first day I phoned Ron at home in Longforgan he was getting dressed for a rather more sombre occasion. "What a coincidence this is," he'd said "I'm just going out to Ben Roberts' funeral. Ben was the goalkeeper for Coupar Angus Boys and played in the same team as Alan and I."

A few days later he provided me with news of a breakthrough which seemed pretty significant to me. "Remember the funeral I told you about the other day? Well, one of the boys who was there was in the same scout troop as Alan. His name is Ian Mackenzie, he was also Alan's best man when he married Irene Todd."

A day earlier, I had left a message with Ron's wife that I would like to take him up to Coupar Angus to look around. He said he was more than willing to do so. "I'm retired now. I play golf on Mondays and Wednesdays, so a Thursday is fine." There is a caveat, though. "Coupar Angus was the centre of the universe to me back then, you realise, but there's not much to it now."

Earlier, in the kitchen at my B&B no more than a mile away from Dens Park, I discussed Gilzean with the owners, a husband and wife whose son had aspirations of playing for Dundee. The former, a budding illustrator, wanted to chat about the book. There were caricatures of former footballers on the walls of the guesthouse. Kenny Dalglish was represented in his Scotland kit, George Best was playing for United and there were a host of other famous players. He'd never heard of Gilzean.

As I killed time watching Brazil take on the USA in a Confederations Cup match, I realised that I had still not heard from Pat Liney. I was due to meet him the next day, and I had tried twice already that afternoon to contact him without success. He phoned soon after and we spent 25 minutes discussing everything from the origins of his surname to how Alan Cousin taught him to complete crosswords.

He provided me with a story that demonstrated just what that Dundee league-winning team meant to the people of the city and the esteem in which the players who comprised it are still held. "One day I was out in the car and this group of four boys ran into the back of me," he said. "It was their fault and they accepted responsibility straight away. Anyway, we exchanged details and I signed a piece of paper with my name and address and as soon as the young lad who was driving took a look at it, he said, 'Aw, fuck, it's Pat Liney, ma da's going to kill me. He grew up watching you keep goal for Dundee.' "

He talked about Gillie not receiving the credit he deserved at Dundee, how people used to say he was just a goalscorer. But ignorance of his abilities extended beyond Dundee. "We played Spurs in the FA Cup when I was at Bradford. Our manager, Jimmy Wheeler, was making plans for Spurs corners," said Pat. "He was telling Norman, our centre-forward, to come back and pick up Martin Chivers every time. He went through most of the team. And then I said to him, 'What about Gilzean?' and he said, 'Is he good in the air?' To which I said 'Well, he scored over 50 goals one season in Scotland and 40 of them were with his head.' We drew 2-2 with them at home and then they beat us 5-0 in the replay. I couldn't believe how much Alan had changed as a player. He was very creative and set up a lot of goals for Spurs. They had Jimmy Greaves at the time and he was their main goalscorer, but Gillie was the playmaker. I think it says a lot about him that he managed to adapt his game."

Years earlier, Pat had been asked for his recollections about Gillie in The Weekly Post. It was one of the first cuttings I had read when that parcel from Bill Hutcheon, the editor of the Dundee Courier, had fallen through the letterbox.

"It was some time since I had seen him and I didn't know what to expect. We were nobodies … he was a big shot. As it turned out, he was the same bloke I'd always known. I got him a couple of tickets and we had a chinwag after the game. When we went down to White Hart Lane he helped to fix me up with tickets. I admired him as much for that as I did for his ability."

When I finally hung up, I started to ponder the kind of questions I was going to ask Gilzean's friends from Coupar Angus. I decided fairly quickly that I was going to give them the opportunity to walk away if they didn't like what I had to say. I drew up a brief preamble outlining my reasons for doing the book.

It was the same speech I had delivered to Ian Gilzean, Alan's youngest son, just a few weeks earlier when I'd phoned him at his home in Carnoustie. Ian Gilzean had played for east Belfast's Glentoran, leaving in 2000, four years before my brother signed for them. Players at Glentoran still remembered Gilzean and gave me a head start in finding contact details.

He asked me what the book was about and I heard myself rambling: "It's about your father ... obviously," as if he hadn't known. "I want to disprove some of the myths ... like him living as a down-and-out. I've nominated him for the Scottish Hall of Fame and I want to give him his place in Scottish and English football history. I'm a massive Spurs fan and my dad idolised your dad ..."

The words had gushed out and I had the overwhelming feeling of not making much sense. "But there is also a crossover; you played for Glentoran and my brother played against you for Linfield, Chris Morgan?"

"He's a centre-forward, isn't he? He's still playing for Newry City," said Ian. I had been impressed by his knowledge and felt we had found some common ground.

"It's a tenuous link, but you scored the winner in the Irish Cup final back in 2000 and a few years later my brother joined Glentoran and played in a league decider which, if Linfield had won or drawn, they would have won the league. He scored the winner in the 94th minute." Throughout the conversation I noticed him letting out little exhalations, as if he was gently laughing to himself. I took it to be a good sign.

Craig Brown told me that in his days as Scotland Under-18 manager he used to hang pictures of Alan in the dressing room before matches in an attempt to motivate Ian. I asked him about it and he laughed again. He had spent a lifetime in his dad's shadow. "He might have done, but I don't remember it," he had said in a broad Cockney accent. "I'm really busy with work at the moment but if you give me your number I'll phone you back in a few weeks and we can see about meeting up then."

I came away from the conversation quietly optimistic but, when I hadn't heard back from Ian a few weeks later, I knew that he wasn't keen. He sounded vaguely hostile when I tried him again at home on a Saturday afternoon, as I watched England playing a World Cup qualifier against Kazakhstan. "I'm not really interested in helping out," he said. I asked for his reasons and he told me that he didn't know what the book was about, whether it was about his dad's life in football or his life after football and that his dad had had offers to do books before and opted not to take them.

"It's not really up to me whether you do the book," he added. "It's my dad's call and he's chosen to keep a low profile and I want to respect that. If that's his decision then he is the person you should be speaking to. He had the career, not me. I can offer to give him your details, if that helps."

I told him that I could understand his reticence, that it was something I had already contemplated – the intrusion on someone's private life. But I also pointed out that his dad's privacy had more than likely cost him his place in the Scottish Football Hall of Fame. I also told him that I was interested in his own side of the story too and that I wanted the book to be as accurate as possible.

"I understand that it's sensitive, but I'm going to write the book anyway and I'd rather do it with his and his family's blessing," I heard myself saying.

"It's nothing to do with whether it's sensitive," countered Ian. "What's known about my dad is out there. At the end of the day, the family knows the truth, so it doesn't matter what's written in a book."

Something I had said had made him mellow, yet I still felt like I had lost him. As a last resort I offered to send him the first chapter and he agreed to take a look.

That following Monday, after I spoke to Ian Gilzean for the second time, I happened upon a news brief in one of the national newspapers which reported that he had taken over as manager of Carnoustie Panmure, an East Region Junior team and the club where Bill Brown started his career. The report added that he had taken his first training session the previous Saturday – presumably just hours before I had spoken to him. Clearly, he had more to concern him than a book about his father.

Ian Gilzean's footballing career was one of frustration. His early days at Tottenham were promising; he scored 25 goals in 38 games as the youth team won the South East Counties Division One, in a side that also included Vinny Samways. A further title followed the following season, before Gillie junior made the step up to the reserves in season 1988-89, when he netted 10 times in 28 appearances as Spurs won the Football Combination. The following season injury struck and he was never quite the same. He played just 34 times between the start of the 1989-90 season and the end of 1991-92. He played 144 times for Spurs reserve and youth teams, scoring 60 goals.

I had heard all the pejorative comments and the unfair comparisons with his father. Like so many sons of famous fathers, the albatross hung heavily around his neck. Over a career spanning 12 clubs – including a brief spell at Dundee – he did not achieve a scintilla of the success that Alan had, but things might have been different were it not for injuries. In 1990, he had seven operations, culminating in surgery to reconstruct both knees.

He signed for Spurs as a trainee in July 1986 after he was spotted playing for Raglan Junior School in Bush Hill Park, near the family home. He was capped at youth level by Scotland – a feat Alan never achieved – and played for Enfield district, Middlesex and London schools. Kevin, Gillie's elder son, was playing for Stansted in the Essex Senior League.

Ian was featured in the Spurs programme five times during his spell at the club, for the league games against Nottingham Forest in March 1988 and January 1989, Sheffield Wednesday in October 1989 and Arsenal in January 1991. His final appearance came in the programme for the European Cup Winners' Cup tie against Porto in October 1991. By summer of the following year, he had been released. Reading through those programmes one thing is clear: Ian Gilzean is under no illusions as to the weight of expectation attached to his name. He comes across as a personable, level-headed young man, revealing that his father, who according to the programme was working now as the national manager of a tyre company, would watch Ian whenever he could. "[He] points out where I am going wrong. I have a lot to live up to having followed my father here, but although I respect all that he did, it's up to me to do the job for myself," he said in March 1988.

"When people hear my name, they immediately make the connection between my father and myself," he said in January 1989. "Perhaps it helped to get me noticed when I was a youngster trying to get into a big club, but now it can make life difficult, because to make comparisons between us is unfair at this stage of my career."

In the programme for the Sheffield Wednesday game, he was still basking in the afterglow of a hat-trick against Reading for the reserves. "This has to be the season I start moving nearer to the first team," he says. "I really want to make it at Spurs and I'll be doing all that I can to see that happen. My great aim now is – and always will be – to play for Scotland. Although I was born in England, both my parents are Scottish and I feel Scottish. I suppose it's just in my blood."

The final two entries are littered with phrases such as 'breakdowns', 'treatments', and 'comebacks'; 'surgery', 'grafts' and 'rehabilitation'. Gilzean documents his torturous attempts to return from injury and ambitions of playing for Scotland have been set to one side in favour of less lofty goals. "My aim for the season is obviously to not get injured," he says in October 1991, but by summer 1992 he had been released.

Ian Gilzean did not have the same impact at Dens Park or White Hart Lane as his old man, but linked a new generation of Dundee and Tottenham fans with the past. I remember my father, brother and I walking along Tottenham High Road brimming with anticipation on a summery Wednesday evening in 1987. There was an excited buzz in the air. It was the first home game of the season and big things were expected of the Spurs team which had finished third the previous season and reached the FA Cup final. Flicking through the programme as the teams warmed up before the Newcastle game, my dad stumbled upon a familiar name. "Ian Gilzean. I wonder if that's Alan's son?" he exclaimed. He said it with such surprise that I wondered if this Ian Gilzean was the second coming of Christ. "Was Alan Gilzean good?" I asked.

"Yeah, he was brilliant," said my dad, with a heavy emphasis on the 'yeah'.

§

I'm not sure exactly how many people are turning up to meet me at the Red House Hotel, but the car park is deserted. Admittedly, I am half an hour early and it gives me a chance to survey the scenery. The town is bigger than I had imagined, but not huge; two youths are sitting waiting on a bus across the road; a car drifts past every once in a while. Coupar Angus is what it is: a market town which once had a vibrant community but which is starting to fray around the edges. I look out towards the horizon and the hills and take in their splendour.

I spy two likely looking candidates at the entrance to the hotel restaurant on my left. One is Jim Lindsay, a Coupar Angus contact through a work colleague, who used to pick berries with Babs Gilzean. The other is Norrie Currie, one of Gillie's former team-mates from the Coupar Angus Boys Club. Jim tells me that Ian Mackenzie, Gillie's best man, is running late, but he will be along soon. Ron Ross arrives not long after and we're at a table having a drink when Ian makes his entrance.

The first thing I'm struck by is how young the men – all in their 60s or 70s – look. Ian and Norrie have either spent a lot of recent time on the golf course or are just back from holiday, given their tans. Each is grey haired, except for Ron who has brown hair and is smaller than the others. After a few minutes of small talk, I deliver my preamble. "Does anyone have a problem with any of what I have just said?"

"Well, I do," says Ian, raising his hand slightly. "Alan knows about the book and he's not interested in it, but I came here tonight to hear what you had to say. I feel Coupar Angus has forgotten about him. The least Coupar Angus town council could have done is name a street after him, but the simple matter is that Alan is not really interested in having a book written about him."

I impress again on Ian that I have nominated Alan for the Hall of Fame, I explain that Ian St John has earned his place at Hampden not just because he was a great player, but because his profile was raised by his television series.

"Which show was that?" asks Ian.

"Saint and Greavsie, the one with Jimmy Greaves."

"Of course." I mention the rumours about Gillie being a down-and-out.

"It's not true," all four men say in unison, shaking their heads. The alacrity with which they do so says one of two things: it's either utterly untrue or a well-rehearsed answer. What I hear next makes me think it is the former.

Norrie Currie tells me another story which demonstrates further the impact

Gilzean's decision to keep a low profile has had on his historical legacy. "There are times when I've gone to Coupar Angus Juniors matches and one of the coaches will say to me, 'Wait 'til you see this player or that player.' And I'll watch the player and afterwards the coach will come to me and ask, 'Well, what did you think?' I'll say, 'He's no Gilzean.' They'll reply, 'Who's Gilzean?' "

An idea is forming: Gilzean's reluctance to put himself in the spotlight has made him an unwitting victim. The dissemination of information on the Internet is a vast, unfettered practice. I had discovered plenty of wild rumours: Gillie had been killed in a freak car accident; he lived as a down-and-out; he had earned huge sums of money during the North Sea oil boom when the haulage company he worked for secured a lucrative contract to export equipment to Aberdeen. Another story said that he had emigrated to Canada; one claimed that he had extra-marital affairs and was threatened at least once; another that he placed a bet on Arsenal to win the double in 1971; still another suggested that he hadn't spoken to his brother Eric in decades.

One discrepancy I had been able to clear up was his date of birth, when an envelope from the Scottish public records office arrived in the post one day. It proved Gilzean was born on October 22, 1938 – and in Perth, not Coupar Angus. It was another example of how the Internet was capable of rewriting history, no matter how insignificant the detail or how innocently the mistake had come about.

The great irony was that in attempting to protect his privacy Gillie had merely added fuel to the rumours. This presented me with something of an ethical dilemma, none the less. If it was really Alan's wish not to have a book written about him then where did that leave me? A sanctimonious, self-appointed warrior for the truth on behalf of someone who didn't really care what was being said about him? It made my job just that little bit harder, too. By continuing to bang the drum about inaccuracies in his life, I was setting myself up for a hefty fall. My 'facts' had to be beyond reproach, and the problem when someone doesn't want to talk to you is that substantiating stories becomes doubly difficult. Furthermore, even Gillie got it wrong sometimes. For example, in Jim Hendry's book, Dundee Greats, he told the author he scored six times that day against Queen of the South in 1964 when he got seven. The history books and newspapers could not always be relied upon either. One report I read had Gillie claiming that the goalkeeper when he had scored his goal against England at Hampden had been Ron Flowers, but it was Gordon Banks. I resolved to trust my instincts. It was not my intention to paint a negative picture, far from it, I was attempting to breathe new life into the Gilzean legend.

The aim of the search had been to expose the down-and-out claim to ridicule, but I had uncovered a raft of other unsubstantiated rumours. Worse, Alan's legacy as a footballer had been lost to a generation of football supporters. His decision to shy away from the spotlight had robbed him and football of a lasting testimony. And yet here I was moving in ever-decreasing circles with the end of the book threatening to become a parody of its start.

The ethical debate could wait, though. For now I was enjoying the conversation inside the Red House Hotel.

The chat flits from one topic to another as each man recalls his favourite anecdote. It is an outpouring of memories not unlike the stories told by family members at a wake. Norrie remembers winning half a crown in a bet with a work colleague the day Scotland beat England at Hampden, when Gilzean scored. "I thought Scotland were going to win that day and I thought Alan was going to score. I said as much to my work-mate and he said, 'I'll bet you half a crown they don't.' I said, 'Let's make it a fiver,' but he said no and in the end it was a straight bet on Alan scoring."

John White comes up. "I don't think Alan would have gone to Tottenham if it hadn't been for John White, he had a big offer from Sunderland," adds Ian Mackenzie. "I think he spoke to Bobby Wishart about it and he gave him some tips and told him to move away. I have a great photo of him giving Irene a big diamond engagement ring a few days after he signed for Spurs." Ian pauses, he has realised I have picked up on what he is saying and says, "Alan will be phoning me on Sunday. If he is happy for me to let you have it, I will get your contact details and send it on." I was with Bobby Wishart last night you should try speaking to him." I recount the conversation that I'd had with Bobby in which he feigned amnesia. "Bobby's trying to protect Alan," said Ian. From what? I thought. I ask Ian whether he would be prepared to speak to me again and he says, "That will depend on what Alan says." I receive a similar response from Norrie. Later in the conversation the failed move to Canada is mentioned and again Ian stops without expanding further. It continues along more conventional lines.

"Some people used to think he was tight in Coupar, but he was very generous," says Ian. Norrie adds: "Aye, quite often he would say to me, 'Go up to the bar and buy everyone a drink.' He wouldn't do it himself; he didn't want to be seen as if he was being big time."

"There was never a problem if you needed tickets for the big European games either," says Jim. "You had to pay, but they were like gold-dust in those days."

The idea that Gilzean perceived himself as just one of the lads who happened to play football gets another airing.

Ian: "If you went out with him on the Saturday or Sunday night, he did not talk about football. He never really spoke much about what the job was like."

Norrie: "No, there were never any titbits about what was going on at Dundee."

I mention Hunter Davies' belief that Gilzean treated football like it was a job and didn't really enjoy the game. They agree with the former, not the latter.

I tell them one of the many rumours I have heard is the one about a local man turning down the chance to sign Gillie and The Beatles in the same week. "It's probably apocryphal," I say as the laughter dies down. "It's a true story," interrupts Ron Ross. "His name was Finlay Farquharson, he was my next-door neighbour. One day he came to me and asked whether there were any young players in the area worth looking at. I recommended Billy Forbes and Alan Gilzean. There was a trial match at Alyth and at the end of the game Finlay told me he had signed Billy and not Alan, because he thought Billy was the better prospect. A couple of nights later Finlay got a call from an agent who had this band in Liverpool and they wanted to know if Billy was interested in booking them. The agent asked for Finlay to pay for a night at the Commercial Hotel in Perth and he baulked at the expense. There is evidence of The Beatles having toured north-east Scotland at that time as The Quarrymen."

When it's time to leave I ask Ron if he will stay behind for a few minutes for a chat about how things had gone. "I think you might get somewhere with Ian Mackenzie," he says. "He seemed quite enthusiastic about the idea."

"Yeah, I got that impression, too," I say, as we shake hands in the car park and resolve to meet again for that walk around Coupar Angus.

§

When Gilzean returned to White Hart Lane for his testimonial, just a few short months after he had left, he was already having second thoughts about his move to South Africa. Martin Chivers notes in Big Chiv that when it was his turn to leave Spurs, in 1976, he had an opportunity to join Durban City and spoke to Gillie, who promptly told him he had hated his time in the country.

In 1974, though, Gilzean was still uncertain about what to do next. His testimonial was scheduled against Red Star Belgrade in the autumn and, while he had fallen just short of the required 10 years' service for his club, Tottenham had lobbied the Football Association for special dispensation. There was a wonderful sense of occasion at White Hart Lane for the arrival of the Yugoslav champions, who had waived an appearance fee and still contained a number of the players who had featured against Tottenham when the sides had met in the UEFA Cup, a few seasons earlier.

There was one extra special guest in attendance, too. Bill Nicholson had not been back at the club since he left in such depressing circumstances earlier that year, but he told the Tottenham Weekly Herald that Gilzean's return was something he would not have missed for the world. Asked why he was breaking his self-imposed exile, he revealed that he had received a phone call from Gillie in Johannesburg when news broke of his decision to step down as manager.

"Don't kick up any fuss because I'm returning," Nicholson added. "This is his night. I don't want to be noticed. I just hope he gets the kind of crowd he deserves. If every manager had a team of Gilzeans then I'm sure football in this country would not be in the state it's in. Not just from the point of view of his football ability but also because of the way he honoured his contracts. He was wonderful. He never argued or moaned. Once he signed, that was that. And Greaves was the just the same. He never got a penny more from Tottenham than he was entitled to."

I couldn't help but recall Steve Perryman's comment that Greaves had said Bill Nick expected Tottenham players to play for nothing. It was clear that Nicholson still had a huge soft spot for the G-Men and his comments no doubt were aimed at Chivers, who had been part of a revolt over contracts and bonus payments.

Chivers says Nicholson was furious when the players rejected a bonus system which he had expected them to accept without question. The players finally agreed to a scheme whereby they would receive £2 for every 1,000 supporters in the ground above 35,000. Before every home game, Chivers recalls Gillie would be surveying the stands as the teams ran out, trying to estimate how many were in.

It was further evidence of the blind spot Nicholson had for Gilzean, who was just as anxious as the rest of the players to ensure he got paid what he was worth. But then Nicholson was being interviewed on the eve of Gillie's testimonial and he was only ever going to say nice things. Not that his words were hollow or hyperbole.

Comparing Gillie to Greaves, he says: "They are natural, instinctive players. They have habits, which are virtually impossible to change. But these habits are the type that thrill the crowd. Gillie is expected to do the unexpected – that makes him such a great player."

In Nicholson's observation is something which demonstrates how much more difficult football is for attackers than defenders. The former must "do the unexpected", and so risk failure; defending is about doing what is expected and therefore easier.

There had been a rare, first-person piece from Gilzean in the Weekly Herald two weeks earlier, in which he talked about his experiences in South Africa and his forthcoming testimonial: "I just can't wait. The prospect of playing for Tottenham again makes me tingle with excitement. I've really enjoyed my first season in South African football and I intend to give it another season out there … but there's nothing like playing for a team of Tottenham's class. Everything is so different playing for Spurs.

"I had many happy days at Tottenham and regretted very much the time when I had to leave. Yet the prospects look good out in South Africa. We play in front of an average 15,000 people. But in some of the really big games, particularly when two of the top 'black' teams meet, the gates swell to 60,000. My team, Highlands Park, reached the final of the cup. But we lost. Our keeper made a couple of errors that cost the game – it's a shame I couldn't take Pat Jennings out there with me. At one time we looked as though we would clinch the league, but we eventually finished third. I'm looking forward to the new season, which gets under way at the end of January, which means I'll be back there at the start of the month for training. While you're all freezing in winter, I'll be lapping up the sun. The next season will probably be my last. The game has given me so much I'm seriously thinking of trying to give something back by becoming a coach or even a manager. But more than likely I'll settle for a business partnership with my brother, who is doing so well in America."

Gilzean never made it back to South Africa, however. For someone who enjoyed a drink, it seemed apt that Gillie should end up at a club called Highlands Park, just one 's' away from a famous Scottish malt whisky, but the marriage was a brief one. The set-up at Highlands Park was pretty impressive and certainly one of the best in South Africa at the time. They were the Manchester United of South Africa, even playing in red shirts, white shorts and black socks. This was a period of Gillie's life in which I'd been unable to uncover anything, but after months of searching I managed to track down one of his former team-mates. Martin Cohen was one of his country's best up-and-coming talents when he and Gillie's paths crossed in 1974.

His player biography on the Highlands Park website suggests he's almost worthy of a book himself. Today, he is a director of the largest paint outlet store in South Africa, but in the past he was an excellent midfielder who spent a season alongside George Best at Los Angeles Aztecs and won a number of domestic trophies at Highlands Park. He played for the White XI when South Africa staged a football competition split purely on ethnic lines in 1973. Cohen played with Phil Beal and Best's great cohort Bobby McAlinden at Aztecs. McAlinden introduced Best to Cohen and the pair hit it off instantly. He found it much more difficult to get close to Gillie.

"Alan is Alan," he tells me from his offices in Johannesburg. "He was a lovely person but a little bit strange. You could never get close to him. He never allowed you to get close to him. I still have a relationship with Phil Beal. We still keep in touch, but no-one knows where Alan is.

"He was like a ghost. You wouldn't see him for 89 minutes and then he would score the winning goal and, as he played on the pitch, so he was in life. When he partied, he partied. I didn't really socialise with him. I was 21, he was 30-odd and when there's that much difference in age you tend to stick together with ones your own age. There was a player who was out here at the same time called Barry Bridges. Barry played for Chelsea and he was probably closest to Alan during his time here."

The deal came about when the former East Stirlingshire player, Joe Frickleton, then Highlands Park manager, and one of his players, Charlie Gough (father of the future Scotland and Rangers captain Richard), went on a scouting trip to Britain. Years later, young Richard would wake to find himself staring at the club's latest signing in the bed opposite. "There were always footballers around the house," Gough told the Evening Times in August 2004. "In fact, I can remember waking up one morning and seeing this bald head sticking out from under the duvet in the spare bed in my room. I said to myself: 'Who's that?' It turned out to be the Dundee, Spurs and Scotland legend Alan Gilzean. He had been for a night out with my dad."

It is tempting to speculate on what Gillie said to Gough, whose career would follow a similar path: he played for Dundee United, Spurs and Scotland. Perhaps Gillie recommended he sign for Rangers if he wanted a long international career.

It was something of a culture shock for Gillie. His professional days were at an end, he was in a new country and he was expected to work four days a week for the Highlands Park chairman, who owned a car dealership. "Don't forget," says Cohen, "we weren't full-time players. The guys worked in the day. The players who came from overseas worked selling cars during the day and then they went training at night for four nights a week. Working in the day and training at night."

Why did he leave South Africa after just a few months? Well, it seems fairly incongruous picturing Gillie as a car salesman. He kept himself to himself and, notwithstanding his easy manner and friendly disposition, it was clear he displayed none of the flamboyance or arrogance needed to sell cars.

He was alone too. He was living in a comfortable apartment in the Hillbrow district of Johannesburg. It was a place where most of the nightlife went on in the city. Irene and the kids remained in London, but Cohen said Gillie rarely talked about home. "You could never sit down with him and have a conversation about his family. It was always 'have a joke, have a drink'."

But the one thing that Martin did learn about Alan is that, despite his age, he was still capable of stopping time on the pitch. "I learned so much from Alan Gilzean; he had such a good first touch. People said that Eric Cantona and Glenn Hoddle had so much time and space, Gilzean was like that. I used to wonder why it always looked like he had time on the ball and I quickly realised it was because his first touch was so good. Before the ball came to him, he was always thinking about what he was going to do next and you need a good first touch to do that. He was such a silky player."

Martin ended with the usual request: "Can you pass on my telephone number to him or email me his if you are speaking to him?"

Cohen and other members of the Highlands Park team were in the crowd of 22,239 on the night of November 28 for Gillie's testimonial at White Hart Lane against Red Star Belgrade. The Dundee Evening Telegraph reported that not everything went to plan off the pitch. A fire at half-time in the tea room set aside for the after-match reception resulted in two fire engines being called out. But on the pitch, despite Terry Neill making seven changes during the second half and disrupting the game as a spectacle, it was a night for reflection and for celebration.

The Weekly Herald had run a competition in the build-up which requested readers to write in with their memories of Gilzean, one child admitting that the reason he liked Gillie was because he "was one of the few players who could make my dad shout out in support" and "[he] would always find time to sign autographs and chat to young supporters at the training ground". The best entries would receive a football from the great man before kick-off and Harry Harris, then a jobbing reporter on the local paper, would help with the presentation.

He recalled in his book, Tottenham Hotspur Greats, many years later: "One self-conscious, very nervous individual – myself – walked on to the pitch in front of thousands of Gilly's admirers in the stadium with a bag full of balls. Gilzean, the old grey fox of Spurs now with tufts of grey hair above both ears, stood in the centre circle handing out prizes as the proud youngsters' names were announced. I didn't know it at the time, as I was totally wrapped up in the presentation, but one fan rushed onto the pitch dodging the stewards and police to fall before Gilly … and kiss his boots."

Harris only realised he had missed this incident of worship when he saw the picture in the London Evening News the following day. "The story is not intended to illustrate my journalistic incompetence, but to demonstrate the sheer affection with which Spurs fans held Alan Gilzean."

The match programme contained the thoughts of several influential journalists including those of Ken Jones and Frank McGhee.

"The man is one of those rare ones with a style all of his own, completely original and not the product of some stereotyped coaching system. He reminds me of no other player I've ever seen and I doubt whether I will ever be lucky enough to see another who reminds me of him," said McGhee.

Jones was equally effusive: "The padding run, the glide over the ground which is the hallmark of good movers – as it was with Di Stéfano – sometimes loses its smoothness. But the good days are still plentiful and there is no need to apologise for including Alan Gilzean among my favourite footballers."

But perhaps the most stirring valedictory message belonged to Peter Batt, the eminent London sportswriter and latterly a scriptwriter for the BBC television soap EastEnders. "Of all the British footballers I have seen over the past 10 years, Gilzean gave the most highly-personalised entertainment value that could only be matched by the likes of Greaves, Law and Best ... We may never see the likes of him again. And if that isn't worth a tear or two we should all put the shutters up."

The crowd chanted for Gillie repeatedly that night as Spurs won 2-0. All the old songs were sung and he gave the supporters plenty of reason to cheer with a goal. But this was no mere stage-managed exercise. Gilzean passed up the opportunity to get on the scoresheet in the 61st minute when Alfie Conn was brought down in the penalty area. Steve Perryman ushered Gillie forward, the crowd chanted "we want Gillie", but he declined; Cyril Knowles – by then one of Gillie's best friends at Spurs – scored, following up his saved kick. "I was dead scared I would miss it," Gilzean said. "But Cyril was playing well and I wanted him to have it."

It was typical Gillie – diffidence, generosity and more than a touch of humility. Ten minutes later he got the goal the supporters had been waiting for, side-footing in from Knowles' low cross from the left. "Just look how they reacted after I scored. I was really glad to get that goal," he said.

Meanwhile, the news that Gilzean was home from South Africa permanently came as a surprise to those north of the border who were still following his career with interest, a set of fans who had never forgotten him at Dens Park.

"Contrary to the widely held belief that he has gone back to South Africa to play for Highland Park [sic], the club he was with last season," wrote Tommy Gallacher in the Courier and Advertiser on January 24, 1975, "Alan Gilzean is still in this country and living at his London home. And there is the distinct possibility that the former Dundee, Spurs and Scotland star may not, after all, be going back to South Africa. I spoke to Gillie at his home yesterday and he was still in the process of tying up all the loose ends in connection with his testimonial match in which Spurs played Red Star Belgrade at the end of November. He expected it to take another couple of weeks yet before everything was settled and even after that he still wasn't sure what he would be doing football-wise.

" 'I am in no hurry to decide where my immediate future lies,' he told me. 'I have had offers from America and Australia and, of course Highlands Park want me back in South Africa to play for them again. But I haven't made up my mind and won't be doing so until everything in connection with my testimonial has been settled.' "

Gilzean was well rewarded for his decade with Spurs and his testimonial was reported to be worth around £16,000 to him. He had time to weigh up what he was going to do next. However, he had already ruled out a return north to Scotland because of an injury and was pondering his options outside of football.

"Only last month Arbroath were foiled in an attempt to get Gilzean to play for them even for a few games before he was meant to go back to South Africa," wrote Tommy Gallacher. "But their bid failed because Gillie was suffering from a groin strain. Now that Albert Henderson knows that Gilzean is having second thoughts about returning to South Africa, he will almost certainly be in touch with the player again to spotlight the attraction that playing at Gayfield could have for him, although the north-east coast may not sound as exotic as the other choices at his fingertips."

There was nothing particularly glamorous about his next destination, however. In March 1975, he was being courted by Stevenage Athletic, whose ground was approximately 30 miles away from Gillie's home in Enfield. Jimmy Burton, his old friend from his early days at Tottenham, was the chairman at the Southern League club and wanted a big name to take over as manager. The pair watched a league match against Witney, after which Gilzean, pictured in the local press signing an autograph for a young fan, fag dangling from the edge of his mouth, was noncommittal. "I haven't made up my mind," he said when asked if he was going to take over as manager.

Another report claimed that Gilzean, "currently a licensee of a pub in Enfield", had been invited to take a seat on the board by Burton. While Gilzean confessed to being reasonably impressed with the set-up at Stevenage, he felt he was "too old and that his best days were behind him" when asked by Burton if he would pull his boots on again. The move neared a step closer when the Stevenage manager left a fortnight later. But Gillie was, according to reports, "in the United States".

"Gillie and I have talked at length about the prospects of Stevenage since his visit to Broadhall Way two weeks ago," said Jimmy Burton. "I had hoped he would join us this week but he is still in the United States, so we must wait a little longer. We need a big name in Stevenage and I am doing my utmost to secure at least one."

His powers of persuasion clearly worked. Gilzean eventually agreed to take over at Stevenage on July 1, following further talks. "Gillie has agreed to join us and that is good enough for me … as far as I am concerned he is our new manager."

One journalist, David Leggat, told me there were no sides to Gilzean. Another, Ken Jones of the Daily Mirror, concurred: "When he first came down to Tottenham the players used to go the Astor Club in Oxford Street and it was the haunt of certain unsavoury types. Gillie used to say, 'I'm getting this, I'm getting this,' when it came to buying a drink. I don't mean these people would have taken money out of your pocket, but they knew what they were doing. I had to tell him to watch himself."

He had learned a lesson during his very earliest days in London to steer clear of the hangers-on. But Jimmy Burton was different. He was a mate, they had gone back a long way and it is probably why Gillie ended up as manager of Stevenage. It helped, too, that Ricky Prosser, another mate, was involved with the club. Nevertheless, it seems that Gillie was there more as a favour to Burton than for any great ambitions about becoming the next Brian Clough. He had gone on record in The Glory Game as saying management was not for him. That he ended up at Stevenage, a club with no money and in the depths of non-league football, seemed all the more incongruous.

Phil Ravitz, sports editor of the Stevenage Comet for more than 20 years, remembers his time in charge as disastrous. "He knew as much about Southern League football as I know about aeronautical engineering. One day we were due to play a game at Ashford in Kent and he turned up at Ashford in Middlesex. It was quite embarrassing. He had been a tremendous player, but he could not transfer the skills of being a top-class footballer to the specific demands of non-league football. It was a shambles, but in fairness to him the club was in a bit of a state when he took over."

Stevenage had finished the 1974-75 season 11th in the Southern League Division 1 (North) and there was optimism over Gilzean's appointment, but his reign got off to a bad start when Burton was convicted of handling counterfeit money at the Old Bailey and was sentenced to two years in prison. An administrative oversight involving player registrations ended with three key members of the squad defecting to Cambridge City, while the failure to fulfil a fixture against Merthyr Tydfil resulted in a £100 fine and almost cost the club its place in the league.

It was as abysmal on the pitch. After an average start, Stevenage failed to record a single league win between November and April and when they lost 8-0 at Merthyr Tydfil in the last game of the 1975-76 season it confirmed what had been long known: they were the worst team in the league and Gilzean was out of his depth.

When Burton was released from prison, there was talk that he was trying to reunite the G-Men by signing Jimmy Greaves, but talk is all it was. Stevenage's wage budget for the entire club was £30. Ravitz says that Burton had surrounded himself with some "dubious characters". Their presence helped drive the club out of existence. When we speak, a reformed Stevenage team have just won promotion to the English football league for the first time in their history.

"They will finish in the top-10 next season in League Two, they might even go up and they will get 3,500 every other week. It's an upwardly mobile place and it's a growing town. It's also 35 miles from London, so there are no big clubs on the doorstep," says Ravitz. "The potential at the club is massive and even Jimmy Burton recognised that 35 years ago."

Gilzean lasted less than a year during which time one of Burton's acolytes, a

Maltese businessman named Javier Revuelta, assumed control of the club. Gillie, though, had long gone by the time that sorry saga had run its course. He announced on August 11, 1976 that he was leaving, citing the club's uncertain future. On the same day, Revuelta admitted that he was going to sell Broadhall Way. He had plans for the redevelopment of the ground which included a Sunday market and the installation of a dog track. When a few diehard club members tried to keep the football team going, the businessman ordered excavators to dig a foot-deep trench through the middle of the pitch. Ultimately, with the club in significant debt, it spelt the end. A new entity, Stevenage Borough, would eventually emerge from the rubble.

Graeme Aslett, a player during Gilzean's tenure at the club, remembers his time in charge with fondness, but concedes his memories have little to do with football. "Sometimes Gillie would announce after 10 minutes that it was too cold and that training would be held in the bar," he says. And when I ask him what Jimmy Burton thought of all this, he adds: "He would have been in there waiting on us. I think it must have been a favour to Jimmy Burton. He could be very persuasive, Jimmy. I can't imagine Alan would have applied for the job if it had come up."

Despite the lack of training sessions, there were times when Graeme caught glimpses of the ability which had made Gilzean a terrace idol. "I'm a Spurs fan and Gillie was a hero of mine," says Aslett, who recalls that Gilzean was working for a haulage company in Edmonton at the time. "He played in the first match I ever watched against Arsenal at Highbury, so I loved him being manager. He must have been about 36 but he was still a class player. We were playing five-a-side once and there was this ball hit up from the back. I thought, 'He's not getting that.' I just tried to get close to him, anyway, and then he was down on his knees and nodding the ball straight into my path and I didn't even have to move. It was the kind of precision that a snooker player gets on the ball. It was incredible."

Aslett recalls the players being asked to play in a match at Aylesbury prison, where Burton was serving his time. "It was a home game for them," jokes Graeme. "Terry Venables played for us and so did Malcolm Allison. Tommy Harmer, the former Tottenham forward from the 1950s, was referee. I remember looking across at Terry Venables and Malcolm Allison in the dressing room thinking, 'What are you doing here?' But he was a popular character, Jimmy, we all liked him. We must have done to go and play a game at a prison for him."

§

Not long after my meeting with Gillie's Coupar Angus pals, I receive an email from

Ian Mackenzie, his best man, subject 'Alan G'. It reads:

Just a quickie. Alan phoned me today. After some discussion I think I can say he is quite amenable to progressing the book proposal. I gave him your home and mobile numbers and he will get in touch with you.

He will be up here at the end of the month (staying with Ian) so it would seem a propitious time to meet him.

I'll email some early photos to you and these can be used as, and if, required. I would think you will have access to those footballing ones already in the public domain. I'll pen some 'early day' biographical notes and again you can use these as you think appropriate or not at all!

I've attached two scout ones just to see if this emailing of them is okay at your end.

Regards, Ian

PS Alan is the "wee lad"

When I open the attachment, I am overwhelmed. There are two Alan Gilzean 'originals'. I feel like an art collector who has just uncovered two Picassos in a thrift shop. One shows Gillie kitted out for Coupar Angus Boy Scouts. 'Wee' doesn't do the picture of Gillie justice. He looks like a 10-year-old called up to play for the Under-18s. Indeed, the average age of the squad appears to be 30. Old photos have that curious quality of making the subjects look much older than they are – or perhaps that was symptomatic of harsher times. The second picture captures Gillie and Ian at Sandringham for a jamboree to mark the coronation. There is a wide-eyed innocence about Alan as he smiles for the camera, hand on hip. It is not unlike the pose on the cover of this book.

Then it happened one Saturday afternoon. It was the day after I had been to see Ian Ure and I was just heading out for a game of golf. The phone rang and I knew who it was going to be. I can't explain that, now; I just knew.

"Hullo, can I speak to James Morgan," said a hoarse yet soft, voice which was undeniably from the east coast of Scotland.

"Speaking," I said, absolutely certain now of what was coming next.

"It's Alan Gilzean," came the reply at the other end of the line.

13

RETURN OF THE KING

Tuesday 21, July 2009. I am driving north past the same road signs that I've passed many times before: Stirling, Perth, Longforgan, Coupar Angus, Dundee. I could do this drive in my sleep. It is a few weeks after I spoke to Gillie's Coupar Angus pals and I've already made this trip to speak to Alan Cousin and Pat Liney. I will embark on it many more times in the months that will follow.

The reason for my trip is to ask Alan Gilzean for permission to write a book about him. It feels onerous when it should feel like fun because I'm worried about what he might say. We had three conversations in the weeks after that initial phone call and in two he said he didn't want to be involved.

"I can tell you this now. I'm not interested in doing a book," he said on the first day we spoke.

I had been caught off guard by the phone call, even though I knew it was coming. I told him I was trying to get him into the SFA Hall of Fame. Gillie asked who was in the Hall of Fame and I struggled to tell him, surreptitiously looking up their website. John White was as far as I got.

"Great player," he said before asking if Jim Baxter was there.

"I'm not sure, I replied, I'll have a look on the website."

"Ach, it doesn't matter," he said.

His voice was surprisingly high-pitched, rising and falling as he emphasised certain words. Age and cigarette smoke had taken their toll. I had run through this conversation in my head many times. On each occasion, Gillie was a gruff, no-nonsense Scot. I couldn't have cast him any less accurately.

I asked him about Tottenham. "Great club. They're the first result I look for every Saturday. I look for three teams: Dundee, Hibernian, because they were my team as a boy, and Tottenham. Harry Redknapp's done a great job this season in keeping them up. I'd love to see them back in the top four."

I asked him if he had been back at Spurs and was surprised by the answer. "Yeah, I went back to see Ian play and was there for Bill Nicholson's testimonial. I never really enjoyed watching football, it was never the same as playing. I loved playing."

I could hear cars drifting past in the background and had this mental picture of Gillie huddled into a phone box at the sea front at Weston-super-Mare.

"Are you up in Scotland?" I asked.

"No, I'm down in Weston-super-Mare. I'm going be up at Ian's for six weeks over the summer. I'll come and meet you then."

We'd ended the call with me fairly optimistic that he was onside but, the following day, Alan phoned again and asked whether I was writing a book about his life.

I said, "Yes, sort of".

"Well, I was speaking to my pal and he says you are out of order, he said that you haven't asked for my permission and that you didn't even offer me terms."

I asked if he thought I was out of order and he didn't really answer me. "I had offers 30 years ago, people you've probably never heard of. Reg Drury of the News of the World, and I've had recent offers from Norrie Price, the Dundee club historian, and a guy I used to play cricket with, Ian Pattullo, his son Alan is a journalist."

I told him that it was not my intention to stitch him up, that I was writing the book for the right reasons. His low profile had denied him his rightful place in the Hall of Fame and that if someone like Ian St John, who hadn't won as many trophies and hadn't scored as many goals for Scotland, was there then he should be too.

"I don't know about that. Ian St John was a great player. Your father was a Spurs fan and you're a Spurs fan. You're biased. It's not really for you to decide who should be in the Hall of Fame," he countered. But he was wrong.

"It's exactly for people like me to decide," I replied. "I can vote for you. The Hall of Fame invites nominations from members of the public and then the committee members sit down and discuss the nominations."

That seemed to be a bit of a breakthrough. I asked for his telephone number and he refused, but he seemed more open to the possibility of the book now.

"Only seven people in the country have my telephone number," he said. I reckoned I had spoken to at least three: Ian Gilzean, Bobby Wishart and Ian Mackenzie.

"Well, I don't expect to be invited into that select group," I replied.

"You never know, one day you might have my number … if we do the book."

The previous day I told Gillie how he'd been one of my father Jim's heroes.

"Pass on my regards to your father," he said.

"My father died 10 years ago this year," I replied. My father is the reason I support Tottenham. It was only after I left Northern Ireland that I realised the incongruity of supporting a team I could never watch live, and was not part of my community.

"I'm sorry to hear that," Gillie said. "You have my condolences on that."

"That's part of the reason why I'm writing the book."

"Look, I'll come and speak to you and you can try to persuade me."

We've agreed to meet in Ian Gilzean's house at midday, but I'm 10 minutes early. I draw up at a set of roadworks and think about the meeting ahead. I'm trying to detach myself: I'm here as a journalist, not a Tottenham fanatic. There are so many strands of his story that remain dangling and, like a prissy housewife, I am just dying to tidy them up. I have literally hundreds of questions to ask Gillie but I'm aware that this isn't going to be one of those meetings. I have already resolved to leave my notebook in my bag. This isn't an interview, it's a sales pitch and how that pitch goes will most probably depend on whether he gives his full co-operation to the book. If he does, the interviews can start then. When I draw up to the house, I try to compose myself; my hands are sweaty as I make my way to the front door and ring the doorbell.

I hear a gate unlocking at the rear of the house and I edge around the corner of the porch to see Gillie sauntering towards me. It is the saunter Steve Perryman would reference months later when I met him in Maidenhead. You see, in many ways this was the end of my search, even though it had happened near the start. The phone call to my home was Alan Gilzean finding me, rather than the other way around. I'd already met Gillie when old John with the hook nose told me that Alan was a very sick man and didn't want a book written about him.

Gillie doesn't look sick. He looks like Gillie. He sticks out a hand and says, "Alan Gilzean." A large labrador accompanies him and barks angrily a few times. "He can be funny sometimes around people he doesn't know."

We go through the garden gates and up the back steps into Ian Gilzean's kitchen. One of the first things I notice is Gillie's shoes. He's wearing an expensive pair of Karrimor walking boots. They are not the shoes of a down-and-out. He's wearing a pair of deliberately faded jeans and a blue and white striped t-shirt. The hair is almost gone completely, save for a few white tufts at the sides. He wears a pair of those glasses that change shade depending on the light.

"Do you want a cup of tea?" he asks.

"I'd love one," I reply. "Do you have any dogs?" I ask, thinking back to Alan

Pattullo's article in The Scotsman which said Gillie spent his days walking on the beach in Weston-super-Mare with his dogs.

"I used to have one, but it died. Do you want a biscuit?"

"No, I'm okay."

"Are you sure?"

"Yeah, thanks."

He stirs some powdered milk into my cup and offers me the sugar. I decline.

"We'll sit down over there," he says pointing towards a pine table and chairs.

"I don't think there's a market for a book," he begins. "Too much time has passed since I played."

"I think it could be a great book. You were a great player. Jimmy Greaves says you were one of the greatest players he ever played with."

"That's Jimmy. He said that because he's just a nice man. I was a good player, but I wasn't a great player. Wayne Rooney is a good player, Cristiano Ronaldo is a great player."

Cristiano Ronaldo has just joined Real Madrid for a world record fee, while Rooney has had a 'good', but not 'great' season. Rooney will end the following campaign as player of the year.

"But there are people who would want to read a book about Wayne Rooney."

"Aye, maybe. Ian thinks I should do a book, Kevin doesn't mind either way. I wasn't sure where you were going with your first chapter."

My original first chapter was a fairly self-indulgent piece about me, the death of my father and how my brother became a big name in the Irish League. When I reflected on it, I realised no-one other than me would be interested in it.

"You've read it? I didn't expect to speak to you. What I was trying to do was detail how I arrived at the point where I was writing a book about Spurs and here I am now speaking to you." I'm not making much sense.

"What happened to you as a footballer?" he asks.

A few training sessions with Bangor and Crusaders. A scout from Reading watched me four or five times.

"I was too interested in having a drink and women, but I wasn't good enough, if I'm honest. My brother was much more dedicated."

"There was a kid at Spurs, Paul Shoemark. He was an England youth internationalist. Big, big things were expected of him, but he couldn't make the step up. You get that with some players," he says to me.

Paul Shoemark made one reserve team appearance for Tottenham. It was significantly closer than I ever got to making it as a footballer.

224

The talk turns to newspapers. "I haven't spoken to the press for years," he says. "A journalist wrote an article one time in which he quoted me as saying that Tottenham were right to get rid of George Graham because he had done nothing at Spurs. The journalist never even spoke to me. So, now, when journalists look for me I tell them I'm not interested. I didn't really speak to the press as a player. I tell Ian just to say I'm not interested. What did he say to you?"

He's looking at me directly, now. He doesn't look much older than he did when he was at Spurs. An advantage, I suppose, of looking older when you're younger.

"He said that to me, but I think I might have had a bit of leeway because he knew my brother."

"Possibly."

I show Gillie an excerpt from a play about Jock Stein and Bill Shankly which had aired on Radio Scotland a few weeks previously. He is genuinely surprised when I tell him he was mentioned favourably in it. "Was ah?" he asks, his voice once again rising in that peculiarly east coast of Scotland manner.

Stein: Bob's a good man.

Shankly: He is, yes.

Stein: That team he put together at Dundee, beautiful stuff, the way
to play.

Shankly: Gifted players ...

Stein: Great wing-men

Shankly: Playing for the jersey

Stein: And Gilzean ...

Shankly: Aye, what a player ...

I show Gillie print-outs from the SFA Hall of Fame. He expresses surprise that Gordon Smith, his team-mate at Dundee, is not there. I risk a question not related to the nuts and bolts of the book. Ian Ure told me to ask Gillie who his favourite player was. Ian felt sure Gillie would say Dave Mackay.

"Naw, it was Jimmy Greaves. He was a class player. There's a picture of us playing England and Ian Ure and Jimmy are running for the ball. Every muscle is standing out on Ian's neck and Jimmy is just starting to move away from him. He was like lightning. He had this lovely style of pushing the ball away from him, just a yard. You know the way Messi just keeps it ahead of him but no-one can get near him? He was the best player I ever played with. Some of the goals he scored were unbelievable. It was a sad day for everyone at Spurs when Jimmy Greaves left."

We talk for almost two hours, the conversation bouncing about. I ask him about Bill Nicholson and he tells me that he was "just a great man" and that there were three other managers who had impressed him most.

"The first was Tommy Walker, the Hearts manager. He spoke to me once before a game at Dens, before I had broken into the first team. I was gathering up balls during the warm-up and as I came off the pitch he started asking me how I was.

"The second was a Celtic manager, Jimmy McGrory. I remember him standing on the sideline and puffing on this great, big pipe. He was holding court with everyone around him in this real Irish brogue. I'll always remember what he said: 'It's great to see all these people here. We're really looking forward to the game, I think both teams are going to put on a real show of good football for them.' And then, as I walked past, he said, 'Hello there,' as if I was an old friend. I wasn't even in the first team at this stage. He didn't need to do that, but it was a measure of the man.

"And the last manager was Matt Busby. I'd just signed for Spurs and I was walking towards the entrance of White Hart Lane, when all of a sudden, he appeared beside me with his arm outstretched and said, 'I just wanted to congratulate you on your move and to wish you all the best.' Those three, as well as Bill Nicholson, will always stand out in my mind because each of them took the time to speak to me at a time when I wasn't as well known as they were. I didn't want to go into management. I saw what it did to Bill Nicholson and thought, 'It's not for me'. I tried it at Stevenage when I came back from South Africa but I didn't enjoy it."

It is easy to see why Steve Perryman was so enchanted with Gillie's tales from the past. He has an easy story-telling style; it is not hard to picture the scenes, and they have an added lustre simply because they are coming from him.

I have the Hunter Davies article from the New Statesman with me. The theory was that it might provoke him into agreeing to do the book. The point size of the text is tiny and he holds it close to his face as he squints to read it.

"I've never been dead lazy in my life … 'Jump in the car for a paper' … that's just not true."

"I think this is your chance to answer him back," I tell Gillie.

"I don't want to stoop to his level," he says. "Frank Lampard phoned a radio station in London recently after he was criticised for walking out on his partner and two children. In the end, I think he just dropped to their level.

"Hunter Davies came to see me at my house when he was writing The Glory Game. We sat in the back garden and had a beer and he said to me, 'I see they've signed Ralph Coates. Are you worried about your place?' I think he was trying to get a reaction out of me. But I said to him, 'No, I'm not worried about my place. He'll not get my place.' And he didn't. They said Ralph was the next Bobby Charlton. He was a good player but he didn't come close to Charlton.

"We were coming back on the train from an away game and all the boys had had a few cans of beer. Suddenly the doors opened and in walks Hunter Davies. We were sitting either side of the carriage and there was a table at the window. The table was in front of me and all the boys were putting their empty cans on it to make it look like I had drank them all. He put it in the bloody book."

Alan had other problems with The Glory Game. Davies paints the picture that he had access all areas and that the players came to regard him as one of them. Gillie remembers it differently. "Mike England had a party one night. Olivia Newton-John was there and she was with a singer, I can't remember his name. Hunter Davies was there; I don't know how he got there, whether Mike had invited him or he had just invited himself, but we were all saying to each other, 'What's he doing here?' "

But journalists had not been all bad to Gilzean over the years. In the course of the conversation I happen to mention Jim Rodger's name and Gillie's eyes light up.

"Ah Jim Rodger," he says. "They called him Scoop. He was this wee fat man who always wore a bowler hat. He got me my move to Spurs. He got a lot of players moves to English clubs. He told me that Spurs and Arsenal were interested in me. He said he had spoken to Billy Wright about me but years later I asked Billy if he'd ever spoken to Jim and he told me no." He laughs at the memory. He's enjoying himself and later in the conversation he tells me as much.

"I must say it's nice to talk intelligently about football for once," he says.

I repeat the question about going back to Tottenham and it's clear he still retains huge affection for the club. "I still watch Spurs. On Sky, whenever they are on live.

"It's a mixed squad. I like Jermaine Jenas but he should score more goals. I like Woodgate, he's very good. Wee Lennon, I thought he would go on to become like wee Jinky [Jimmy Johnstone] but he's never really developed – his final ball is too wayward. Modric is a bit too lightweight."

When we meet, Spurs are being linked with Arjen Robben, the Real Madrid winger who would, that summer, join Bayern Munich, but Gillie is dismissive. "He won't come. When I was down there, there were five teams who were always at the top: Liverpool, Manchester United, Tottenham, Arsenal and Everton. Now it's four."

It is July 2009. By the end of the forthcoming season Spurs will have qualified for the Champions League. Jonathan Woodgate and Jermaine Jenas will play little or no part in the campaign through injury, while Aaron Lennon and Luka Modric will play instrumental roles in securing the very thing that had prevented Tottenham from signing players like Robben over the years: Champions League football. The closest

Tottenham got to a marquee signing in the wilderness years since their FA Cup win in 1991 were Jürgen Klinsmann, David Ginola and, arguably, Dimitar Berbatov.

"What do you think of Berbatov?"

Gillie's eyes narrow slightly as if he's savouring the question. "Yeah, very good," he says. "Great touch."

Gillie looks like he's starting to tire and I tell him I've taken up enough of his time. I hand him an envelope with details from the publisher about terms and conditions. He skims through it before setting the pages down and saying: "I'm very impressed by everything you've had to say. I'll have a word with my boys and see what they think. I go back down south in the middle of August. I will let you know my decision on the first. To be honest, I'm not really interested in the Hall of Fame. It doesn't really matter to me. I would have played football for my local team, Coupar Angus Juniors, if I hadn't played for Tottenham or Dundee."

I feel certain Gillie is being disingenuous. Why had he shown so much interest in the Hall of Fame when we first spoke about it? That aside I'm quietly pleased with how things have gone. My hundred-odd questions can wait for another time. We stand outside in the driveway chatting for a short while afterwards. Me not wanting to miss out on a single story, and him enjoying the chance to relive the past.

Ian Ure and I had a debate about which foot Gillie used. I said right, he said left. It was a testament to how good both were that neither of us could say definitively; not me from watching old footage, nor Ian from having played with him for five years. "I was right-footed," he tells me, "but I worked and worked with my left until it was stronger than my right." Another one in the eye to the theory that he was lazy.

As I replayed the conversation over and over again in my head, I was delighted with how it had gone. But there would be no explanation about how his marriage with Irene ended or why he finished up in Weston-super-Mare.

And so I waited, replaying the conversation in my head. When August finally arrived I had convinced myself that it was only a matter of Gillie signing the contract. I was to be disappointed. When I reflect on it now, though, I realise Gillie meeting me had been out of character. Saying 'no' was more like him. "I've given it a lot of thought and it's not for me, but I'll have a think about it over the next couple of months and if I change my mind you'll be the first person I come to."

A few days later, I phoned Gillie back and tried to convince him one last time. "I know you have spent a lot of time on this, but I wouldn't like to go into a bookstore and look up at the shelves and see a book about me," he said.

The following Saturday, Alan Gilzean took in Dundee's first league game of the new First Division season against Morton. A new, wealthy owner was in situ at Dens Park and plenty of money had been lavished on the team. Gillie, who attended the game with his grandson, saw his former club win 1-0 but, unlike Tottenham, it would be a season that would end in heartache for Dundee, who missed out on promotion to the Scottish Premier League despite leading the table for most of the season.

Like Norrie Price when he had discovered Gillie had signed for Tottenham, I tried to erase him from my mind. But I could not. I weighed up the ethics of writing a book about someone who did not want a book written about him. The only way I could reconcile this was by convincing myself that carrying on was the right thing to do, and that my reason for writing it was a worthy one.

§

As he stepped forward to accept his SFA Hall of Fame award at Glasgow's Hilton Hotel on November 15 2009, Alan Gilzean told the guests that it was the best night of his life in sport.

I missed it as I was convinced that he would be a no-show. I gave up a ticket and decided to work at my office instead. At 9pm, I took a call from our Chief Sportswriter, Hugh MacDonald, who said Alan was there and what he had said. Gilzean's opinion of the Hall of Fame contrasted greatly from what he had told me and yet I knew which I believed. He had been too persistent when he asked questions about it for there not to have been a part of him that was proud of the achievement.

Graeme Souness, his former Tottenham team-mate, told the story about the time Gillie had pulled him aside and told him the two Scots had to stick together. Craig Brown, his former Dundee colleague, was on the stage and one of the first things he said was that Gillie was too modest. He was right.

I waited for my break at 11 o'clock and then made my way to the Hilton Hotel. I stood outside the main doors for 20 minutes waiting for Hugh to pick up my voice messages and get me in, not sure whether to just brass-neck it. An assortment of faces from Scottish football filed past – Souness, Mo Johnston, Gordon Smith, the then SFA chief executive (Gillie's old team-mate of the same name died in 2004), and others. Then I recognised Kenny Strang, the collections manager at the SFA museum, where I had spent two long days collating match reports.

"He's here," said Kenny. "Do you want me to introduce you?"

"Yeah, I've heard. Does he know about the book?"

"Yes, he was talking to Ian St John about it earlier."

"What did he say?"

"Well he told me he wasn't really that fussed about it, but then I heard him talking to Ian St John and I thought 'Hold on, perhaps maybe he's okay with it.' I'll tell him you're here."

"No, hold on a minute. I want to go and see for myself."

It took me all of two minutes to find Gillie in a banquet hall of over 300 people. There was a small group crowded around him, hanging on his every word. I wanted to stride forward and say, 'Hi Alan,' but my feet were stuck in cement.

Again, I looked at his shoes. They were expensive-looking, made from Italian leather from what I could tell. He was the picture of sartorial elegance in his tux.

I sought out Kenny again and I found him having a pint at the bar.

"What did he say when you phoned him about the Hall of Fame?" I asked.

"He asked me if I was sure I had got the right guy?"

"What did you say to that?"

" 'Fuck's sake Gillie, you're a legend,' " said Kenny, laughing. "Come on, I'll introduce you."

The group was still gathered around him asking questions, all wanting a bit of him. For the first time, I was aware of what it must be like. Someone always wanting you, pulling on your sleeve, patting you on the back or even asking to write a book about you. We shook hands and exchanged pleasantries. I told him I was delighted for him and then he excused himself so that he could finish off his conversation.

He turned side-on to me, so that I was on his left and the group was on his right. I noticed him looking out of the corner of his eye just to check that I was still there and when he finished talking he turned to face me.

"Have you been working hard?" he asked. I think he meant the book, but I had told myself that I wasn't going to talk about the book. This was his night and I didn't wanted to appear opportunistic.

"I'm actually working tonight," I told him.

"Are you?" he asked in that lilting voice. "I was looking for you at the start of the night. I thought you would be here. I thought it would be ex-footballers here but it's mostly press men."

"I'm on my break, I just came down to tell you how chuffed I am for you," I said, sounding like a Spurs fan rather than a press man. "I hear Graeme Souness made a nice speech about you. He was a sore one for us to lose. Apparently he gave Bill Nicholson a hard time demanding a first-team place."

"Aye, he was never out of that office," Gillie said, smiling at the memory.

A drunk ambled his way towards us, swaying from side to side before dropping his pen. He offered Gillie a scrap of paper.

"You're drunk. I've already signed it for you," said Gillie, stooping for the pen.

He attempted to take a picture of Gilzean, but couldn't work his camera phone. All the while, he was looking at me and, just as I thought he was going to ask me if I wanted a fight, he turned to Gillie and said: "Is this your laddie, Mr Gilzean?" Alan and I exchanged a look. What was it? Both identifying the pathos in this drunk's performance. Two relative strangers briefly united in a moment of farce. I have known of this man for most of my life and, during the course of my search, I have gotten to know him more intimately, so why does it feel like I know nothing about him?

It was the day after I watched Dundee v Queen of the South with Bobby Waddell and I told Alan of our meeting, and of Bobby choosing to sit with the away fans.

"Does he?" asked Gillie, sounding genuinely surprised. "I'm going back up to Dundee at the end of the month for a sportsman's dinner, I'll see him there. You know he had a heart operation a few years back. He got on the bus at Dundee, went down to Glasgow, had the operation and then when he was better, got back on the bus and went back to Dundee."

It's my turn to be surprised, but then, having spoken to Bobby Waddell, I know him to be full of beans.

"Yeah, he goes to a different game every Saturday," I said. "He gets to the bus stop on a Saturday and decides where he's going to go. You know he told me that when you beat St Mirren 9-2 in 1964, the keeper was on the take for bets?"

"Was he?" asked Gillie.

"Yeah, Bobby said he threw one ball out to him and he volleyed it back into the goal and thought something was up."

And at that we laughed.

"Are you driving back to Hamilton tonight?" asked Gillie, looking at my pint of Guinness.

"I've just had the one."

Kenny Strang joined the company and asked Gillie if he wants a drink.

"I can't," said Gillie. "I've got reflux. I can't even have a glass of wine."

When it's time to leave there was no symbolic parting of the ways, no demonstrative gestures or promises. We shook hands and I left him standing there. Another crowd quickly formed around him. Kenny told me that Alan has promised to call him in the coming days. I asked him to tell me when he does and to sound him out about the book. A week later I emailed Kenny and he told me he hadn't heard from Gillie again. I resigned myself to the fact that I probably never would either.

But one didn't have to look too far for Gillie in the aftermath of that Hall of Fame dinner. The next morning, Sky Sports News carried an interview with him. The reporter, clearly unaware of the significance of the event, pressed Alan for his opinions on Jermain Defoe's candidacy in Fabio Capello's England squad for the 2010 World Cup, rather than ask the obvious question about where Alan had been hiding away for all this time. It was another indication of how his legacy had faded.

I returned to my research but the more bits of clay that I added to the sculpture the more it became ill-defined. Only one person – or perhaps one of the seven with Gillie's telephone number – could answer my questions. The pictures of Gillie at the sportsman's dinner appeared soon after on the internet, as did those from the Hall of Fame night. They caused quite a stir among Spurs fans who had assumed he had fallen off the face of the planet. One blogger started a campaign to get Gilzean back on to the pitch at White Hart Lane because, despite his reappearance at Dundee, he had still not been back at Spurs. Gillie told me he had been back to watch Ian and for Bill Nicholson's testimonial. Nicholson had two testimonials: one against West Ham in 1983 and the other against Fiorentina in 2001. Phil Beal told me he had not seen Gillie at the latter, but perhaps he had been at the former.

There was only one thing left for me to do and that was establish what happened to Gillie when his playing days came to an end and he had to join the real world. I had maintained email contact with Ian Mackenzie but we had agreed to communicate along pre-determined lines. Instead, I was forced to do some detective work.

The start point was an article which appeared in the Evening Times in April 1980. It read: "When Alan Gilzean, the King of Tottenham, abdicated in 1974 he wanted to take over a pub. Now he's manager of the Blue Dart in London. But it isn't a pub, it's a transport company."

"I wouldn't have a pub now," he is quoted as saying. "You're tied to it seven days a week, whereas at present I start at 8am, finish before 5pm, Monday to Friday, have a very good salary and few problems."

I contacted a website for truckers and swapped emails with someone who had worked with Alan at Blue Dart. The correspondent was attached to the Manchester depot while Alan worked in Enfield. He saw Gillie regularly around the yard and when he left Blue Dart he would meet up with George Hill, who was at Dundee at the same time as Gillie. But his dates were all wrong, claiming that Alan was working for the company at a time when he was still turning out for Spurs. The man's stories seemed authentic, but there seemed little point in repeating them when I couldn't put an accurate timeframe on them.

I uncovered another former work colleague. Trevor Curling worked with Gillie for a year in the mid-1980s at another Enfield-based transport company. His dates seemed much more reliable. "We worked together in a company called Leggett Freightways where Alan was transport manager for around about a year in 1985. Leggett's was owned by three East End brothers and one of them was passionate about Leyton Orient. He was the life president.

"Leyton Orient played Spurs in the League Cup in 1985 and Gillie and I were invited along because the company had sponsored the match. It was strange to see him in his environment because I was used to seeing him in work. Gillie was my idol. He was always in the Stag and Hounds in Bury Street when he was a player. He would go there after training. I seem to remember that he was first to finish training and first to get away. I would see him in there talking to people but I never plucked up the courage to have a conversation with him.

"Then, from being a starstruck fan in my younger days, to seeing him years later in front of me in the office, sitting at a desk with his bald head bent down in front of me was surreal. I'd look at him and think, 'How many times have I seen you scoring goals or flicking one on for someone else with that bald head of yours? And now you're sitting in front of me.' It seemed strange to see him working longer hours than me, taking all the aggravation that went with it.

"Bobby Robson, the England manager, was at the Leyton Orient match. It was just before Mexico '86 and he was having a drink with Alan and talking about the forthcoming World Cup. Bobby Robson was saying things like, 'if we qualify' and Alan was quite abrupt with him and told him to cut out the nonsense."

It was the same old Gillie that I had heard of ad infinitum. Still joking, still reluctant to open up ... and still looking after his feet.

"One thing I remember is that he always had good shoes. They were always very expensive and it looked like his feet were comfortable. But if you saw him sitting at the desk you wouldn't see the shoes, and his other clothes looked ordinary. He had a Jag but that was the only indication that he had had this other life.

"I never really felt he was comfortable with people recognising him and he would never open the conversation. One day I was talking to him about the 1967 FA Cup final and he said he would bring in his medal. It was sitting in his drawer and the box was a bit battered and didn't look well cared for. He probably treasured it, though."

And then one day, Gillie just didn't turn up for work. Trevor says he wasn't surprised, it was the sort of thing that happened all the time. "The brothers were pretty ruthless. They weren't the Krays or anything, but they didn't muck about and I think they ruled through fear. But Alan wasn't afraid of them. And, then one day, he wasn't there. He just didn't come in to work. Whether he didn't get along with them or whether they had had an argument, I don't know. Certainly, it wasn't unusual for people just not to turn up for work the next day. Perhaps they just got rid of him. They did it to me a few years later.

"It was very much a routine, average job. It was mundane, and pressurised and he was doing it for an ordinary wage. In his case, he was there early in the mornings and late at night. It was bloody hard. He was on the phone all the time organising drop-offs and he would have had a lot of people swearing at him. Those days were hard and that company was hard and people came and went. One minute he was there and the next minute he was gone. But it was obvious that something had happened."

I did some more digging and turned up a number for Ricky Prosser, Gillie's friend from his days at Tottenham. He confirmed the names Blue Dart and Leggett Freightways and added another, Langham Transport.

"He didn't really know what he was doing," Ricky said. "Blue Dart gave him a job just because he was Alan Gilzean and the next thing I know he was transport manager of Leggett's. Gillie used to have to phone me and say, 'Rick, what should I charge?' if he was sending a certain weight to Manchester or wherever."

There was still a whole chunk of Gillie's life that remained unaccounted for. The rumours remained just that, and some were so fanciful as to be irrelevant. But I heard others more than once. Ultimately, only one person could ever discredit them fully.

This presented me with difficult questions about the very essence of writing a life story. How could it ever be a true representation of the subject? There are moral and ethical questions that must be answered in order to find the truth and yet, without knowing the individual, or at least without their consent, it is impossible to understand them. I was blatantly missing any significant input from Gilzean himself. Even then, the process is fraught. They might not remember or even know why they chose a particular course of action. It is not as if life presents us with straightforward choices. Even the monochrome picture on the wall in Dens Park has shades of grey.

Alan Gilzean has maintained a quiet dignity. It is inherent in his refusal to dignify some of the rumours with responses, but also in his insistence on privacy.

The modern sports biography is almost always confessional – chock-full of lurid details and exposés. They dwell on the prurient and unseemly when they are meant to be a celebration of the person's life, a testimony to their achievements. Instead, we are subjected to pages upon pages of footballers shitting themselves after one too many, or banging everything that moves. Maybe the most interesting subjects are those who preserve a bit of themselves.

They might leave questions unanswered, they might come across as enigmatic, but that's part of the charm, and it's an increasingly rare quality in this media age where every detail is picked over and where the internet peddles myth without means of redress for the wronged individual.

I hope, if this book is not one of those warts and all biographies, it serves as a celebration of Gilzean's life as a footballer. It is after all why I took the time to write about him. It is the memory those who idolised him want to preserve.

All a biographer can do is shine some light on the enigma. And in Gillie's case, the enigma has remained intact.

§

In some small way, though, the penny had dropped. Gillie told me there was little demand for a book about his life, but he was wrong. In April 2010, I appeared on a programme entitled Scotland's Greatest Team, which asked viewers to pick the best Scotland international XI since 1967. On the back of his nomination for the SFA Hall of Fame, Gillie was included in a shortlist of six strikers, alongside Kenny Dalglish, Joe Jordan, Denis Law, Maurice Johnston and Ally McCoist. I supplied one of the programme's producers, Craig Coughlan, with details of how to contact Gillie and other team-mates from his time at Spurs.

I argued that Alan was the forgotten star of Scottish football, but that pearl of wisdom didn't make the edit. There were other talking heads who were much more qualified to give their opinions on his impact as a player than me.

Not least Gillie himself. Again, I was surprised to hear that he had agreed to be interviewed. But he was making a gradual return to the spotlight. His next appearance was at the Dundee Hall of Fame night in March 2010, a year after he had missed his own induction. It appeared as if he had undergone some kind of epiphany and that he was now giving something back to the fans after so many years in the shadows.

When Gilzean showed up for his interview in Bristol, Craig Coughlan told me, he was wrapped up in a scarf, hat and overcoat. Craig asked Gillie if he had been able to get a parking space okay, and Gillie told him he'd got the bus. "I had this mental picture of this legend sitting at the front of the bus, in a big overcoat and hat, and everyone on that bus being oblivious to who he was," Craig said.

I was greatly intrigued by the discovery, too, that Steve Perryman had been interviewed on the same day and met Gillie. Craig said the meeting was very affable as the old team-mates caught up. But Steve handed over his phone number while Gillie managed to avoid reciprocating. Perhaps the explanation was really simple, perhaps it was just down to the passage of time: he had moved away, lost touch with the old crowd and the longer the years had gone by the harder it had been to go back to

White Hart Lane. But that still didn't explain why Gillie had been at Dundee, for example, and not Spurs. What he said that night at the Hilton Hotel as he picked up his Hall of Fame award made his reasons for staying away all the more curious.

"When you move in football you have got to go into a club where you feel it's right for you and at Dundee and Tottenham everything was right for me," he said.

In Scotland's Greatest Team, Martin Chivers and Steve Perryman gave a flavour of what Gilzean meant to the Spurs fans. "If Alan Gilzean came back to Tottenham, and he was to come out onto the pitch, it would take the roof off," Chivers said and Perryman was just as praiseworthy as he had been that day in Maidenhead. "Gillie was one of those top, top class players that did something that you weren't going to see anywhere else. That matched his personality because he was a very special man and a very special player."

When the man himself was interviewed, there was an assurance about him, a clarity about what he had achieved as a player. "I went to four cup finals and we won four," he began. "The FA Cup, two League Cups and the UEFA Cup, so I was very happy with that. In Tottenham's history, there have only been five players who have scored over 100 goals for the club. Jimmy Greaves, Martin Chivers, Teddy Sheringham, Robbie Keane and myself."

He hesitated slightly as he said it, probably because he knew it wasn't quite right. There were other players in Tottenham's history who had scored over 100 goals but this was as close as Gillie had ever come to blowing his own trumpet. "He was, and still is, a very modest guy," says Ian Mackenzie, his best man. "In all the socialising we did he never once capitalised on his fame in conversation. When asked by admirers he would speak about the football, almost reluctantly, and was quite adept at differentiating between 'hangers-on' and genuine admirers."

He was ahead of his time and if he had not always received the credit for it when he was a player, there seemed to be a dawning realisation on a personal level that what he had given to football was worth remembering. But this was not confined just to Gillie. In the aftermath of the programme, numerous friends and colleagues approached me to say that they had had no real grasp of just how brilliant Gilzean had been. Many admitted they had never heard of him before the show. And that said everything one needed to know about whether his legacy had been restored or not.

At Dens Park, the King had returned to pick up his crown, but they were still waiting for him to return to his throne at White Hart Lane.

ACKNOWLEDGEMENTS

I have been overwhelmed by the help received from individuals who owed me nothing. In many ways, it spoke volumes about how Alan Gilzean was perceived as a man and how his retreat from the spotlight had pricked their curiosity as it had mine. Most are listed below, but there are many others who gave up freely of their time and to whom I am indebted that they did so. To the others I may have forgotten, those who have contributed a telephone number here or a cutting there, my sincere apologies and heartfelt thanks.

I spent long periods with my head burrowed in offprints from various libraries. Special mention must go to Claire McGugan at the Mitchell Library in Glasgow, all the staff at Dundee City Library, Clare Stephens and Bill Rust at Bruce Castle museum and Christian Algar at the British Newspaper Library

The chapter on Coupar Angus would not have been possible without the help of Ron Ross and Ian Mackenzie, whose energy and local knowledge proved invaluable, so too Ron MacDonald, Jim Lindsay and Norrie Currie.

Many of Gilzean's Dundee team-mates proved particularly helpful and my gratitude goes to Craig Brown, Bob Seith, Kenny Cameron, and Alan Cousin. Special thanks for Ian Ure, Pat Liney, Bobby Waddell and the late Hugh Robertson for their generosity and hospitality.

Dundee supporters Norrie Price and Stephen Borland were also very helpful by providing pictures, stories and contact details while Kenny Ross gave me a clearer image of life at Dens Park during Gilzean's time. Journalists Bill Hutcheon, Ronnie Scott and Jim Hendry provided much-needed help during the early stages.

The publisher and I would also like to thank DC Thomson for the kind permission to use many of the photographs pertaining to Gillie's time at Dundee and SNS for helping out with the SFA Hall of Fame photo.

As a Spurs supporter, it gave me particular pleasure to sit down with many of the former players whom I grew up reading about and watching and my sincere thanks go to Phil Beal, Alan Mullery, Cliff Jones, Steve Perryman and Pat Jennings, Jimmy Greaves, Eddie Baily, Mike England and John Duncan.

At Spurs, thanks go to John Fennelly and Andy Porter while others who contributed material on Gilzean's time in London and beyond include Nick Hawkins, Nick Forsyth, Marcel Brown, Morris Keston, David Leggat and Ken Jones.

Gillie's latter years proved particularly difficult to pin down and I am extremely grateful to Steve Miller, Martin Cohen, Lloyd Briscoe, Graeme Aslett, Phil Ravitz, Ricky Prosser and Trevor Curling for their insight and help.

Richard McBrearty and Kenny Strang at the Scottish Football Association Museum took the time to help out when they were far busier with other things and again I want to extend to them my thanks.

Apologies to all on The Herald sports desk who had to listen to my bellyaching and pontificating on all things Gilzean for well over a year. Special thanks goes to Donald Cowey, my sports editor, for turning a blind eye when necessary, Hugh MacDonald for his guidance and Martin Sheach for his pep talks, overwhelming enthusiasm and encouragement when I needed it most. There are a number of other journalists and former journalists to whom I am indebted for contact details, support and advice including Darryl Broadfoot, Richard Winton, Graeme Elder, Gordon Stevenson, Darren Fullerton and Kenny Hodgart.

Martin Greig, Neil White and James Porteous always listened, were always open minded and were always available to discuss ideas. Particular thanks goes to Martin, who gave me the belief to carry on when it seemed easier to give up.

I want to thank my Scottish and Irish families for all their support. My mum Mina for offering suggestions for rewrites and, like she has done all my life, correcting my grammar, and to my late dad Jim who provided the inspiration for this book.

Finally, I want to thank my wife Helen for the unconditional love and support she gave me throughout the writing of this book and at a time when I should have been helping her out with our newborn son instead of chasing a childish fantasy. It was truly appreciated, sweetheart.

– James Morgan, May 2010